PHILOSOPHY AND EDUCATION

PHILOSOPHY AND EDUCATION

Eightieth Yearbook of the
National Society for the Study of Education

PART I

By

THE YEARBOOK COMMITTEE

and

ASSOCIATED CONTRIBUTORS

Edited by

JONAS F. SOLTIS

Editor for the Society

KENNETH J. REHAGE

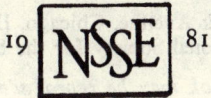

Distributed by THE UNIVERSITY OF CHICAGO PRESS • CHICAGO, ILLINOIS

The National Society for the Study of Education

Founded in 1901 as successor to the National Herbart Society, the National Society for the Study of Education has provided a means by which the results of serious study of educational issues could become a basis for informed discussion of those issues. The Society's two-volume yearbooks, now in their eightieth year of publication, reflect the thoughtful attention given to a wide range of educational problems during those years. A recently inaugurated series on Contemporary Educational Issues includes substantial publications in paperback that supplement the yearbooks. Each year, the Society's publication contain contributions to the literature of education from more than a hundred scholars and practitioners who are doing significant work in their respective fields.

An elected Board of Directors selects the subjects with which volumes in the yearbook series are to deal, appropriates funds to meet necessary expenses in the preparation of a given volume, and appoints a committee to oversee the preparation of manuscripts for that volume. A special committee created by the Board performs similar functions for the Society's paperback series.

The Society's publications are distributed each year without charge to approximately 4,500 members in the United States, Canada, and elsewhere throughout the world. The Society welcomes as members all individuals who desire to receive its publications. For information about membership and current dues, see the back pages of this volume or write to the Secretary-Treasurer, 5835 Kimbark Avenue, Chicago, Illinois 60637.

The Eightieth Yearbook includes the following two volumes:

Part I: *Philosophy and Education*
Part II: *The Social Studies*

A complete listing of the Society's previous publications, together with information as to how earlier publications still in print may be obtained, is found in the back pages of this volume.

Library of Congress Catalog Number: 80-83743
ISSN: 0077-5762

Published 1981 by
THE NATIONAL SOCIETY FOR THE STUDY OF EDUCATION

5835 Kimbark Avenue, Chicago, Illinois 60637
© 1981 by the National Society for the Study of Education

No part of this Yearbook may be reproduced in any form without written permission from the Secretary of the Society

First Printing, 8,000 Copies

Printed in the United States of America

Officers of the Society
1980-81

(Term of office expires March 1 of the year indicated.)

JEANNE CHALL

(1981)
Harvard University, Cambridge, Massachusetts

MARGARET J. EARLY

(1982)
Syracuse University, Syracuse, New York

ELLIOT W. EISNER

(1983)
Stanford University, Stanford, California

JOHN I. GOODLAD

(1983)
University of California, Los Angeles, California

PHILIP W. JACKSON

(1982)
University of Chicago, Chicago, Illinois

A. HARRY PASSOW

(1981)
Teachers College, Columbia University, New York, New York

KENNETH J. REHAGE

(Ex-officio)
University of Chicago, Chicago, Illinois

Secretary-Treasurer

KENNETH J. REHAGE

5835 Kimbark Avenue, Chicago, Illinois 60637

The Society's Committee on Philosophy and Education

JONAS F. SOLTIS

(Chairman)
Professor of Philosophy and Education
Teachers College, Columbia University
New York, New York

DONNA H. KERR

William Heard Kilpatrick Professor of Philosophy and Education
Director, Institute for the Study of Educational Policy
University of Washington
Seattle, Washington

JANE ROLAND MARTIN

Professor of Philosophy
University of Massachusetts
Boston, Massachusetts

DENIS C. PHILLIPS

Professor of Education and Philosophy
Stanford University
Stanford, California

Associated Contributors

CLIVE M. BECK

Coordinator of Graduate Studies
Ontario Institute for Studies in Education
Toronto, Ontario, Canada

HARRY S. BROUDY

Professor Emeritus of Philosophy of Education
University of Illinois
Urbana, Illinois

ASSOCIATED CONTRIBUTORS

ROBERT H. ENNIS

Professor of Philosophy of Education
University of Illinois
Urbana, Illinois

MAXINE GREENE

Professor of Philosophy and Education
Teachers College, Columbia University
New York, New York

JAMES E. MC CLELLAN

Professor of Philosophy and Education
State University of New York
Albany, New York

KENNETH A. STRIKE

Professor of Philosophy and Education
Cornell University
Ithaca, New York

Acknowledgements

This venture needed lots of helping hands. It began with the Board of Directors of the National Society for the Study of Education, who saw merit in the project. A good colleague, A. Harry Passow, was on that Board and has served faithfully as this yearbook's good friend, liason officer, and shepherd. A number of philosophers of education consulted and argued over important matters long before the present editor and format were chosen. Among them in the ad hoc discussion groups I attended in 1976 were Joe Burnett, Harry Broudy, Phil G. Smith, Robert Heslep, Philip Phenix, and Maxine Greene. There were many, many others too numerous to mention here who talked and thought this volume into existence. I hope they will forgive me for not including so long a list of able colleagues here.

I must also thank Douglas Sloan, Editor of *Teachers College Record*, who invited me to be a guest editor for a special issue of the *Record* on "Philosophy of Education Since Midcentury." That issue was designed to introduce the format of this yearbook to educators prior to its actual publication. I must thank Harry Broudy, Richard Pratte, Joe Burnett, Donald Vanderberg, and Tom Green for their contributions to that effort.

Finally, I thank Kenneth J. Rehage for his sage advice and the handling of the technical editing chores; Ellen Fendrich, Pat Pheanious, and Jo Ellen Thomas for first-class secretarial assistance; Harry Broudy for his wise counsel; the contributors to this yearbook who conscientiously met deadlines and strove to attain the purpose of our joint venture; and most especially my editorial committee, Donna Kerr, Jane Martin, and Denis Phillips, whose advice, support, and hard work made my chairing of this project a very satisfying adventure in good colleagueship.

JONAS F. SOLTIS, Editor
New York, January 1981

As is the case with all volumes in the Society's series of yearbooks, this volume is the product of considerable thought and planning over a number of years. Our debt is particularly great to

Professor Jonas Soltis, whose vigorous leadership has been a major factor in bringing the work to completion, and to the members of the editorial committee who have so ably assisted him. All of the authors have been most generous in devoting their time and talents to the preparation of their manuscripts, to thoughtful attention to comments on their various drafts, and to the attention to detail as the book has gone through the editing process. Without the kind of professional commitment to which their work testifies, the Society would be unable to produce volumes like this one.

KENNETH J. REHAGE
Editor for the Society

Table of Contents

	PAGE
THE NATIONAL SOCIETY FOR THE STUDY OF EDUCATION	iv
OFFICERS OF THE SOCIETY, 1980-81	v
THE SOCIETY'S COMMITTEE ON PHILOSOPHY AND EDUCATION AND ASSOCIATED CONTRIBUTORS	vii
ACKNOWLEDGEMENTS	ix

CHAPTER

I. INTRODUCTION, *Jonas F. Soltis* 1

Philosophy of Education 12

II. BETWEEN THE YEARBOOKS, *H. S. Broudy* 13

Introduction. The Constituencies of Philosophy of Education. The First Two Yearbooks. The Third Yearbook. What Have Educators a Right to Expect from Philosophy of Education?

Curriculum Theory 36

III. NEEDED: A PARADIGM FOR LIBERAL EDUCATION, *Jane Roland Martin* 37

The Forms of Knowledge Theory. Ivory Tower People. The Epistemological Fallacy. An Untenable Dualism. Toward a New Paradigm. Agenda for the Future.

Theory of Teaching 60

IV. THE STRUCTURE OF QUALITY IN TEACHING, *Donna H. Kerr* . 61

Introduction. A Question en Route to Theory of Teaching. Theory of Teaching as Theory of Practice. Practical Applications. Concluding Note.

Epistemology 94

V. EDUCATION AND THE CONCEPT OF KNOWLEDGE, *Jonas F. Soltis* . 95

Educators and Knowledge. The Sociocentric Perspective. Language and Human Knowledge. Forms of Human Knowledge. Dynamics of Knowing. Conclusion.

Aesthetics 114

VI. AESTHETIC LITERACY IN GENERAL EDUCATION, *Maxine Greene* . 115

Neglect of the Arts by Educators. Art Education, Art Appreciation, and Beyond. Philosophy and the Art World. Perspectives on the Aesthetic. Aesthetic Educating.

TABLE OF CONTENTS

CHAPTER	PAGE

Logic 142

VII. RATIONAL THINKING AND EDUCATIONAL PRACTICE, *Robert H. Ennis* 143

Introduction. An Outline of a Conception of Rational Thinking. Five Cases. A Detailed Conception of Rational Thinking. Summary.

Ethics 184

VIII. THE REFLECTIVE APPROACH TO VALUES EDUCATION, *Clive M. Beck* 185

Overview. Insights from Educational Philosophy. Some Approaches to Values Education in the Schools. The Reflective Approach in Values Education. Some Philosophical Roots of the Reflective Approach. Conclusion.

Social Philosophy 212

IX. TOWARD A MORAL THEORY OF DESEGREGATION, *Kenneth A. Strike* 213

Introduction. A Moral Theory for *Brown*. An Empirical Interpretation of the Moral Theory. A Second Empirical Interpretation of the Moral Theory. A Second Moral Theory for *Brown*. Synthesizing the Moral Theories. Conclusion.

Philosophy of Science 236

X. POST-KUHNIAN REFLECTIONS ON EDUCATIONAL RESEARCH, *D. C. Phillips* 237

Introduction. The Kuhnian and Wittgensteinian Perspectives and the Emergence of Relativism. Fruitful Applications to Education, I. The "New Methodology" of Science. Fruitful Applications to Education, II. Concluding Remarks on Epistemology.

Metaphysics 262

XI. FIRST PHILOSOPHY AND EDUCATION, *James E. McClellan* . . 263

How to Get to Basics. Excerpts from the Historical Canon of First Philosophy. We Seek a First Philosophy. Toward a Scientific First Philosophy. Practical Applications.

NAME INDEX 289

SUBJECT INDEX 293

INFORMATION ABOUT MEMBERSHIP IN THE SOCIETY 297

PUBLICATIONS OF THE SOCIETY 299

CHAPTER I

Introduction

JONAS F. SOLTIS

This yearbook has had a long gestation. More than a decade ago, the Board of Directors of the National Society for the Study of Education recognized that considerable time had elapsed since their 1942 and 1955 yearbooks on philosophy of education and so commissioned the writing of a 1972 yearbook that eventually was titled *Philosophical Redirection of Educational Research*. That yearbook filled the hiatus, but its narrow focus on topics related to educational research did not satisfy the felt need of educators to get some broader view of what contemporary philosophers of education had to offer them and what philosophy of education as a scholarly field of inquiry had become. True, the "redirection of research" volume accurately reflected the movement in the field away from the "systems of philosophy" approach of earlier yearbooks and toward attacking an array of particular educational problems piecemeal by the use of rigorous philosophical method and logical argument. But it made no attempt to provide a framework for displaying the full range of philosophical concerns with educational matters across the field as a whole, and for good reason, for philosophy of education was in a period of growth, transition, and development that had not yet crystallized into a perceptible form.

In 1976, the NSSE Board decided to try again. It tested the waters with a letter to a number of prominent philosophers of education asking if a more general volume on philosophy of education was needed and feasible and, if so, what form it should take. The responses were uniform in affirming need, but quite disparate regarding feasibility and form. There seemed to be no generally acceptable formula for representing the field as a whole. Over the next year a number of informal *ad hoc* meetings were held by different and overlapping mixes of the philosophers contacted, and several competing ideas for the projected volume were transmitted to the NSSE Board. At its February 1978 meeting, the Board formally approved a plan that has resulted in the production of the yearbook in this form. In it, we attempt to provide the broader representation of philosophical work felt to be needed. We who have worked to put it together believe that it provides a good general way to reflect the potential uses of philosophy for educators.

To signal the expanding view of philosophy of education that has been developing since midcentury, we have called this volume "Philosophy *and* Education." We believe that such a title highlights the growing interpenetration of philosophy and education that currently characterizes the field and will force readers consciously to attend to a different way of thinking about philosophy of education. But even though we believe it is essential for educators to come to see and appreciate a newer and still developing multifaceted view of philosophy of education, we also believe that it is essential that they see it *as* philosophy of education, and not as some mutant worthy of a different name. So while we deliberately call this yearbook "Philosophy and Education," all the chapters have been written by contemporary philosophers of education and reflect the kind of work they do in the field. The main purpose of this introduction as well as the entire volume, therefore, is to help the readers readjust their conceptions of what philosophy of education is and to come to see the many ways in which philosophy and education can be connected.

The key to our finding a suitable structure for representing the field of philosophy of education at this stage in its development was the recognition of a serious professional mismatch between expectation and delivery. Quite frequently, it seemed to us, the philosophical expectations of educators were not being met by what was being delivered by professional philosophers of education. In the 1960s and 1970s, preservice initiates with a commonsense view of philosophy and educators schooled in the "schools of philosophy" approach were finding philosophers arguing over what appeared to be the meaning of words or dealing with very esoteric philosophical problems rather than describing or defending comprehensive views of the world and the place of education in it. Learned labels like idealism, realism, pragmatism, or perennialism, progressivism, essentialism were becoming less and less helpful for understanding what many philosophers of education were doing. Even the newly added labels of "phenomenology" and "linguistic analysis" seemed to name odd methodologies and philosophical research programs rather than world views and systematic educational ideals. Thus, for many people the very meaning of having a philosophy of education as the holding of a world view that supports a systematic set of beliefs about educating was being violated or at least seemed to be disregarded by philosophers who were busy analyzing concepts, bracketing the world to obtain pure phenomenological descriptions, or just plain philosophizing about some narrow and particular topical educational idea or issue.

What had happened to bring about this incongruous state of affairs setting expectation and delivery at such odds? The answer is increasing professional specialization along with many other less central things too numerous to mention here.* But it was clear to us that somehow we had to reflect the new state of affairs in the field in a way that could meaningfully restructure the expectations of educators with regard to the relation of philosophy to education, and vice versa, if philosophy of education was to have any

---

* Early on a basic decision was reached *not* to use the yearbook to trace and describe developments in the field since the publication of the earlier yearbooks. To do such a history competently would have taken all the space allotted to us. It seemed more important to us to try to use philosophy to illuminate educational matters in a way that would help contemporary educators see and appreciate the potential relationships between philosophy and education. Still, we sensed a genuine need to try to fill the historical gap, however incompletely. The editor's notes preceding each chapter are designed to suggest ways in which our contemporary work is part of the philosophical tradition in education. In chapter 2, Harry S. Broudy sketches in very broad strokes some of the developments in the field between yearbooks of the National Society that dealt specifically with philosophy of education. A special issue of *Teachers College Record*, volume 81 (Winter 1979), was designed to precede the publication of this volume and to fill in more of the historical gap by treating "Philosophy of Education Since Midcentury." It is recommended to readers who desire more historical perspective than we offer here. Of course, the full history of the development of philosophy of education as a professional field in the twentieth century has yet to be written. We hope some enterprising scholar will consider the topic worthy of serious research.

value for educators in the decades ahead. To do that, we would have to help people grasp the relevant shifts that had occurred in the field, help them understand why their idea of philosophy of education, while still valid, was too narrow a conception of what philosophers have to offer educators, and provide them with a wider scheme for generating useful expectations about the field as a whole. This chapter and those that follow are designed to fill that tall order.

To illuminate one major characteristic of the shift in philosophy of education between yearbooks, the distinction between the noun "philosophy" and the verb "philosophize" is helpful. In the noun sense, philosophy is a thing, a product of philosophical thinking such as the philosophy of Dewey or of Marx, or like pragmatism, Thomism, or existentialism. The verb, philosophize, comprises a set of activities of elucidation, argument, critique, clarification, analysis, synthesis, and so forth aimed at reflecting on how we think about the world and our actions in it.

In recent years philosophers of education, following the trend in general philosophy, have been less inclined to build or interpret systems of philosophy and have been more engaged in examining a number of topics and ideas relevant to educating by the use of their highly honed philosophical skills. Thus they have tended to view philosophy less as a noun and more as a verb, less as system building and more as ways of thinking critically about some important aspect of educating, such as moral education, equality of educational opportunity, and the nature of educational research. They have tried to use the techniques of philosophy to help educators think more clearly about what they are doing. Through the activity of philosophizing, they have provided elucidations, reflections, critical appraisals, and conceptual frameworks for ordering ideas, analyzing educational situations, considering options, designing curricula, making judgments, and in general understanding what the many bits and pieces of the complex educational enterprise are about. Clearly, if an educator is looking for a comprehensive view of education and finds numerous philosophical discussions dealing only with discrete topics, no matter how cogent they are, those discussions will still fall short of the mark. The many parts are always less than the whole.

Does this mean that philosophers of education no longer pay any attention to world views and broad educational theories? Not at all. It means that while some do, they and others also do much, much more. What this really means is that viewing philosophy of education from this single perspective of world views is too narrow and cuts educators off from a richer perception of the wider field of philosophical endeavor that has developed in recent years.

Does this trend toward more *doing* of philosophy mean that the labels identifying schools of philosophy and of education are useless? No, they still name some very basic intellectual and valuational postures toward the world and educating that are useful as interpretive frameworks. For the purpose of reading this volume, however, it is important to see that they do not name *all* that can be called philosophy of education or prepare people to understand all that philosophers of education do.

Does all this mean that only philosophers can *do* philosophy of education? Cannot any person develop a philosophy of education or publicly recommend adoption of a comprehensive view of educating? Of course, making sense of the whole and developing a consistent set of educational values, beliefs, and goals is still a highly desirable and lifelong enterprise for educators, but once again, it is important to see that it is not the only way educators can be philosophical or make practical use of philosophy. It is only one of many ways. As for philosophy of education in this its broadest public sense, anyone, including politicians, journalists, intellectuals, citizens, *and educators*, should be deeply concerned and thoughtfully reflective about fundamental aspects of educating in our time. This is not the singular province of those professionals trained in philosophy of education, nor should it be. Education is such a central social and cultural enterprise that the rational design and appraisal of it should be and is open to any who would aspire to provide thoughtful leadership for our society and its schools and are willing to test their ideas in public. Public philosophy of education is everybody's business.

But there is also a *professional* sense of philosophy of education that reflects another important shift in the field. In this century, for the first time in the history of education, philosophers have been trained singularly and directly in the field of philosophy of education, have developed a scholarly literature of their own, and have assumed as their major professional responsibility the bringing of technical philosophical perspective to bear on educational theory, policy, and practice. This has brought with it an increasing emphasis on training in the parent discipline of philosophy and the mastery of its methods and content, which in turn has provided philosophers of education with another source for generating philosophical topics, problems, and ideas. Thus they take philosophical grist for their mills from three sources: from education itself, from the literature of philosophy of education, and from philosophy. Some examples should help make this broad source of topics for philosophers of education clearer. From contemporary education itself, philosophers have become concerned with such things as accountability, competence, equality of opportunity, and so forth, and these in turn have become part of the literature of philosophy of education along with a traditional literature dealing with such things as the idea of liberal education, teaching, and moral education. From philosophy, recent work in the philosophy of science has had special impact on educational thinking in research and curriculum, and the resurgence of interest in social philosophy has had its correlative revival in philosophy of education. Thus, the base for philosophizing about education has been considerably broadened.

And just as we do not expect every historian to rewrite the history of civilization or every psychologist to be the next Piaget, so it would be unrealistic to expect each and every professional philosopher of education to invent a new philosophy of education, to provide the definitive critique of contemporary educational practice, and to set once and for all our national educational goals. As professional educators, we appreciate the scholarly work of historians, psychologists, sociologists, and other such scholars precisely to the degree that they help us see, understand, and make better sense of some aspect of what we are doing. So too ought it to be with the professional educational philosophers who bring their technical knowledge, training, and skills to bear on relevant educational-philosophical matters, even though those matters may be substantially less than a comprehensive view of educating.

How best can we capture the results of these shifts in philosophy of education and change the expectancy set to include this broader spectrum of professional philosophical work in education without forcing a premature crystalization of a field that is still in the process of becoming? We believe we have found a solution that has these important characteristics: it provides a simple, understandable order; it is comprehensive; and it has the flexibility to adapt to changes and new concerns inevitably to be found in both philosophy and education in the near future. The basic idea for the solution is drawn from the way in which philosophy in general is ordered in colleges and universities today, namely, by means of its subfields of philosophical inquiry (for example, ethics, logic, aesthetics, philosophy of science, of history, and of language). Each of these subareas has a special literature and a set of concepts, arguments, theories, major figures, and philosophical problems that provide a rich context for locating and dealing with important philosophical and (for our purposes) educational issues, topics, or ideas. Moreover, as philosophical, societal, and educational winds shift, certain subareas of philosophy become temporarily more relevant to the elucidation of some equally timely educational topic, as attested by the recent heightened interest in such philosophical subfields and correlative educational topics as philosophy of science and educational research, ethics and moral education, philosophical psychology and Piagetian views of development. Such a mode of organization allows us to show the multiple ways in which philosophy can be linked to the concerns of educators by philosophers of education and assures us of providing a volume with breadth. Even so, we will only be providing a sampling of the vast potential for producing a useful mix of philosophy and education by professional philosophers of education.

The major advantage of adopting a structure for the yearbook based on a subarea of philosophical inquiry schema is to set the reader to expect something less global than *a* philosophy of education of every work in the field and to focus attention on some particular dimension of education, for example, the moral, the social, the aesthetic, the epistemological. The positive aspect of this focusing is more important than the extinction of the more general expectation. An educator deeply concerned about principles of social justice and equity in education might hope to find them dealt with in a literature of social philosophy and education but surely would not expect their treatment in a chapter or book on philosophy of science and educational research, nor would a general work on philosophy of education necessarily include that topic. Thus, we believe that a structure based on subareas of philosophy provides for a better match of expectation and philosophical delivery with this more accurate labeling of philosophical focus and context.

Clearly, it would have been impossible to treat every subarea of philosophy in the yearbook. The major subareas of aesthetics, ethics, epistemology, logic, social philosophy, and metaphysics have been chosen because they form a basic and comprehensive division of philosophy in general. The subarea of philosophy of science was also included because of the recent strong interest in it among both philosophers and educational researchers. One other accommodation to the subarea framework had to be made to reflect the fact that philosophy of education is itself a subarea of philosophy. As such, there is a part of it that focuses philosophical inquiry directly on the unique aspects of education as a human institution and phenomenon in its own right and produces theories about such things as curriculum and teaching per se. Just as a literature has grown up regarding concepts of scientific method in philosophy of science and theories of art in aesthetics, so philosophers of education have developed a literature dealing with such discrete educational phenomena as teaching, learning, curriculum, and the aims of education. To reflect this central aspect of philosophy of education, two chapters, one on curriculum theory and one on theory of teaching, were included in the yearbook. The content of the yearbook can now be briefly described.

The authors were asked to begin the development of their respective topics by first thinking of an educationally important problem, issue, or phenomenon that could be illuminated by and located in the context provided by a subarea of philosophy. We were not interested in presenting in textbook fashion either an academic definition and description of the subarea or a review of the literature in the subfield. Of course, reference to major works, figures, prominent themes, or the use of standard concepts or arguments found in the subfield and relevant to the educational topic at hand was encouraged if to do so would illuminate that topic. Authors were encouraged to engage the reader in some philosophical thinking. The point of a chapter was to demonstrate the philosophical perspective and the clarification that could be provided by locating an educational topic in a subarea of philosophy.

The chapter by Harry Broudy is introductory in nature and is designed to provide a brief sketch of some of the developments in philosophy of education since the 1942 and 1955 yearbooks. It also aims at setting the stage for a better match of reader expectation to the philosophical reflection on topics educational that follow. The next two chapters, one by Jane Martin and the other by Donna Kerr, deal with curriculum theory and theory of teaching respectively. Martin's essay questions the received view of curriculum embodied in Paul Hirst's "forms of knowledge" theory of liberal education by challenging its narrowness, noting the "epistemological fallacy" on which it is based, and questioning the adequacy of the view from a perspective of a participatory democratic social theory. Kerr focuses upon the idea of quality in teaching. She develops a philosophical description of teaching as practice, defining quality in ways useful to thinking about teaching competence, research, evaluation, and professional education.

The six remaining chapters locate a number of educational topics predominately in one of the subareas of philosophy and, in some cases, link these topics to more than one subarea. Taking epistemology as his context in chapter 5, Jonas Soltis treats individual and collective forms of knowledge from a "sociocentric" perspective. He argues that our view of knowledge is being transformed in the twentieth century and that reflective educators can use the emerging conception of knowledge to great advantage. Maxine Greene follows with a chapter on aesthetics and aesthetic education, in which she distinguishes "aesthetic literacy" (the development of aesthetic concepts, language, and sensitivity) from art appreciation and calls for more attention to the need to develop aesthetic literacy in general education. Urging that educators embrace a fourth R, rational thinking, Robert Ennis uses the subarea of logic in chapter 7 as a context from which to speak to the relation of rational thinking to all forms of educational practice. He provides a detailed characterization of the rational thinker in action. Clive Beck uses ideas drawn from the philosophical subarea of ethics in chapter 8 to illuminate his argument for a "reflective approach" to values education. In the next chapter, Kenneth Strike provides an analysis of the moral arguments implicit in recent Supreme Court decisions regarding segregation and locates these issues in the broader context of social philosophy and social justice in education. Denis Phillips in chapter 10 writes from the perspective of recent developments in philosophy of science. The aftermath of Kuhn's treatments of scientific revolutions provides a framework for Phillips to speak to such diverse things as the legitimacy of Kohlberg's cross-cultural research on moral development, forms of knowledge, curriculum theory, competing educational theories, and the nature of scientific educational research. James McClellan in chapter 11 brings the perspective of metaphysics to bear in doing "first philosophy" and assessing our traditional beliefs about the nature of such educationally fundamental ideas as knowledge, belief, truth, reality, and values.

Organized in the way that it is, the yearbook reflects the increasing specialization to be found in all academic fields as well as in the professions during the last half of the twentieth century. We believe that such specialization need not be narrow and technical and that it can provide important focus and resolution for the practitioner. We also believe that there is a growing recognition on the part of educators that philosophy, as well as the social and the behavioral sciences, has much to offer the highly specialized contemporary educators by way of *particular* knowledge relevant to developing a broad and basic perspective on their work. Without denying the need for some fundamental and general thought about education as a phenomenon in its own right, it is becoming increasingly clear that the practice of a specialized professional can best be sensibly informed by carefully selected study in different subareas of different disciplines taught in schools of education by people well trained in the disciplines and genuinely interested in educational phenomena. This yearbook does not fully reflect this high level of specialization. It was not our intent to do so. But we do believe that the volume provides a transitional framework for trying to think this way about the special relationship between philosophy and the work of practicing educators. In terms of philosophy of education, moreover, we believe that this volume provides a better way to match what philosophers of education do to what educators might expect to gain from a particular bit of work in philosophy of education because it links some part of philosophy to some part of education in a way that can be easily seen. In doing so we hope that we have demonstrated the importance of philosophical perspective for many contemporary educational concerns and that we have given the reader a more effective way to conceive of philosophy of education.

Philosophy of Education

In the course of the emergence of philosophy of education as an institutionalized field of study in this century, philosophers of education frequently have given serious consideration to the nature and definition of their own subarea of philosophy. The 1942 and 1955 yearbooks of the National Society, edited by John S. Brubacher, did much to crystalize one dominant view of the field by linking it to various schools of philosophy. But there were other views. Articles by Kingsley Price and Harry S. Broudy in the *Journal of Philosophy* (1955) on the nature of philosophy of education inspired a special issue of the *Harvard Educational Review* in 1956 that was devoted entirely to a discussion of "Philosophy of Education: Its Aims and Content." It contained the differing views of no less than twenty-five philosophers. A quarter of a century later, neither the debates nor the development of the field is over. In the following chapter, Professor Broudy, one of the most respected and dominant figures in the field for over fifty years, reflects on the nature of the changes in professional philosophy of education between yearbooks. His chapter does not purport to be a history of educational philosophy, but does highlight some of the events and developments in the field during this period. An earlier version of this chapter appeared along with five other articles in a special issue of *Teachers College Record* (Winter 1979) on "Philosophy of Education Since Midcentury." Each article treated in detail substantive developments in the field on which Broudy can only touch here. Readers interested in obtaining more historical perspective on analytic, existential, and phenomenological contributions; on educational policy studies; on the legacy of John Dewey; and on the role of philosophy in the education of educators should consult that issue. (Editor)

CHAPTER II

Between the Yearbooks

H. S. BROUDY

Introduction

Opinions differ as to whether education is a craft, a profession, an institution, or just another name for proper nurture of the young. However, if it is to be regarded as a profession coordinate with other professions, it shares two tasks with them. One is to find a theory (*logos*) that explains its procedures (*techné*). The other is to formulate "philosophy of" that explicates and justifies its claim on society for prestige, privilege, and remuneration. Assuming optimistically that science-like disciplines will provide the makings of a theory, where is education as a putative profession to find its philosophy? Clearly from philosophy. But what if philosophy is too remote from the particulars of professional practice?

A volume published in 1945 entitled *Philosophy in American Education* asked:

Is our education as a whole moving in the right direction? Is philosophy playing the part it should in that education? Are those of us who teach it teaching it as we ought, and if not, is it because we are too technical, too hortatory, or too ignorant, or too historical, or too cut off from the world? Has philosophy any guidance to give on the great problems, moral, religious, economic, and political, that are going to trouble men's minds when they try to put together again the pieces of their world?[1]

Many pages later, the authors suggested that

If the philosopher will accept the responsibility of making his ideas fit the particular subject matter in which the specialist is working, and if the specialist in his turn is willing to think through his own assumptions to the point at which their philosophical meaning can be clearly stated

1. Brand Blanshard et al., *Philosophy in American Education* (New York: Harper and Brothers, 1945), p. 9.

and responsibly judged, they will jointly have something to say in the interpretation of their common subject that will be worth hearing and worth teaching.[2]

In 1942, the Forty-first Yearbook of the National Society for the Study of Education, Part I, entitled *Philosophies of Education*, had already anticipated this suggestion, and a second yearbook of the Society (the Fifty-fourth, Part 1, published in 1955) called *Modern Philosophies and Education* carried it further. In launching a third yearbook, we are asking once more what philosophy and philosophers of education can say that is helpful and important to educators. Why do we need another yearbook? What has happened in education and/or philosophy to make us think we need one now?

In this interval the tide of school and college enrollments soared and receded. The civil rights legislation of the mid-1960s was enacted and translated into educational mandates. Human rights and the push for equality among races and sexes in employment affected all levels of schooling. The counterculture of the 1960s attacked not only our participation in the Vietnam war but also the public school as part of the "WASP" establishment that was to be brought down. Even as this yearbook was being planned, however, countertrends to the counterculture were developing. Perhaps twenty-five years is too long to wait between yearbooks to hear from philosophers on important educational topics. But do philosophers have anything to say to educators? What can educators reasonably expect from philosophy and the philosophers of education that is not already in the previous volumes?[3]

Before trying to answer such questions, a little historical perspective is in order. Philosophy of education did not wait until 1942 to be born, but in the teacher education curricula, courses

2. Ibid., p. 234.

3. In 1903, the Second Yearbook of the NSSE was called *The Relation of Theory to Practice in Education*, and presumably raised some philosophical problems. There was also the Seventy-first Yearbook, Part 1 *Philosophical Redirection of Educational Research*, ed. Lawrence G. Thomas (Chicago: University of Chicago Press, 1972), to which philosophers of education contributed. Chapter 1 of the present volume is addressed to the task of setting expectations of readers in a way different from all earlier yearbooks and should be read to get an overview of this yearbook.

bearing that name in the first half of this century were not uniformly related to formal philosophy. Even though formal theories of education (for example, those of Plato, Comenius, Froebel, Herbart, and Rousseau) often found their way into courses on the philosophy of education, philosophy of education most commonly referred to one's set of beliefs about life and schooling. Sometimes these beliefs were the results of "being thoughtful or reflective about education." Often they embodied proverbial wisdom about the young or long experience in the schools. School personnel were expected to have a set of beliefs of this kind, and candidates for teaching and administrative positions were often asked: "What is your philosophy of education?"

The major achievement of the yearbooks noted above was a conscious effort to relate very general ideas about life and school to types of philosophical thought and thus provide a more systematic idea of philosophy of education. But since 1955, philosophy of education has developed new modes of inquiry, new constituencies, and has diversified its tasks; it has become more than a system of general beliefs about schooling or a way of classifying such beliefs according to philosophical typology. However, these changes and the increasing complexity in the field have created practical problems in connecting the work of philosophers of education with the needs and expectations of professional educators. The present yearbook is designed to repair the connection. This chapter reflects on the climate between yearbooks and sets the scene.

The Constituencies of Philosophy of Education

Today philosophy of education, Janus-like, is facing two ways at once. It speaks to philosophers of education, that is, the academic guild whose members teach courses in the field to prospective teachers and doctoral students, but it also speaks to educators at all levels of schooling. It is concerned with problems of philosophy on the one hand, and with problems of schooling on the other. This duality of audiences and tasks engenders differences in language, interest, and channels of communication.

The language in which philosophers of education write and speak to each other and to their graduate students is more technical and abstract than their discourse with public school teachers and administrators. When talking to each other, they tend to stress the logical aspects of argument and precise conceptualization of problems. With teachers and school administrators, the pragmatic aspects of goals, curriculum, organization, and teaching-learning are primary, not the niceties of argument, and the discourse cannot demand a high level of technical and esoteric sophistication.

Presumably, the primary audience and the focal problems of philosophy of education are educational, but the inevitable tensions between obligations to practitioners and to the field as a domain for academic inquiry were heightened as the study of philosophy of education in the 1950s and 1960s became more philosophically technical and increasingly a field for specialization in doctoral study.

Philosophers of education communicate with their diverse constituencies through different channels. They reach educational personnel in courses that are preservice or in-service components of baccalaureate and graduate programs. There was a time when virtually all "professional" programs *required* some study in the foundations, including the philosophical foundations. During the campus turmoil of the 1960s, foundations courses often provided platforms for social activists promulgating the spirit of the counterculture. This spirit was not conducive to stability of course content or structure. Some courses were organized on the views of various philosophical schools; some by issues; some by books—classic or contemporary; and some were no more than group discussions of current social issues—ideological exchanges—for credit. In short, the introductory course in philosophy of education could be and often was anything the instructor during a particular semester thought it would be important or interesting to do. As a result, some embarrassing questions were asked about courses without stipulated uniform content being required as too important for any prospective educator to miss. But the flood of college students in the 1960s kept enrollments in schools of education and in foundations courses comfortably high. It also provided jobs for doctoral students to teach these courses.

Outside of formal courses, school people learn what the philosopher of education has to say through articles that occasionally appear in the professional journals to which they subscribe. There is little reason to believe that many of them subscribe or read journals devoted to the philosophy of education. Occasionally, philosophers of education may be heard at conferences attended by administrators, college teachers of education, and classroom teachers. As some philosophers of education move into policy studies, they may be heard from more frequently both in journals and conferences outside their own field of specialization. In the great societal and educational controversies of the last decade, however, neither philosophers nor philosophers of education were consulted in high places, nor did their views command much attention in the educational establishment.

Philosophers of education communicate with each other through the meetings and proceedings of a national organization, the Philosophy of Education Society, regional groups, and journals devoted to studies in the field. Philosophy of education communicates with its parent discipline through the doctoral program. For as doctoral programs increased in number and popularity, a greater proportion of the requirements for the Ph.D. degree was allocated to courses in the philosophy department, and philosophers were often asked to serve as members of doctoral committees. This had a dual effect. First, it attracted bright young people with an aptitude for the kind of abstract thinking required for the study of philosophy. For some of these, as might be expected, the messy problems of education, which are supposed to be the texts of the philosophy of education, became the pretexts for doing general philosophy, especially in their dissertations and in contributions to their professional publications.

The other effect of the greater ingestion of philosophy by doctoral students was the widespread adoption of the analytical modes (linguistic and logical) for philosophizing by philosophers of education. In time, the doctoral students became professors, and admirable though their desire for logical clarity and linguistic accuracy was, the beneficiaries of their therapeutic analysis did not always discern the relevance of the cure to their disease, which they did not regard as a lapse in language. It became increasingly difficult for philosophers of education to communicate with educators.

School administrators and teacher educators continued to insist on the importance of *a* philosophy, but were likely to mean thereby a set of beliefs about the good life in the good society (usually a democracy). These beliefs, more or less systematized, were supposed to justify ends and means of schooling. The Forty-first and Fifty-fourth Yearbooks supplied such a framework for those who wished to go beyond common sense and conventional moral and pedagogical principles. However, school people did not always understand or appreciate highly technical discussion as to why "applying" a philosophy to schooling was not as simple as it sounded. After the middle 1950s they were increasingly confronted with such discussions by philosophers of education and with works in philosophy of education that did not speak at all to the importance of having a philosophy of education. What had happened between yearbooks to bring about this state of affairs?

The First Two Yearbooks

Readers of the two earlier NSSE yearbooks on the philosophy of education will be struck by the differences in their rationales. In justifying the 1942 volume, Brubacher cited the need for philosophy in the "muddled times in which we live." They were indeed muddled, trailing the Great Depression and ushering in American participation in World War II, although the book says very little about either.

As for the muddled times in education, Brubacher mentioned the impact of science and industrialism on the schools and the questioning of "a long-accepted political ideal of education" as contributing to the confusion about the aims of schooling. Hence the desire for an inclusive theory of education, presumably to dispel the confusion. Brubacher noted that a number of such theories (philosophies) had been developed, but that often educators were acquainted with only one of them. A yearbook setting forth a variety of theories would correct this "professional astigmatism."[4]

The variety included an historical overview by Edward H. Reisner titled "Philosophy and Science in the Western World"; a

---

4. John S. Brubacher, "Introduction: Purpose and Scope of the Yearbook," in *Philosophies of Education*, Forty-first Yearbook of the National Society for the Study of Education, Part 1, ed. Nelson B. Henry (Chicago: University of Chicago Press, 1942), pp. 3-4.

chapter on experimentalism by William H. Kilpatrick; realism by Frederick S. Breed; idealism by Herman H. Horne, Catholicism by William J. McGucken. These were followed by a defense of philosophy of education by Mortimer J. Adler and a chapter by Brubacher comparing the views of the diverse philosophical positions on traits of reality, knowledge, human nature and learning, educational values, school and society, social conflict, communication, and cooperation. Brubacher thus identified themes to which a philosophy did or should address itself. How much consensus this identification represented is hard to say, because he reported that the committee could not agree on target problems, "not even . . . as to what constitutes a problem in the philosophy of education."[5]

In his opening chapter of the Fifty-fourth Yearbook, Brubacher attributed the great interest in educational philosophy to the challenge of Progressive education. It was, as he noted, a challenge not only to traditional schooling patterns but also to the accepted social and philosophical rationales for education. The strife of educational ideologies interrupted by World War II was resumed at its close. The Philosophy of Education Society had been revived, and its annual meetings in the decade after 1945 were animated by the debates between the advocates and foes of the philosophies that had been articulated in the Forty-first Yearbook and some views not there represented.[6]

The main motivations of the Fifty-fourth Yearbook, according

5. Ibid., p. 5.

6. And animated they were. Before concurrent paper sessions were instituted, most of the annual meeting was devoted to plenary sessions at which the various positions were interpreted, defended against misinterpretation and attack, and praised as incorporating the virtues claimed by the other views, but not their vices. Until the late 1950s, the pivot on which most discussion revolved was John Dewey. What he said, what he meant, what he should have said, and, of course, whether it was true, were rarely absent from the argument on the floor or in the corridors. The Ohio State University versions of the doctrine were represented by Henry Hullfish and defended resolutely by Ernest Bayles, who was a perennial watchdog against any interpretation of the doctrine that had the faintest odor of absolutism; about the evils of absolutism Bayles was absolutely certain. And until high administrative posts preempted his time, if not his interests, R. J. Henle's urbane pleas for the insights of Thomism were a feature of the meetings. In the early 1950s the young language analysts began to demand a session at the annual meeting. James E. McClellan, Robert H. Ennis, and B. Paul Komisar were among the early rebels, and they badgered program chairmen until they did get a place on the program, a place that became a popular fixture in subsequent years.

to Brubacher, were (a) anxiety that modern education was adrift, (b) a belief that current aims of education were either vague or conflicting and did not generate strong loyalty, (c) anxiety over a "serious letdown in standards of instruction as a result of modern educational procedures," (d) lack of confidence in a democratic conception of education, (e) concern that schools allowed children too much freedom, and (f) concern that schools were neglecting religion.[7]

Neither yearbook committee seemed to doubt the potential of philosophy for dealing with muddles and relieving anxieties. Despite increased diversity in philosophical theorizing, the committee for the Fifty-fourth Yearbook still believed that the best way to get an overall view of the problems of men and education was to examine them through the stencil or lens of a philosophical system.

The Fifty-fourth Yearbook embodied several significant changes, however. First, it entrusted the writing of the chapters to "real" philosophers, but provided each with a philosopher of education to keep him relevant, so to speak, to problems of education. In the second place, the inability of the committee for the Forty-first Yearbook to define problems of philosophy of education presumably was overcome, and the writers were instructed to include (a) an opening section to develop a general philosophical orientation; to be followed by sections on (b) aims, values, and curriculum; (c) the educative process, its methods, motivation, and the like; (d) school and society; (e) the school and the individual; and, finally, (f) religious and moral education.

The third difference was in the positions chosen for presentation. Realism was represented by John Wild, Thomism by Jacques Maritain, Idealism by Theodore M. Greene, who wrote "A Liberal Christian Idealist Philosophy of Education." Experimentalism was represented by George R. Geiger, Marxism by Robert S. Cohen, Existentialism by Ralph Harper, the linguistic approach (to be distinguished from ordinary language analysis) by Kenneth Burke, logical empiricism by Herbert Feigl. The concluding chapter by

7. John S. Brubacher, "The Challenge To Philosophize about Education," in *Modern Philosophies and Education*, Fifty-fourth Yearbook of the National Society for the Study of Education, Part 1, ed. Nelson B. Henry (Chicago: University of Chicago Press, 1955), pp. 15-16.

James K. Feibleman was called "An Ontological Philosophy of Education."

The decision to have the chapters written by philosophers rather than by philosophers of education reflected an awareness on the part of some of the prominent figures in the Philosophy of Education Society that philosophy of education needed more philosophy. This, in turn, was the result of studies (including one by R. Bruce Raup) and general observation that philosophy of education courses were often taught by instructors relatively innocent of training in formal philosophy.[8]

The Forty-first and Fifty-fourth Yearbooks reflected the view that philosophy of education should be a field of scholarly inquiry, writing, and teaching. It was more than being thoughtful about education and more than the proverbial wisdom about schooling. It was different from, if not more than, the history of educational institutions. It also was different from psychology and sociology of education. The differences were marked by the word "philosophy." Some knowledge of what is included in the college catalog under that rubric was thought to be essential to philosophy of education. It was to be expected that this trend in educational philosophy would reflect developments in general philosophy. What, then, was the situation in that field in the 1940s?

In 1945 the Commission on the Function of Philosophy in Liberal Education published its report to its parent organization, the American Philosophical Association.[9] The original proposal for the report was made in 1943 and as part of its inquiry the Commission interviewed educators, public figures, and philosophers, including some philosophers of education. The volume, therefore, is a valuable statement of how general philosophy was being perceived at that time by philosophers and philosophers of education. And it came at the time when philosophy of education was experiencing a new, postwar impetus.

8. Beginning in the middle 1940s, Brubacher, Kenneth Benne, George Axtelle, Louis Antz, R. Bruce Raup, and Theodore Brameld were especially active in trying to promote more scholarly work in the field. I am sure there were others, but this group met with some regularity in New York and was more familiar to me. Robert Ulich was at Harvard and a regular attendant at the New England regional meetings.

9. Blanshard et al., *Philosophy in American Education*.

Blanshard summarized the "reproaches to philosophy" (mostly from within the ranks of philosophers) as follows. First, it was ensconced in an ivory tower, busy with such "trifles" as sense data, the meaning of meaning, reduction of the number of primitive propositions required by deductive logic, and whether all or some a priori statements are tautologous. Furthermore, where was philosophy in times of crisis? For example, the "three most prominent schools of ethical thought . . . hold respectively that the moral philosophy of the past 'rests on a mistake,' that moral standards are group customs with no validity beyond the group, and that moral judgments have no significance at all."[10]

The critics charged that there was no agreement on what philosophy says, that its knowledge was imperfect, that it could not unite the disciplines nor achieve competence in them, and that philosophers were negative "artists of demolition of belief." Finally, philosophers were crabbed in expression, needlessly technical, unlike John Stuart Mill and William James, who could talk to plain men.

It is natural enough that young writers who feel uncertain of themselves should stud their text with technicalities; they want the record to show that they know the tools of their trade; and if it does show that, they are content to forget for the time that a "platitude is not turned into a profundity by being dressed up as a conundrum." But when this and worse are done by veteran philosophers, supposed in virtue of their profession to be connoisseurs of clear and orderly exposition, readers are not likely to be tolerant.[11]

These criticisms of philosophy were not new. They reflected the high expectations nurtured by speculative idealism, which dominated the closing years of the nineteenth century in which philosophy in America first won wide recognition as an autonomous field of study. It was the time of Howison, Royce, Creighton, Wenley, and their associates. The philosopher was the "judge and critic of both science and theology," and the philosophical criticism was to be based on "speculative insight into the nature of ultimate reality."[12]

10. Brand Blanshard, "The Climate of Opinion," in Blanshard et al., *Philosophy in American Education*, p. 32.

11. Ibid., p. 38.

12. Arthur E. Murphy, "The Situation in American Philosophy," in Blanshard et al., *Philosophy in American Education*, p. 45.

Murphy remarked:

> Their [the Absolute Idealists] warrant to speak for Absolute Reality . . . has been called in question. But in presenting to their confused contemporaries the ideal of rational wholeness and of comprehensive justice to all aspects of experience . . . they performed an essential philosophical function.[13]

It is important to note that the Pragmatism of William James and John Dewey had already challenged speculative idealism, and that by the time the book was published various types of Realism and Naturalism had been challenging both Idealism and Pragmatism. It was an age of isms, and thinkers could take their choice of them.

In the late 1920s and most of the 1930s, the Commission noted, the college student was introduced to philosophy by a study of types or isms in which the instructor maintained a more or less neutral stance. It was this pattern that was adopted by both yearbooks. However, the relation of the yearbooks to the content and modes of inquiry in general philosophy is harder to match upon the basis of the Commission report. For example, Murphy notes that in the 1940s philosophy had already witnessed a strong interest in formal or symbolic logic. Logic was to be studied as a discipline, but also as a tool to get rid of many "pseudo" problems in metaphysics. He adds, however, that:

> Meanwhile the battle of the positivists and the metaphysicians has bred a suspicion of symbolic logic in the traditionalist camp and a contempt of historical philosophy among the analysts.[14]

One does not get a strong impression of these developments in the Forty-first Yearbook, and if I am not mistaken, even the Fifty-fourth Yearbook does not reflect the extent to which general philosophy had become devoted to the logical purification of philosophical discourse, despite the inclusion of Feigl's chapter on logical empiricism. On the other hand, it is a bit surprising that the Commission Report published in 1945 did not include in its index the names of Wittgenstein, Kierkegaard, Husserl, and Heidegger, possibly because they had not yet become established in the general introductory courses in philosophy.

One is hard put to decide whether Murphy was premature or

---
13. Ibid., p. 47.
14. Ibid., p. 57.

prescient in his estimate of the effect of the strong critical emphasis in philosophy. He concluded that "this dialectical achievement has failed, so far at least, to eventuate in any corresponding philosophical wisdom or to make effective connection with the public mind." He continues:

> Nor is the reason for all this at all hard to find. Most men who turn to philosophy for guidance [and surely educators must be included here] want not arguments but conclusions; they are concerned not so much to avoid error as to arrive at truth. . . . What seems to be established is that the major philosophies so far devised have involved grave lapses in logical or linguistic propriety, and that while, properly translated into an analytically purified language, they might possibly be true, there is no good reason to suppose that in any case they are. The better we understand logic, Bertrand Russell has characteristically remarked, the less we find that we can prove and the more, consequently, that we must accept on nonlogical grounds, if we are not to land in a rationally immaculate but unlivable skepticism.[15]

The failure of philosophy to make effective connection with the public mind did not disturb professional philosophy unduly; nor did it abandon its concern with logical and semantic purity. For that matter, it did not discourage a similar concern among the younger generation of educational philosophers in the late 1950s and 1960s.[16] Unfortunately, school people cannot operate with "a rationally immaculate but unlivable skepticism." One must say "unfortunately" because there is no denying the intrinsic satisfaction that theory people get from just "playing" with ideas, whether they "work" or not. Philosophers of education can and should experience this joy also, and happy is the society that can afford to let them do so, but no "philosophy of" can be *all* games and no work, something that graduate departments of education and doctoral candidates will have to face.[17] Philosophy of education must

15. Ibid., p. 55.

16. Perhaps the most easily accessible sources to support this assertion are the Proceedings of the Philosophy of Education Society. See also Harry S. Broudy et al., *Philosophy of Education: An Organization of Topics and Selected Sources* (Urbana, Ill.: University of Illinois Press, 1967).

17. What Russell's remark comes to is that the better our logic, the narrower the context of the statement being examined becomes and existential situations resist such narrowing. It is difficult to find human situations to which the educational context is totally irrelevant; and it is almost as difficult to find educational contexts to which anything is irrelevant.

connect with education. This Eightieth Yearbook tries to make the connection by way of linking educational concerns to various subareas of philosophy.

It would take a careful historical study to establish the precise synchrony between the views entertained by general philosophers and philosophers of education and perhaps it is not too important to do so. In any event, the expansion of the doctoral program in the philosophy of education, as has previously been noted, greatly reduced whatever lag had existed. More important is that as philosophy of education shifted more of its attention to the logical and linguistic analysis of educational concepts and problems, it shifted away from the "isms" approach. Israel Scheffler's development of views on the nature of knowledge and teaching based on Gilbert Ryle's theory of mind, R. S. Peters's work on the nature of motivation and education as a form of initiation, Paul Hirst's writings on the forms of knowledge, and Philip Phenix's realms of meaning, to cite a few, illustrate that shift. In another direction, B. O. Smith's project at Illinois on the analysis of classroom discourse introduced a number of graduate students into the literature of the British analysts. Moral reasoning, which attracted a good deal of philosophical attention during the 1950s and 1960s, also had its reverberations among philosophers of education, as did philosophical discussions of scientific inquiry. The shifts in the philosophizing about education also reflected the organization of topics in departments of philosophy along the lines of subareas of philosophy such as the philosophy of science, ethics, aesthetics, and social philosophy, suggesting the framework for this yearbook.

The shift was most rapid in colleges of education located in research-oriented universities that concentrated on advanced graduate study; somewhat less rapid in schools devoting their major efforts to undergraduate teacher preparation; and much less in the minds and discourse of school personnel, who learned their philosophy of education from texts that used the "isms" format. What effect will a yearbook not organized by "isms" but by subareas of philosophy have on school people who may very well constitute an important segment of the school establishment? This volume is designed to provide them with another way to conceive of philosophy of education and to match their concerns to its literature.

However, there are bound to be problems in trying to alter a deep-rooted conception.

Aside from the circumstance that courses in philosophy frequently had been organized by the isms in college departments—although much less so now—there was a belief that each philosophical system as it formulated an epistemology, metaphysics, and ethics would ground beliefs about the real, the true, and the good. Hence the notion that an ism or a well worked out system of philosophy would yield a rational guidance to life and education seemed obvious. The layman, one can be sure, will continue to identify philosophy with a search for and love of wisdom, even though college catalogs almost never include wisdom among offerings of departments of philosophy.[18] Likewise, the layman will continue to look to a philosophy of education for more than logical purity, wholesome skepticism, and focused concern on a single subarea like logic or philosophy of science. People are not and do not want schools to be neutral about the life they want for their children as citizens, workers, and persons.

Whether there is a logical warrant for finding such guidance and norms in systems of philosophy is another matter. During the 1950s there was much heated debate among philosophers of education as to whether a value "ought" could be deduced from a factual "is," and whether prescriptions for educational practice could be determined from a theory about the good in general.[19] The positivists were pushing the fact-value distinction for all that it was or was not worth, depriving assertions of value of all empirical truth claims—and no others were regarded by them as legitimate. Doubt was expressed that the nature of man could be arrived at rationally by any system of inquiry or definition, and that even if the *telos*, the natural end of man, could be discovered, it would still leave open the question as to whether it was good. But all of this took place in the academy and had relatively little effect on the educational practitioner's convictions that some forms of con-

18. Wisdom, as the late W. Oliver Martin observed, is studied in the English department, and language in the philosophy department.

19. See the papers published in the *Harvard Educational Review* 26 (Spring 1956) and 28 (Fall 1958) and in the *Journal of Philosophy* 52, no. 22 (1955).

duct were more consonant with the ideals of humanity than others. The layman is incurably metaphysical, and if the philosophy of education ignores or merely makes fun of this need, it will be satisfied from nonphilosophical sources. How to deal with this demand philosophically without resorting to a comparison of isms was a paramount problem for this yearbook.

However, we believe we have entered and gone some way into a period in which both general and educational philosophy have turned more of their attention to substantive questions that have always engaged systematic philosophies but from another avenue of approach. These problems are the current versions of the perennial conflict between freedom and necessity, individuality and the common good, personhood and the mass society, justice and compassion, mores and morals, mass and class, truth and credibility, and have brought with them renewed vigor to work in social philosophy and ethics.[20] The concern with social justice, the environment, peace, the third world, and many other agitations of the late 1960s and the early 1970s have given impetus to neo-Marxism, a variety of existentialisms, cultism, and even occultism in academia, not excluding the departments of philosophy and philosophy of education. Humanism and the problems of humanity that students discussed in courses organized according to isms are once more in the forefront of scholarly attention, albeit the new and the old humanisms do not always sound like variations on the same theme.

Concern with modern science and its epistemology has affected theories of critical thinking in school work. Piaget's work on genetic epistemology has had reverberations in the philosophy of education both with respect to the development of levels of cognition and with levels of moral reasoning. Ethics has exfoliated into medical ethics, business ethics, and professional education in general. Circumstances have virtually forced all our major professions and institutions to respond to ethical questions, and the writings in philosophy of education reflect these concerns. Indeed, philosophy of education, once reserved for the foundational work in teacher preparation, now is becoming part of the curricula of

20. A notable example was the widespread attention given to John Rawls, *A Theory of Justice* (Cambridge, Mass.: Belknap Press, 1971).

medical schools, schools of law, commerce, and engineering. This yearbook reflects the variety, increased specialization, and scope of contemporary work in philosophy of education.

The Third Yearbook

It may be of some significance that twenty-five years will have elapsed between the last yearbook on the philosophy of education and the current one. Only thirteen years separated the first two. Surely it does not signify a lack of writing in the field that needed summarizing. On the contrary, an examination of the *Proceedings of the Philosophy of Education Society, Educational Theory, Studies in Philosophy and Education*, text materials, and the like reveals a high volume of work in the 1950s and 1960s.

A more plausible conjecture is that between 1955 and 1970, the year when another yearbook might have been expected, the styles of doing philosophy of education and the problems facing philosophers of education had both changed too radically to permit a definitive summarization. The movement away from the isms approach had begun, but the analysis of particular topics or concepts for meaning or validity of usage had not yet captured the field. There was still much debate at the annual meetings and in the journals as to the proper role and method of philosophy of education. The older isms were being abandoned, but new ones, such as existentialism, phenomenology, and Zen, were rising in popularity and a new humanism was struggling to acquire philosophical shape. Equality, self-hood, justice were being treated by analysis on the one hand, and from within the perspectives of the new humanism on the other. The concept of alienation, for example, was a target for existential and linguistic analysis, Hegelian interpretation, psychoanalytic theory, and revolutionary literature of the left. By 1970 these various currents of thought had not fully defined themselves and the social changes that gave rise to them had not yet reached their culmination.[21] More of the writing was devoted to the analysis of individual concepts (for example, needs, interests, teaching, action, indoctrination) and less to the develop-

21. For items published up to 1974 see the bibliographies compiled by Thomas W. Nelson in *Studies in Philosophy and Education* 9 (Summer 1975): 166-206.

ment of a system of ideas grounded in this or that philosophical tradition. A number of collections of such analyses were published and were used as texts of supplementary readings in courses in the philosophy of education.[22]

The length of the interval may also be a result of problems created by the new relationships between school administrators, teachers, institutions that prepare teachers, and the bureaucratic workers in the U.S. Department of Health, Education, and Welfare and in the National Institute of Education, and half a hundred other federal and state agencies that funded, regulated, or monitored schools after the mid-1960s. In 1965, civil rights legislation marked a watershed in schooling at all levels. There followed a great upheaval on campuses about matters that touched fundamental issues in truth and value, the relation of school to society. The public schools had lost the steadying momentum furnished them by the mores and aspirations of the middle class. Democracy, the work ethic, the perfectibility of humankind through education, social mobility for those who were willing to work and study, justified public and relatively free education from kindergarten through the university. In the aftermath of the Vietnam war, this momentum was not fully restored. Many members of the middle class themselves accepted liberation from the mores, notably those associated with sex and self. The human rights legislation loosed a flood of litigation not only by dissidents of one kind or another but for all citizens who were alerted to golden opportunities by armies of lawyers for whom every new piece of legislation created new potential clients. Individualism, cultural pluralism, the new hedonism—the need to do one's own thing—have undercut the foundations that permitted the American public school to go about the business of instruction without worrying about or even giving explicit attention to the social and moral assumptions on which it operated. The curriculum, the organization, and style of instruction today are more responses to specific

22. Among the earlier volumes of this sort were Israel Scheffler, *The Language of Education* (Springfield, Ill.: C. C. Thomas, 1960), *Language and Concepts in Education*, ed. B. Othanel Smith and Robert Ennis (Chicago: Rand McNally, 1961, and R. D. Archambault, *Philosophical Analysis and Education* (New York: Humanities Press, 1965). The latter volume was expressly designed to make American readers familiar with the British writers on the philosophy of education.

legislative mandates for the mainstreaming of handicapped children, bilingual education, special education of various kinds than expressions of an ethos or philosophy.

It would be strange indeed if the schools were not affected by these changes and if they would not reflect the ambiguities of parents and citizens toward their children, their spouses, their new life-styles.

The rapid shifts at about five-year intervals from a curriculum devoted to excellence in science and mathematics to one that concentrated on compassion for and understanding of the newly enfranchised minorities and thence to a return to basics were symptoms of shifts in social ideology. The accountability movements and the efforts of the federal government to implement civil and human rights legislation were matters of morality as well as economics and law. The rapidly changing "life-styles" revived once more demands for moral education, which were also cries to philosophers for help. In answering these cries, or at least discussing them, philosophers of education were splashed by more existential mud than they might have wished and more help was expected than they could deliver.

It is not surprising, therefore, that philosophers of education began to address these problems. In one book of readings called *Philosophy for a New Generation*, for example, the section headings included: The New Generation, Philosophy and the Ideology of the University, Morality: Old and New, Love and Sex, Hedonism and Beyond, Rules and Situations, Up against the Law, Third World Liberation, Political Flux: Freedom, Violence, and Revolution, the Impact of Technology, Search for Self and Identity, God and Religion, Flight from Meaninglessness.[23]

Paulo Freire's *Pedagogy for the Oppressed* and *Education for the Critical Consciousness*[24] together with Ivan Illich's writings on deschooling society were of a piece with the complaints of Paul Goodman, Edgar Z. Friedenberg, Jonathan Kozol, and John Holt

23. Arthur K. Bierman and James A. Gould, eds., *Philosophy for a New Generation* (London: Macmillan, 1970).

24. Paulo Friere, *Pedagogy for the Oppressed* (New York: Herder and Herder, 1970); idem, *Education for the Critical Consciousness* (New York: Seabury Press, 1974).

against the public schools and of revisionist historians who demythologized the virtues claimed for them and their advocates. Philosophers and quasi-philosophers of education, as well as educational journalists, contributed to the discussion; the distinctions among them are hard to fix, but one might suppose that the contributions of the philosophers were more sensitive to the niceties of logic and language in expressing sentiments they shared with the others.

These topics were continuous with the traditional concern of philosophers of education about the problems of school and society. They differed in their intensity, variety, and their relation to activist movements on and off the campus. In any event, the climate of theory and opinion was more unsettled and turbid than the general anxieties that inspired the Fifty-fourth Yearbook, and how could the yearbook committee have arrived at consensus on organizing them in any definitive and even mildly authoritative way?[25]

In other words, the developments of the last quarter of a century do not fit comfortably within the organization of the first two yearbooks, and in this yearbook the shift from that organization reflects it. There is little doubt that the departure from the isms approach to a categorization by subareas of philosophy will disturb many educators who were introduced to the philosophy of education and perhaps to philosophy itself through introductory courses of the isms kind. At least one important professional group is currently spending considerable time and money classify-

25. An attempt to make some sort of judicious selection of philosophical writings bearing on problems of education was made under a grant from the U.S. Department of Health, Education, and Welfare. Its form was a precursor to that of this Eightieth Yearbook, being arranged both by educational theme (aims, curriculum, organization, teaching-learning) and by subareas of philosophy. With the help of a task force made up of philosophers of education and many consultants, the selection was accomplished and published. Broudy et al., *Philosophy of Education: An Organization of Topics and Selected Sources.* A supplement was issued by Broudy and Christiana M. Smith in 1969, and still another by Ronald P. Jeffrey in 1971. The more specialized interests and activities of philosophers of education is also reflected in the Seventy-first Yearbook of the Society, Part 1, *Philosophical Redirection of Educational Research,* ed. Thomas, and in the volume of the American Educational Research Association on the same topic in its series on research, Harry S. Broudy, Robert H. Ennis, and Leonard I. Krimerman, eds., *Philosophy of Educational Research* (New York: John Wiley and Sons, 1973).

ing its own goals, policies, organization, and procedures according to five isms. Logical niceties about the validity of the approach do not weaken their conviction that each of the five philosophies is a distinctive way of looking at knowledge, reality, and value, and that seeing education through these lenses will reveal something important about their own field. They also believe that the view through each lens or stencil will have a certain internal consistency, so that the left hand will know what the right hand is supposed to be doing. The workers in curriculum, for example, because of this consistency, will not frustrate the workers in policy or methods of teaching. Somehow this wholeness of view and internal consistency need to be preserved, and a yearbook that does not organize and classify the domains of education will leave many educators disappointed.

I believe that there is no alternative to study of isms *somewhere* in general education.

To know the chief rival attitudes toward life, as the history of human thinking has developed them, and to have heard some of the reasons they can give for themselves, ought to be considered an essential part of liberal education. Philosophy, indeed, in one sense of the term is only a compendious name for the spirit in education which the word "college" stands for in America.[26]

Speculative philosophy is the endeavor to frame a coherent, logical, necessary system of general ideas in terms of which every element of our experience can be interpreted.[27]

The history of these systems is part of the cultural tradition, and if one could insist on some work in the history of philosophy prior to admission to professional education curricula, this background could be presupposed in courses in the philosophy of education. In a college of education that took professional preparation of teachers seriously such courses would be included in the preprofessional prerequisites, thus obviating the need of what have often been denigrated as watered down courses in the parent discipline.

26. William James, *Some Problems of Philosophy* (New York: Longmans, Green and Co., 1911), p. 6.

27. Alfred N. Whitehead, *Process and Reality* (New York: Macmillan Co., 1929), p. 4.

Given such basic familiarity with the history of philosophy and philosophical problems, the course in the philosophy of education could concentrate on the philosophical treatment of educational issues or problems.

But this is just another way of saying that philosophy of education can help the educator think through the major educational problems and issues of the day and the days to come. If the philosophy of education does not provide a set of *Weltanschaungen*, it can provide a literature that pushes the implications and presuppositions of educational policies and practices to the very brink of such views—where what is really real, good, and true are relevant questions.

Philosophy of education has no consensus on ultimate truth, albeit this does not prove that ultimate truths do not exist nor that some minds may have access to them. If this volume does not set forth an array of world outlooks or alternative philosophical stances, it can do for educators what the Blanshard Commission concluded philosophy could contribute to a "faith for living," namely (a) "[it could contribute] a reflective, discursive, rationally examinable inquiry into the warrant of beliefs which lay claim to ultimate or final validity" and (b) "[it could] be the intellectual conscience of the community—to measure all special interests, half-truths, and half-hearted ideals which claim final authority or ultimate validity, by the most penetrating and comprehensive standards of truth and adequacy that can rationally be maintained." [28] It is to be hoped that this volume will indicate where and how this work is being done, where philosophy of education has been, and where it plans to go.

What Have Educators a Right to Expect from Philosophy of Education?

1. They have a right to expect that philosophers of education will address themselves to problems of education in general and how those problems impinge on schooling. Problems arising in the formulation of aims, curriculum, organization, teaching-learning, and the methodology of research qualify as educational problems. Not all educational problems are philosophical, however. Some are

28. Blanshard et al., pp. 79, 80.

technical; some economic; some are administrative; some have to do with matters of fact; some appeal to theories of empirical science. It is only when an educational problem has a philosophical dimension that philosophy becomes relevant. Indeed, one of the more useful services philosophers of education can render is to point out just what sort of philosophical perspective or method is relevant to some educational problem. In this connection the educator has a related right not to be expected to cope with technical problems in philosophy or educational problems couched in highly technical philosophical language.

Yet there is a limit to what the philosopher can do by way of translation for school people who have not had some work in the philosophy of education and preferably in general philosophy as well. This is why courses in philosophy of education should be part of the professional preparation of all educational personnel and some work in general philosophy should be required as a preprofessional prerequisite.

2. Educators have a right to expect from philosophers of education a clarification and elucidation of concepts and arguments used in educational literature, especially in the literature of educational controversy. Voucher systems, minimum competency testing, equality of educational opportunity, integration are examples of such concepts and issues. The educator can expect from the philosopher of education (a) reasoned proposals to use terms in one way rather than another so that ambiguity, equivocation, and vagueness can be eliminated, (b) reasoned proposals that a controversy be adjudicated in one way rather than another. What school people cannot expect is consensus on usage or judgment from the philosophers. (Aside from the fact that philosophers are not likely to agree on philosophical issues, issues cease to be philosophical when such agreement is reached—at least they cease to be of philosophical interest once they are settled.)

3. School people have a right to expect from the philosopher of education a careful examination of proposals and policies with respect to their consequences and possibilities, in the round, so to speak. This the philosopher of education does by examining issues in a variety of contexts: social, moral, ideological. For example, the moral dimension of the *Bakke* decision is properly a

philosophical problem, but it is also the business of the philosophy of education to explicate its political and educational consequences as well.[29]

4. Educators also have the right to expect from at least some writers in the philosophy of education a synoptic, systematic, coherent set of beliefs and arguments about education that deals with the educational enterprise as a whole and that makes connection with a philosophy of life.

5. Finally, educators have a right to expect from philosophy of education a strong and steady advocacy of rational discussion, freedom of inquiry, and instead of a fixed faith "an interest and standard from which reliable beliefs can spring."[30]

One cannot expect everyone writing in the field to fulfill all of these expectations. There is bound to be a diversity of interest with a corresponding variety of literatures from which courses in the philosophy of education will be composed. But it is fair to expect that good courses in philosophy of education will introduce students to the philosophical aspects of the major issues in education.

29. Allen Bakke was denied admission to the Medical School of the University of California at Davis. The U.S. Supreme Court upheld Bakke's contention that a quota system kept him out in favor of minority candidates with lower admission scores.

30. Blanshard et al., p. 108.

Curriculum Theory

Two major themes in twentieth century curriculum theory have been the philosophical elaboration of the nature of knowledge and the restatement and elucidation of the dominant Western ideal of a liberal education. During the past fifty years, generations of educators have been introduced to the idea of a liberal education by reading the works of such philosophers as Whitehead, Newman, Hutchins, Adler, Maritain, and the famous "Harvard Report," *General Education in a Free Society* (Cambridge, Mass.: Harvard University Press, 1945). After Sputnik, the increasing emphasis on the structure of knowledge as the key to curricular thinking was given voice by Jerome Bruner, Joseph J. Schwab, and Philip H. Phenix, was translated into the "new curricula" of the late 1950s and early 1960s, and was presented systematically to educators by B. Othanel Smith, Harry S. Broudy, and Joe Burnett in their volume *Democracy and Excellence in American Secondary Education* (Chicago: Rand McNally, 1964). In this chapter, Jane Martin addresses these two persistent philosophical themes of the idea of a liberal education and the attempt to ground curriculum theory in the nature of knowledge. (Editor)

CHAPTER III

Needed: A New Paradigm for Liberal Education

JANE ROLAND MARTIN

The Forms of Knowledge Theory

Curriculum, in the sense of decision making about what should be learned, is here to stay. There was a time in the late 1960s and early 1970s when its disappearance was momentarily expected. But in fact, even if the educational reforms proposed during those years had been generally adopted, curriculum would not have vanished. It was thought that it would disappear if students were in charge of their own learning; it was not realized that curriculum need not be compulsory and does not require for its survival that some knowledge be essential for all. It was thought that it would disappear once we deschooled society; it was not realized that curriculum can outlive schools. So long as people try to educate one another, or even simply themselves, decisions about what is to be learned will remain a central fact of life.

I draw attention to the persistent character of curriculum because educational fashions change so quickly. As I write, discussions of the basics, of liberal education, of minimal competency testing—all of them in large part discussions of curriculum—are in the news. By the time this is read, educational issues with less obvious ties to curriculum may have replaced these in the public consciousness. If so, curriculum will still demand our serious consideration.

Sad to say, contemporary philosophers of education have not given curriculum its due. I am not sure why. They have not, in the manner of the radical school reformers, expected curriculum

---

I wish to thank Ann Diller, Nancy Glock, Michael Martin, Beatrice Nelson, the editorial committee for this volume, and my colleagues for helpful comments on two drafts of this chapter.

to disappear. Perhaps they have taken it for granted, perhaps they have underestimated its importance, perhaps they have found it too hot to handle. Whatever the reason, contemporary philosophical investigation of curriculum has for some time been in a rut: it has focused on a very limited range of curricular questions and has endorsed a theory of curriculum that is seriously deficient.

The curricular theory to which I refer was first expounded by Hirst in a widely read article.[1] It has since been elaborated by Dearden,[2] by Peters in collaboration with Hirst,[3] and by Hirst himself in a number of papers in his volume *Knowledge and the Curriculum*.[4] Anyone who remembers the movement for curricular reform of the post-Sputnik era and Bruner's popular book entitled *The Process of Education*, or is acquainted with the curriculum theory set forth by Phenix, or with that presented by Broudy, Smith, and Burnett will find the broad outlines, if not all the details, of Hirst's "forms of knowledge" theory familiar.[5] I have chosen to discuss Hirst's theory here, rather than one of these others, because his is the one that has come to dominate the thinking of philosophers of education. To use Kuhn's language, Hirst's theory has become one of *the* paradigms in the field of philosophy of education. Just as scientists articulate the paradigms of what Kuhn calls "normal science,"[6] so Hirst with the help of both

1. Paul H. Hirst, "Liberal Education and the Nature of Knowledge," in *Philosophical Analysis and Education*, ed. Reginald D. Archambault (London: Routledge and Kegan Paul, 1965), pp. 113-38. Reprinted as chapter 3 in Paul H. Hirst, *Knowledge and the Curriculum* (London: Routledge and Kegan Paul, 1974). (All page references to Hirst appearing in parentheses in the text are to this latter volume.)

2. R. F. Dearden, *The Philosophy of Primary Education* (London: Routledge and Kegan Paul, 1968).

3. R. S. Peters and Paul H. Hirst, *The Logic of Education* (London: Routledge and Kegan Paul, 1970).

4. Hirst, *Knowledge and the Curriculum*.

5. Jerome S. Bruner, *The Process of Education* (Cambridge: Harvard University Press, 1961); Philip Phenix, *Realms of Meaning* (New York: McGraw-Hill, 1964); Harry S. Broudy, B. Othanel Smith, and Joe R. Burnett, *Democracy and Excellence in American Secondary Education: A Study in Curriculum Theory* (Chicago: Rand McNally, 1964).

6. Thomas S. Kuhn, *The Structure of Scientific Revolutions* (Chicago: University of Chicago Press, 2d ed., 1970). For a critical discussion of Kuhn's theory and an application of it to Hirst, see chapter 10 in this volume.

colleagues and critics has clarified and modified his forms of knowledge theory of liberal education.

Behind Hirst's theory lies a conception of liberal education as the development of mind and the identification of the achievement of knowledge with that development. Upon this foundation rests Hirst's thesis that a liberal education is an initiation into the forms of knowledge.

In his original statement of the theory Hirst distinguished seven forms of knowledge: mathematics, physical sciences, human sciences, history, religion, literature and the fine arts, philosophy (p. 46). He has since taken history and the human sciences off the list, replacing them with moral judgment and understanding of our own and other people's minds. In doing so he has made clear what some readers did not realize, namely that the original list did not refer to disciplines, but that the forms of knowledge are to be understood as classes of true propositions. Thus, history and the human sciences have been dropped from the list not because Hirst now questions their disciplinary status, but because he has come to believe that their statements are not *sui generis:* some of them are truths about the physical world, some are truths of a mental or personal kind, and some presumably are moral or even aesthetic judgments (pp. 86-87).

Hirst takes the seven forms to embrace commonsense as well as technical knowledge (p. 90). He also takes the forms to be irreducible (pp. 84, 89-90). He does not mean by this that they have nothing in common, that they share no concepts and logical rules with one another; his claim seems simply to be that each form has *some* unique concepts *and some* distinctive network of relations between concepts. The forms are not, however, eternal and immutable in Hirst's view (p. 92). They are human creations and as such are open to change; indeed, Hirst holds not only that each form can change, but that new forms can be created (p. 95).

Hirst makes it very clear that the forms of knowledge theory is compatible with different patterns of curriculum organization: for example, a curriculum with subjects like mathematics, physics, literature, and philosophy; or a curriculum organized around what he calls fields (as opposed to forms) of knowledge such as geography and engineering; or even a curriculum involving practical projects of design and building. Decisions about the organization of a curriculum are to be made on a variety of practical grounds, which he does not attempt to specify. For these decisions to be in accord with Hirst's theory of liberal education, it is essential that the curriculum organization in question serve to initiate students into each of the seven forms (p. 51).

Initiation must not be confused with the acquisition of encyclopedic information or the expertise of a specialist. A liberal education, in Hirst's view, is neither a technical nor a specialized one. Hirst characterizes initiation as sufficient immersion in the concepts, logic, and criteria of a form of knowledge for a person to come to know the distinctive way in which it works; a coming to look at things in a certain way is what is wanted, and along with this an outline of the major achievements in each area so as to grasp the range and scope of experience that it has made intelligible (pp. 47-8).

The many critics of Hirst's theory of liberal education have concentrated on his analysis of knowledge. Thus, they have questioned his classification of art, religion, and morality as forms of knowledge;[7] they have challenged the criteria he uses to differentiate the various forms;[8] they have taken him to task for claiming that the forms can change;[9] they have argued that common sense should be recognized as a distinct form.[10] Important as

---

7. See, for example, A. J. Watt, "Forms of Knowledge and Norms of Rationality," *Educational Philosophy and Theory* 6 (March 1974): 1-11; Robin Barrow, *Common Sense and the Curriculum* (London: George Allen and Unwin, 1976), chap. 2; James Gribble, "Forms of Knowledge," *Educational Philosophy and Theory* 2 (March 1970): 3-14. See Hirst's reply to Gribble, "Literature, Criticism, and the Forms of Knowledge," *Educational Philosophy and Theory* 3 (April 1971): 11-18. Reprinted in Hirst, *Knowledge and the Curriculum*, chap. 10.

8. See, for example, Gribble, "Forms of Knowledge"; D. C. Phillips, "The Distinguishing Features of Forms of Knowledge," *Educational Philosophy and Theory* 3 (October 1971): 27-35; idem, "Perspectives on Structure of Knowledge and the Curriculum" in *Contemporary Studies in the Curriculum*, ed. Peter W. Musgrave (Sydney: Angus and Robertson, 1974).

9. Allen Brent, *Philosophical Foundations for the Curriculum* (London: George Allen and Unwin, 1978), chap. 3.

10. John P. White, *Towards a Compulsory Curriculum* (London: Routledge and Kegan Paul, 1973), chap. 6.

criticisms of this sort are, they do not get at the heart of the matter, in part because so many of them seem to share Hirst's basic and mistaken assumption that the nature and structure of knowledge determines the nature and structure of a liberal education and in part because the form in which he presents his theory makes deeper criticism seem inappropriate.[11] Hirst's assumption about knowledge will be examined in the third section of this chapter, and in the fourth section the implications of the sharp separation between mind and body implicit in the forms of knowledge theory will be discussed. First, however, I want to make clear the extent to which that theory is narrow and intolerant.

Kuhn has shown us that when a scientific paradigm faces serious problems the time for scientific revolution has come. I hope to show here that Hirst's theory has major flaws that no modification or clarification will remedy. It is a paradigm in need of a revolution. The object of this chapter, then, is to get philosophical investigation of curriculum out of its rut by challenging the existing paradigm, thereby extending the range of questions to which philosophers should devote attention. In the last sections I will sketch in the bare outlines of an alternative paradigm and will argue, even as I do so, that philosophical investigation of curriculum must go beyond liberal education.

Ivory Tower People

The forms of knowledge theory conceives of liberal education as the acquisition of knowledge and understanding. In so doing it ignores feelings and emotions and other so-called "noncognitive" states and processes of mind.[12] Except for what Hirst calls "the arts and techniques of different types of reasoning and judgment"

---

11. In *Epistemology and Education* (New York: Harvest, forthcoming), Michael Matthews does get to the heart of the matter after providing an especially clear, comprehensive account of the development of Hirst's theory. Some of the points to be made here were reached independently by Matthews.

12. I qualify my introduction of the term "noncognitive" in this way to indicate that, although I am following ordinary usage, I do not mean to commit myself to the view that there is a hard and fast distinction between the cognitive and the noncognitive.

(p. 47), it also ignores *procedural knowledge* or *knowledge how*.[18] Complex conceptual schemes are to be acquired, but aside from the "know how" involved in using them, knowing how to do something (for example, playing the violin, riding a bicycle, writing a well-organized essay, or managing a political campaign), is not primarily a matter of having learned concepts, logic, and criteria. Rather, it is a matter of having learned skills and procedures.

Needless to say, as a result of its identification of liberal education with initiation into the forms of knowledge, the received curriculum theory of our day places physical education and vocational training beyond the pale of a liberal education. What is perhaps less apparent, but equally important, is that it also excludes from a liberal education the development of artistic performance, the acquisition of language skills including the learning of a second language, and education for effective moral action as opposed simply to moral judgment.

A natural criticism to make of the forms of knowledge theory is that it is unduly narrow. As Hirst himself has said, it excludes all objectives other than intellectual ones and even the intellectual ends it seeks are limited (p. 96). He has made it clear, however, that his is a theory of liberal education, not the whole of education. Thus, feelings and emotions and procedural knowledge are not barred from a person's education; they simply fall outside the boundaries of a liberal education. When the fact that Hirst calls his concept of liberal education "stipulative" (p. 96) is added to the restricted domain of his theory, he seems to have an airtight defense against the charge of narrowness. We cannot claim that liberal education is not by nature as narrow as he suggests it is, for he is stipulating its nature—making it up, if you will—and he surely has the right to do this in any way he sees fit. We cannot claim that the things the forms of knowledge theory leaves out

13. Hirst himself points this out (p. 57). For a criticism of Hirst based on this point, see Ormond Smythe, "On the Theory of Forms of Knowledge," in *Philosophy of Education 1978*, Proceedings of the Thirty-fourth Annual Meeting of the Philosophy of Education Society (Champaign, Ill.: the Society, 1979), pp. 28-39. For the classic account of *knowledge how*, see Gilbert Ryle, *The Concept of Mind* (London: Hutchinson's University Library, 1947), chap. 2.

are important to learn whereas the theory deems them to be unimportant, for Hirst never says they are not important; he simply leaves them for other theorists of education to consider. Small wonder Hirst's critics have focused on his analysis of knowledge. He has left nothing else open to attack.

Still, we ought not to ignore the fact that Hirst has chosen to call the conception of education he has formulated "liberal education," for this label is not neutral. Over the years liberal education has been thought of as an education having great value, indeed as an education having greater value than any other; we look down on education that is illiberal, some of us even refusing to call it education at all. It seems as if we cannot condemn Hirst's theory for being narrow because it is not a theory of all education. Yet as Hirst must realize, "liberal education" is an honorific title. Suppose he had used the label "intellectual education" instead. Would his theory have been taken as seriously as it has been by philosophers of education? Would it have come to dominate thinking in the field so that to all intents and purposes it has become a theory of the whole of education deemed valuable? Surely not.

Philosophers of education today never ask the question, "What is left over when we subtract a liberal education from the whole of education?" Seldom, if ever, do they try to develop theories to supplement Hirst's. Hirst is not to be condemned either for devoting his considerable philosophical talents to elaborating a theory having limited intellectual objectives or for the uses to which others have put that theory. At the same time we should recognize that his theory has taken on a life of its own at least in part because Hirst has traded on the label "liberal education." The forms of knowledge theory has become the received theory not just of intellectual education but of that education deemed valuable, at least in part because Hirst has presented it as a theory of liberal education and liberal education is thought to exhaust that education which is valuable. In judging the forms of knowledge theory, therefore, we need to remember the limited claims Hirst has made for it, but we must also feel free to go beyond Hirst's explicit intentions. Granted he does not claim to be setting forth a theory of education in general, we must still ask if the forms of knowledge theory provides a tenable account of all education deemed valuable. Granted his concept of liberal education is stipulative, we must ask what the programmatic implications of Hirst's stipulations are.[14]

The great irony of Hirst's theory of liberal education is that it is neither tolerant nor generous: it conceives of liberal education as the development of mind, restricts the development of mind to the acquisition of knowledge and understanding, and restricts knowledge to true propositions. Because the gap between liberal education and the whole of education tends to be obscured and liberal education has come to be equated with that education deemed valuable, this series of restrictions has grave practical consequences. The best way to grasp them is to envision the "products" of a liberal education conceived of as an initiation into the forms of knowledge.

The received theory's liberally educated person will be taught to see the world through the lenses of the seven forms of knowledge, if seven there be, but not to act in the world. Nor will that person be encouraged to acquire feelings and emotions. The theory's liberally educated person will be provided with knowledge about others, but will not be taught to care about their welfare, let alone to act kindly toward them. That person will be given some understanding of society, but will not be taught to feel its injustices or even to be concerned over its fate. The received theory conceives of a liberally educated person as an ivory tower person: one who can reason, but has no desire to solve real problems in the real world; one who understands science, but does not worry about the uses to which it is put; one who grasps the concepts of biology, but is not disposed to exercise or eat wisely; one who can reach flawless moral conclusions, but has neither the sensitivity nor the skill to carry them out effectively.

We make fun of ivory tower people—their interests are so

---

14. For a discussion of programmatic and stipulative definitions, see Israel Scheffler, *The Language of Education* (Springfield, Ill.: Charles C. Thomas, 1960), chap. 1. The reader is referred also to Robert H. Ennis, "Rational Thinking and Educational Practice" in this volume and to Ennis's discussion of impact equivocation in his presidential address to the Philosophy of Education Society in 1979. See *Philosophy of Education 1979*, Proceedings of the Thirty-fifth Annual Meeting of the Philosophy of Education Society (Normal, Ill.: The Society, 1980), pp. 3-30.

narrow, their inability to cope with the realities of life is so pronounced. Yet those who allow the received theory to dominate their thinking about curriculum may be said to encourage that life-style. In fact, there is nothing objectionable about a world in which *some* individuals choose to live in an ivory tower, but imagine a world populated by the people envisioned by Hirst's theory.

It will be said that this portrait of the forms of knowledge theory's liberally educated person depends for its validity on the false assumption that no other education will be received. To be sure, the portrait is a caricature. Some people educated according to the theory will no doubt become competent doers and makers; some will become moral agents and some social reformers. From the standpoint of the theory in its role as paradigm of education deemed valuable, however, this will all be accidental, for what matters is simply that the forms of knowledge be acquired. To be sure, the theory does not require an educated person to live in an ivory tower. Yet by failing to address the question of how best to educate for effective participation in the world, the theory-become-paradigm stands guilty of sanctioning a world filled with ivory tower people.

A supporter of the forms of knowledge theory of liberal education might argue that its "products" will not be ivory tower people because an education in the forms of knowledge sets people on the right track. Given an initiation in Hirst's seven forms of knowledge we can relax, they will say; competent action, moral agency, altruistic feeling will all fall into place. In a society whose dominant institutions fostered virtues such as caring about others, a sense of justice, honesty, and benevolent action, faith in the sufficiency of an initiation in the forms of knowledge might be justified. In a society whose institutions encourage conformity of thought and action, a desire for instant riches and worship of self—that is, in our society—I am afraid that such faith is nothing but a pious dream.

A supporter of the forms of knowledge theory with a rather different orientation might argue that ivory tower people are not to be despised; that, on the contrary, detachment, disinterestedness, and freedom from passion are ideals to be cherished. No doubt they are in some circumstances. However, when a country is fighting an unjust war, there is nothing admirable about a detached citizenry; when a regime is exterminating an ethnic or religious minority, a people free from passion is scarcely the ideal; when a government is caught in a web of corruption, a disinterested electorate is a foolish electorate. There is a time and place for the cool virtues of detachment, disinterestedness, and freedom from passion and also for the warmer ones of feeling, fervor, and taking a stand. The trouble with the ivory tower people of the forms of knowledge theory is that the cool virtues will not have been tempered by any warmer ones.

No theory of education can take everything into account. Does not the fact that the forms of knowledge theory ignores education for feeling, emotion, and effective participation in the world simply mean that it is incomplete? Does it really *sanction* nonparticipation? It must not be supposed that every theory endorses or sanctions everything it fails to address. This would be absurd. However, when a theory functions as the forms of knowledge theory does, namely, as a theory of that education deemed valuable, it surely must be held responsible for ignoring the development of such central aspects of human existence as action, feeling, and emotion.

The Epistemological Fallacy

Basil Bernstein, the British sociologist of education, has said, "The battle over curricula is also a conflict between different conceptions of social order and is therefore fundamentally moral."[15] He is surely right. Yet Hirst and too many of his colleagues and critics do not see the battle in this way. For them it is fundamentally epistemological: a conflict between different conceptions of knowledge.

According to a sympathetic critic of Hirst's theory, it is a principle of educational theory "that upon one's analysis of the structure of knowledge depends what one will admit into a curriculum

---

15. Basil Bernstein, *Class, Codes, and Control*, vol. 3 (London: Routledge and Kegan Paul, 1975), p. 81.

and what one will leave out."[16] This critic has fallen victim to a fallacy that preys all too successfully on those who theorize about curriculum. The epistemological fallacy, as I will call it, consists in arguing from a theory of knowledge to conclusions about the full range of what ought or ought not to be taught or studied. Some years ago William Frankena warned against the epistemological fallacy, although he did not call it by that name. "Suppose we hold that music is not knowledge," he said. "Does it follow that it should not be taught? Not unless we also accept the normative premise that only knowledge should be taught."[17] His point was that decisions about curriculum content and objectives necessarily rest on value judgments. Theories of knowledge are relevant to curriculum theory and planning, but they are not in themselves decisive.

Hirst and a number of his critics have paid no heed to Frankena's warning. They seem to think that their respective accounts of knowledge are decisive in determining the broad outlines of curriculum, if not all its details (p. 27).[18] Their approach to curriculum theory is understandable, for it gives them authority in relation to curriculum that otherwise Hirst's own conception of the task of philosophers would deny them. Hirst has argued that philosophy is an analytic pursuit: concerned with the clarification of concepts and propositions, it investigates the meanings of terms and expressions and the logical relations and presuppositions these terms and expressions involve (p. 1). In this view of philosophy there is no place for the making of value judgments. If Frankena is right—if value judgments are an essential ingredient in decisions about what should be taught and studied—then those who accept Hirst's conception of philosophy must also accept a rather limited role for philosophers vis-à-vis curriculum. They can offer analyses

16. Brent, *Philosophical Foundations of the Curriculum*, p. 31.

17. William K. Frankena, "A Model for Analyzing a Philosophy of Education," in *Readings in the Philosophy of Education: A Study of Curriculum*, ed. Jane R. Martin (Boston: Allyn and Bacon, 1970), pp. 15-22.

18. "The question is simply which account of knowledge is correct, for surely that alone can form the basis of defensible curriculum planning." (Hirst, *Knowledge and the Curriculum*, p. 67.) See also chapter 5 by Soltis in this volume.

of the concept of knowledge, but they will have to do so in the realization that currriculum planners may reject them saying, "Who cares if music is not a form of knowledge. On independent grounds it ought to be part of a liberal education." If, however, value judgments can be circumvented, philosophers can accept Hirst's conception of philosophy and also dictate the broad outlines of curriculum.

By virtue of his definition of liberal education and his conception of mind, Hirst's forms of knowledge theory gives the *appearance* of dispensing with value judgments, but it does not in fact do so. His claim that a liberal education consists in an initiation into the forms of knowledge does not seem to require value judgments because liberal education is defined as the development of mind and the latter is identified with the acquisition of knowledge. Since on Hirst's account there are seven forms of knowledge, the conclusion that a liberal education is an initiation into those forms seems unavoidable.[19] Given his definitions, his claim that all the objectives of a liberal education are intellectual seems unavoidable too.

Definitions and analyses are not sacrosanct, however. Hirst's analysis of knowledge is a description of a certain kind. Like all descriptions it is selective; it singles out some aspects of knowledge to the exclusion of others. Assuming that Hirst has given us a true account of the nature of knowledge, alternative ones singling out different aspects of knowledge can nonetheless be constructed. But if alternative analyses can be given, upon which analysis should curriculum decisions rest? In particular, why should we choose Hirst's analysis of knowledge rather than some other, for example, one that divides knowledge into two forms—empirical and nonempirical?[20] We cannot appeal to epistemology for an answer to this question since the answer will depend on our purposes. Given some purposes, Hirst's account of knowledge will be the one to choose; given others, it will not be. Since our choice of an account of knowledge

19. Even with these definitions the conclusion does not follow unless a premise is added that initiation into all the forms of knowledge, that is, comprehensive initiation, is essential for the development of mind.

20. As, for example, Barrow does in *Common Sense and the Curriculum*.

depends on our aims or purposes, we cannot use an account of knowledge to justify these. Their justification will involve value judgments about the kind of life people should lead and the kind of society they should live in.

Those who commit the epistemological fallacy say that the nature of liberal education is dependent on their analysis of knowledge when, in fact, their analysis of knowledge depends on their views of the nature of liberal education. They decide what a liberal education should consist in and tailor their accounts of knowledge accordingly. It is because they think the arts ought to be part of a liberal education that they take the trouble to argue at such length that they constitute a form of knowledge. It is because they believe that religion and moral judgments ought to belong to a liberal education that they worry about their cognitive status. In effect, being worthy of inclusion in a liberal education is sufficient for something to be knowledge for them.

Hirst assumes that a liberal education consists solely in knowledge. This is why he has to tailor his theory of knowledge to fit the arts and other fields, such as religion, whose cognitive status is in doubt. But this assumption is not required by a conception of liberal education as the development of mind. To be sure, Hirst identifies the development of mind with the acquisition of knowledge, but just as there can be alternative analyses of knowledge so too there can be alternative conceptions of mind. We have feelings and emotions, moods and attitudes. These and other non-cognitive states and processes can figure in an account of mind. Thus, when a conception of mind enters into a curriculum theory, once again a choice must be made. Why should Hirst's conception of mind in terms of knowledge alone be adopted, rather than one which, for example, embraces feelings and emotions too? A choice is involved that rests not on the nature and structure of mind, but on one's educational purposes.

Actually, no matter what account of mind is adopted, an education intent on developing mind need not develop only those characteristics thought to define it. So long as noncognitive states and processes of mind exist, educators have the option of developing them. Indeed, even if they did not exist, an education of the mind could try to bring them into existence and develop them. Philosophical analyses are not as powerful as they seem. For Hirst's account of mind to determine curriculum we would have to agree not simply with his conceptions of liberal education and of mind, but with the assumption that liberal education ought to develop only the aspect of mind he singles out as definitive, namely knowledge.

As I have already made clear, Hirst conceives of the forms of knowledge theory as a theory of liberal education, not the whole of education. Liberal education is concerned, he says, with "those elements in a total education that are logically basic" (p. 96). Since in his view noncognitive mental states are dependent on cognitive ones, he concludes that the latter are the most fundamental or basic curriculum objectives.[21] Noncognitive states are not thereby barred from a person's education; as objectives they simply fall outside the boundaries of a liberal education.

Once again, however, we find Hirst in the clutches of the epistemological fallacy. From the fact, if it is one, that noncognitive states are dependent on cognitive ones and hence that cognitive states are logically basic, it does not follow that cognitive educational objectives are logically basic. If it were the case that once mind was developed, feelings and emotions, attitudes and sentiments would take care of themselves, there might be reason to consider cognitive objectives as in some sense primary. As we have seen, however, no such case can be made in relation to our society. Hirst does not himself subscribe to the view that an initiation in the forms of knowledge *simpliciter* makes one a person for all seasons. In his view an education in the forms of knowledge is necessary, not sufficient, for the development of desirable noncognitive states and processes. It lays the groundwork, so to speak. Thus he says, "Only in so far as one understands other people can one come to care about them and actively seek their good." [22] Even this more modest thesis is false, however. Do children first understand their parents and then care about them? Do we not

---

21. Peters and Hirst, *The Logic of Education*, p. 62.
22. Ibid.

often discover as adults that we cannot understand those we care about? Furthermore, if we grant Hirst his premise, it does not follow that an education in the knowledge required to understand others is therefore more basic or important than an education in caring for others and actively seeking their own good.

In sum, neither curriculum content nor curriculum objectives are determined by the structure we attribute to knowledge. In choosing them we make value judgments about our educational purposes and we set these, in turn, in relation to the moral, social, and political order we believe to be desirable.

An Untenable Dualism

John Dewey spent his life trying to combat the tendency of educators to separate reason from emotion, thought from action, education from life.[23] The forms of knowledge theory of liberal education resurrects the dualisms Dewey thought he was laying to rest. It does so by banishing both knowledge how and non-cognitive states and processes from its conception of mind, and hence from the realm of liberal education. But this is just a part of the story. The theory relies on a conception of liberal education that divorces mind from body. It thus makes education of the body nonliberal, thereby denying it value. Since most action involves bodily movement, education of and for action is denied value also.

Ivory tower people are a legacy of the dualisms that Hirst's stipulative concept of liberal education presupposes. Lest it be imagined that the received theory's value judgments stop there, I refer the reader to the work C. B. Macpherson has done on the life and times of liberal democracy.[24] Through the use of historically successive models, Macpherson has revealed the assumptions about people and about the whole society implicit in democratic theory. Thus, the democracy of John Stuart Mill, John Dewey, and A. D. Lindsay viewed people as exerters, developers, and

23. See, for example, John Dewey, *Democracy and Education* (New York: Macmillan, 1961).

24. C. B. Macpherson, *The Life and Times of Democracy* (Oxford: Oxford University Press, 1977).

enjoyers of their own capacities. Developmental democracy, as Macpherson calls it, took the good society to be one that permits and encourages all people to act as exerters, developers, and enjoyers of their own capacities. The model that has replaced developmental democracy is quite different. Equilibrium democracy, the democracy of Joseph Schumpeter and Robert Dahl, is not a kind of society or set of moral ends; it is simply a mechanism for choosing governments. The citizen's role is not to decide political issues, but to choose between sets of politicians. Voters are consumers rather than active participants in the political process. Indeed, equilibrium democracy requires and encourages apathy.

Equilibrium democracy is the kind of democracy that prevails in our society. The equilibrium it maintains is one of inequality. The consumer sovereignty it claims to provide is an illusion. Equilibrium democracy, in other words, is not very democratic. Nevertheless, the received theory's liberally educated person is tailor made for equilibrium democracy, since that theory encourages neither the development, enjoyment, and exertion of one's capacities nor participation in political and social life.

The strength of the connection between the forms of knowledge theory and equilibrium democracy must not, of course, be exaggerated. Hirst's theory is compatible with those political models other than equilibrium democracy that also require apathetic citizens. Equilibrium democracy, in turn, is compatible with other curriculum theories that also yield apathetic people. But the ivory tower people of the received theory are *not* compatible with developmental democracy. Nor are they compatible with the participatory democracy, which Macpherson sees as a desirable successor to equilibrium democracy. In short, while the forms of knowledge theory by no stretch of the imagination entails equilibrium democracy, acceptance of it commits one to political models that require, or at least desire, people to be passive rather than active participants in the political process. Ivory tower people are, after all, apathetic people.

Suppose Hirst's conception of mind were broadened to include noncognitive states and processes. A world populated by liberally educated people would then be a slight improvement over the one envisioned earlier: the people in it might care for others even if their caring did not prompt altruistic action; they might be concerned about injustice and the fate of modern society even if they did nothing about either; they might have a desire to solve the problems of the real world even if they had none of the requisite skills. However, as long as a conception of liberal education drives a wedge between mind and body, as Hirst's does, and liberal education is equated with the whole of valuable education, a liberally educated person will be a lopsided person: a thinker but not a doer, an experiencer but not a maker, a feeler but not a moral agent. And consequently a world populated by liberally educated people had better be perfect to begin with for the individuals in it will not act to make it better; even if it occurs to them to do so, they will not know how.

A conception of liberal education as the development of mind is not peculiar to Hirst; many educators conceive of liberal education in precisely this way. So long as the rest of education is slighted, Hirst's or any curriculum theory that singles out mind as the sole focus of liberal education implicitly sanctions a world inhabited by lopsided, apathetic people and, in so doing, a social, economic, and political order that will accommodate them.

Toward a New Paradigm

A conception of liberal education as the development of a person can provide the basis for the much needed curricular revolution. A person consists in reason and emotion. A person is a thinker and an actor. More important, reason and emotion are inextricably bound together in persons and so are thought and action. To be sure, nothing follows about the content and aims of a liberal education from these facts about persons; an analysis of the concept of a person no more determines the general outlines of curriculum than does an analysis of knowledge. One could conceive of liberal education as the development of a person, but define a person in terms of mind alone and identify the development of mind with the acquisition of knowledge. That is to say, one could adopt an alternative starting point to Hirst's yet end up with his forms of knowledge theory of curriculum. However, a conception of liberal education as the development of a person can serve as the bedrock of a curriculum theory quite different from Hirst's.[25]

Begin with a conception of liberal education as the development of a person, add to it an analysis of the concept of a person in which mind and body are inseparable, mix in the value judgment that the purpose of a liberal education ought to be to develop us as persons and not simply as minds. Guidelines for a liberal education that drives no wedge between thought and action, between reason and emotion begin to emerge. In such an education the acquisition of conceptual schemes would play an important role but a limited one. Initiation of the sort Hirst proposes into the forms of knowledge could be one of its components, but it would not be the whole thing. There would be initiation into various forms of skill, for example, artistic and athletic, linguistic and mechanical. In this liberal education there would also be room for feelings, emotions, and attitudes to flourish, for creativity and imagination to develop, for making and doing and moral commitment.[26]

Presumably an education is called liberal because it is thought to free us not only from ignorance, but also from the constraints of habit, custom, and inertia. The standard conception of liberal education would free our minds, but not our selves. Surely if being a victim of ignorance and a slave to habit, custom, and inertia are undesirable, then our whole selves ought to be liberated from them.

An education whose purpose was to liberate us as persons

---

25. Langford claims that to be educated is to learn to be a person. See Glenn Langford, "The Concept of Education," in *New Essays in the Philosophy of Education*, ed. Glenn Langford and D. J. O'Connor (London: Routledge and Kegan Paul, 1973), pp. 3-32. My conception of liberal education does not assume, as Langford's seems to, that those being educated are not already persons.

26. Hirst and Peters argue that the central feature of emotions is cognition and that for creativity to be developed initiation into the forms of knowledge is essential. See Hirst and Peters, *The Logic of Education*, pp. 32, 49ff. Supposing for the sake of argument that they are right, it does not follow that the forms of knowledge and limited intellectual objectives should monopolize a liberal education. Moreover, creativity in practical endeavors such as the arts and politics are not served by this argument.

would include within its boundaries a much broader range of things than the classic theory has dreamed of. Some would disapprove of a theory of liberal education developed along these lines for precisely this reason. If anything can go into a curriculum, one commentator on Hirst has said, then the concept of curriculum loses its practical value.[27] But to reject the principle that a liberal education should consist only of knowledge is not to say that anything goes. A theory that countenances more kinds of things than true propositions need not allow everything imaginable into the curriculum.

Others would object to the present proposal on the grounds that most skills and activities, feelings and emotions are picked up in the course of living so that to include them in a liberal education is to devote time and effort to them which could better be spent acquiring knowledge. I do not mean to deny that noncognitive states and processes, as well as skills and ways of acting, will be acquired if they are not included in a liberal education. However, there is no reason to suppose that the attitudes, feelings, and emotions, the skills and ways of acting that are picked up in the course of living will be ones that *ought* to be acquired. If particular skills and ways of acting, attitudes, and emotions are held to be desirable and others are held to be undesirable, then reasons of economy militate against a liberal education that ignores everything but knowledge.

The trouble with this liberalized theory of liberal education is not that it ignores the principle of economy,[28] but that it does not solve a very basic problem confronting the received theory, namely, that it is wedded to an atomistic ideology. Liberal education is supposed to free us from ignorance and the like so that we will be free in the sense of being autonomous individuals. Since autonomy involves action as well as thought, a conception of liberal education as the development of persons is more adequate to this task than Hirst's conception. However, individual autonomy is not the only important value for education to consider. Even as

27. Brent, *Philosophical Foundations of the Curriculum*, p. 31.

28. For discussions of curricular economy see Israel Scheffler, "Justifying Curriculum Decisions," in *Readings in the Philosophy of Education*, ed. Martin, pp. 23-31; White, *Towards a Compulsory Curriculum*, pp. 37, 71-72.

our education develops autonomous thought and action by liberating us from ignorance and the constraints of habit, custom, and inertia, it should bind us to one another and to the natural environment.

The atomistic ideology underlying the received theory of liberal education is reflected not in the fact that the "products" of that theory learn to be apathetic people, but that they learn to be asocial. Because no attempt is made to foster other-directed feelings and emotions, such as caring about the welfare of others and a sense of injustice, or to develop other-directed skills, their social links will at best be weak and their social sensitivity will be nonexistent. Just as the tobacco farmer who, when asked if he experienced any moral conflict about continuing to grow his crop in the face of massive evidence linking cigarette smoking to death, allowed that it never occurred to him to feel guilty because his primary responsibility was to make a living, the liberally educated people of the received theory will see themselves if all goes as planned not as mutually dependent, cooperating members of a society, but as self-sustaining atoms.[29]

A liberal education conceived of as the development of a person can encompass other-directed sentiments and skills. However, so long as a theory of liberal education conceives of persons as self-sustaining atoms who may bump up against one another in passing, but are socially indifferent, it will be deficient for it will ignore the kind of social and natural education everyone should have.

An adequate theory of education needs to go beyond a conception of persons as autonomous individuals not simply because education ought to bind human beings to one another, but because it should bind us to the natural order of which we are a part.[30]

29. For discussions of atomism and education see Elizabeth Cagan, "Individualism, Collectivism, and Radical Education Reform," *Harvard Educational Review* 48 (May 1978): 227-66; Ann Diller and Nancy Glock, "Individualized Instruction: Some Questions," in *Philosophy of Education 1977,* Proceedings of the Thirty-third Annual Meeting of the Philosophy of Education Society (Urbana, Ill.: The Society, 1977), pp. 190-97.

30. On this topic, see Stephen R. L. Clark, *The Moral Status of Animals* (Oxford: Oxford University Press, 1977).

Just as education should foster in us a sense of community, so too, in the interests of future generations, if nothing else, it should foster recognition of our solidarity with other living things. A sense of community requires a change in our consciousness so that we see ourselves not as self-sustaining atoms, but as dependent, contributing members of a group. A recognition of our solidarity with nature requires at least as great a shift in consciousness, for we must begin to see the earth as a cooperative endeavor in which "other lives have lives to live,"[31] indeed, to see the earth as part of a larger order in which other "earths" have lives to live. Changes in consciousness are not enough, however. Natural education should foster restraint, so that the natural environment will not be destroyed, and a willingness to share what there is with other species, even while social education fosters other-directed feelings, attitudes, and ways of acting.

Agenda for the Future

Can the kind of social and natural education I have just sketched in be accommodated by a new paradigm of *liberal* education? This question cannot be answered simply by an appeal to the nature of knowledge or mind or a person or liberal education itself for, as we have seen, an account of each of these will depend on one's purposes. I do not mean to suggest that for every purpose some form or other of liberal education is suitable: for some purposes, liberal education of any sort may be inappropriate. An answer to our question will, therefore, rest on value judgments about the worth of the education at issue and on decisions about the relationship of liberal education to the rest of education. If liberal education continues to be equated with that education which is valuable, then a positive answer to our question must be given. If, on the other hand, liberal education is acknowledged to be one valuable part of education but not the only valuable part, then it may not matter very much if social and natural education fall outside its boundaries.

What does matter is that the received theory of our day—the forms of knowledge theory—be replaced by a more general cur-

31. Ibid., p. 160.

ricular paradigm, whether that be a paradigm of liberal education or not: one that does not ignore the forms of knowledge, but reveals their proper place in the general scheme of things as but one part of a person's education; one that integrates thought and action, reason and emotion, education and life; one that does not divorce persons from their social and natural contexts; one that embraces individual autonomy as but one of many values. What matters, in other words, is that a new paradigm become established that addresses itself, not simply by default, to the whole of that education which is valuable.

With a new paradigm will come new questions for philosophers of education to answer. The nature of social and natural education will have to be explored as will their relationship to education for individual autonomy. The nature of vocational education and its relationship to liberal education will become a respectable concern as will the general problem of the integration of education and life. But this is not all. Because the existing paradigm incorporates the epistemological fallacy, it obscures the links between curriculum theory and social and political theory. A whole range of philosophical questions will become pertinent when that paradigm is discarded: for example, questions about the relationship between philosophy of education on the one hand and social and political philosophy on the other, about the social and political implications of curricular aims and content, about the possibility or impossibility of curricular neutrality.

The epistemological fallacy encourages philosophers to take the structure of knowledge and run. It fosters the illusion that curriculum can be determined without their asking questions about the good life and the good society. It also allows them to ignore the social and historical context of education. Yet to formulate curricular aims and content without taking into account the educational setting and also the practices and beliefs of the larger society is to court disaster. In freeing us from the epistemological fallacy a new paradigm will force us to confront questions about the relationship between a curriculum and both its educational and societal setting. Ultimately, this will lead to questions about hidden curriculum, something philosophers of education have pretended does not exist, and to questions about curriculum, both hidden and otherwise, in nonschool settings.

An agenda for the future cannot be laid out in detail. One thing leads to another in philosophy of education as in any other form of inquiry. It should be clear, however, that the curriculum questions to be addressed come in various guises. Some will call for analysis, some for the making of value judgments. Some will require knowledge of school practices, some will require broader institutional knowledge. Some will lead directly to epistemology, some will lead to ethics and social philosophy. At the outset of this chapter I said that philosophers of education have not given curriculum its due. I trust that once the wide range of relevant topics and variety of questions are recognized—once the philosophical challenge of curriculum is felt—this long standing neglect will disappear.

Theory of Teaching

William Heard Kilpatrick's *Project Method* has probably been the most influential single piece of philosophical writing on teaching in this century, having been reprinted and translated numerous times since its first publication in *Teachers College Record* in September, 1918. It represented to educators the import of Dewey's philosophy and the essence of progressive education. It is exemplary in another sense in that it represents a prescriptive mode of philosophizing about teaching in the context of some larger philosophical view such as pragmatism, realism, or idealism. The writings on teaching of such philosophers of education as Ernest Bayles, Harry S. Broudy, H. Gordon Hullfish, George Kneller, Van Cleve Morris, and many others reflect this "school of philosophy" way of thinking about teaching. But much as empirical research on teaching after mid-century has moved from experimentally trying to find the best way to teach to descriptive studies of the nature of teaching and teaching effects, so too have philosophers turned more toward descriptive analyses of teaching. Work by B. Othanel Smith and Israel Scheffler in the late 1950s and early 1960s on the concept of teaching signaled this shift in philosophy of education and a substantial literature has grown up around the concept of teaching since then. In this chapter, Donna Kerr sketches a descriptive theory of teaching that takes into account the judgment of quality. (Editor)

CHAPTER IV

The Structure of Quality in Teaching

DONNA H. KERR

Introduction

Walking on the tidal flats, I recently came upon a duck and her eight small ducklings. Though little more than balls of down, the ducklings somehow could already do most of those things the mother was doing: peck the beach for insects, scratch the back of the head with a foot, swim, shake off water, and so forth. In fact, save for their propensity to stumble over their own feet, the behavior of the ducklings appeared little different from that of the mother duck. While there surely remain things for those ducklings to learn, one doubts that they will be taught much, if anything. Without any specially designed environment or set of experiences, in time the ducks will just learn how to avoid tumbling over. And such seems to be the case with much of what other animals, including human beings, learn.

A combination of growth and maturation and a "natural" environment that allows for trial and error nurtures a variety of learnings, especially the acquisition of motor skills. Ordinarily, in due time humans and other creatures just learn to walk. And, ordinarily, human beings who grow up in full-fledged linguistic environments just learn to talk. But in those cases where the ordinary day-to-day environment does not itself offer conditions ripe for particular trial-and-error learnings, we sometimes resort to the creation of environments or opportunities for particular experiences that foster specific learnings—environments such as rooms with pianos, sheet music, and opportunities for and expectations of particular kinds of repetition and the like. That is, we resort to teaching.

What must likely be taught to be learned within a given period of time or to be learned at all depends upon the relation of the object of the learning to the usual environment. As a young child I simply learned to understand basic English, but I had to be taught the small bit of Latin that I learned. Had I been reared in Roman antiquity, it surely would have been otherwise. Similarly, I grew up in a linguistic environment where, for the most part, the subjunctive mood was employed properly. Therefore, I simply learned to use the subjunctive correctly and so did not have to be taught it.

If learnings were limited to those motor skills, knowledge, values, dispositions, and the like that can be acquired by maturation or that are likely to be acquired by trial and error in our "natural" environments, then neither the growth of any kind of knowledge nor any learnings beyond our own "naturally occurring" experience would be possible. To the history of humankind and to our biographies as individual persons, the deliberate fostering of learning has been crucial. Teaching is more than a nice aid to learning. It has been humankind's way of breaking through the restraints of individuals' commonplace environments of nature, social roles, traditions, language, and survival patterns.

All of this is another way of saying that teaching is important to us all, individually and collectively. I would not take such care to underscore what some undoubtedly consider obvious, but in the recent wave of calls for deschooling society, I wonder if perhaps the point is misunderstood as a call to abandon teaching. Schooling and teaching are not identical; indeed, one can and often does take place without the other. One can imagine or even point to societies and cultures without schooling, but not without teaching.

Anything so important to our lives as teaching is well worth trying to understand. And it is *theory* of teaching that would provide means for understanding. But theory of teaching has eluded our grasp. Notwithstanding thoughtful and sophisticated considerations both of teaching activities and of theories somehow having to do with teaching, we have come up empty-handed. Well, there are reasons. It is a review of those reasons that will serve to introduce the agenda of this chapter.

First, *theories of phenomena related to teaching* seem to be easily misconstrued as *theories of teaching*. By theories of phenomena related to teaching, I mean constructs that help us predict such things as learning outcomes for persons who have been subjected to particular treatments. In such cases both the treatments and learning outcomes are phenomena and, as such, observable (at least in theory). Now it does seem that any theory allowing us to predict phenomena that might count as learning and the occurrence of phenomena that might count as teaching would somehow be *related* to a theory of teaching. But such theories of phenomena cannot themselves count as theories of teaching, for they *presuppose* theories of teaching.[1] That is, such theories of phenomena assume (at best, stipulate) a view of teaching or, more precisely, a theoretical description of teaching, and so cannot themselves help us understand the full range of actions that constitute teaching. Just such a theoretical description of teaching is central to the program of this chapter.

The second reason that theory of teaching has escaped our grasp lies in the mistaken belief that *theory of teaching* is reducible to *theory of learning* (the reductionist view) or that theory of teaching can be developed merely as an elaboration of theory of learning (the elaborationist view). We see a reductionist view in Bruner's "four major features" of a theory of instruction: specification of (a) experiences that predispose one to learn, (b) the "optimal structure" of knowledge for learning, (c) the most effective sequencing of subject matter for learning, and (d) the nature of carrots and sticks that promote learning.[2] These could as well be labeled the four major features of a theory of learning. Gage, representative of the elaborationists, calls for the development of

1. For illustration of the nature of the task of generating theories of phenomena related to teaching, see Richard E. Snow, "Theory Construction for Research on Teaching," in *Second Handbook of Research on Teaching*, ed. Robert M. W. Travers (Chicago: Rand McNally, 1973), pp. 77-112. Among other things, Snow instructively distinguishes six grades of theories (ranging from axiomatic theories to "formative hypotheses") and points to possible roles for metaphor, models, and metatheoretic issues in the construction of theories for research on phenomena related to teaching. Especially suggestive of the nature of such theory construction is his elaboration of the Bayesian sheepdog metaphor of teaching and its development into a mathematical model of the "ideation rate." Such steps toward theory construction promise to help us predict the learning outcomes of behaviors that Snow calls teaching.

2. Jerome S. Bruner, *Toward a Theory of Instruction* (New York: Norton, 1968), pp. 40-42.

theories of teaching that are to be generated as "implications" of theories of learning. He proposes three "theories of teaching," each of which is intended to mirror a theory of learning (teaching as cognitive restructuring, teaching as model-providing, and teaching as conditioning).[3]

From either view, teaching is fully describable as the application of theories of how people learn. Both assume that the "oughts" of the actions of teaching follow from three premises. The first specifies the nature of learning; the second indicates what learning is desir*ed*; and the third holds that efficacy in the promotion of learning is desir*able*. In this view, quality in teaching consists in getting results. Period. As I hope to demonstrate to the contrary, to be adequate a theory of teaching must have sufficient discriminatory power to distinguish quality in cases of teaching, where quality is at least in part dependent on more than efficacy. And, I submit, the quality issue is crucial. Much as the primary point of theories of phenomena is to improve our understanding of those phenomena for purposes of prediction, the point of theory of practice (or practical activities) such as teaching is to augment our understanding of practice for purposes of improvement. The program of this chapter, then, can be viewed in part as an effort to uncover just what beyond theories of learning any well-formed theory of teaching would entail.

The third reason for our failure to produce a full theory of teaching arises from confounding *theory of empirical phenomena* with *theory of practice*. Such a conflation is apparent in the O'Connor side of the Hirst-O'Connor debate over the nature of educational theory. In particular, O'Connor claims that " 'theory' as it is used in educational contexts is generally a courtesy title" [4] because it does not satisfy the definition of theory of empirical phenomena, that is, it is not "a logically interconnected set of hypotheses confirmed by observation" with "the further properties

---

3. N. L. Gage, "Theories of Teaching," *Theories of Learning and Instruction*, ed. Ernest R. Hilgard, Sixty-third Yearbook of the National Society for the Study of Education, Part I (Chicago: University of Chicago Press, 1964), pp. 268-85.

4. D. J. O'Connor, "The Nature and Scope of Educational Theory," in *New Essays in Philosophy of Education*, ed. Glenn Langford and D. J. O'Connor (London: Routledge and Kegan Paul, 1973), p. 48.

of being both refutable and explanatory."[5] In presenting an opposing view, Hirst argues that as a theory of practice a theory of education must, instead, specify adequate reasons for actions. The general thrust of Hirst's counter, when applied specifically to teaching, is that theory of teaching must be qualitatively different from theory of empirical phenomena, inasmuch as a practice is qualitatively different from phenomena.[6] One suspects that such disputes over the possibility of "real" theory of teaching will continue until we have a clearer idea of how to generate theories of practice. Such is part of the program of this chapter, in which I shall argue that much as the adequacy of any theory of phenomena can in part be evaluated by appeal to theory of (empirical) knowledge, so a theory of practice must in part be judged by appeal to theory of action. By this reasoning, one properly looks to theory of action rather than to theory of empirical phenomena to develop expectations for theory of teaching. In other words, to demand that theory of teaching meet the formal requirements for theory of empirical phenomena (for example, empirical testability and predictive power) is to apply the wrong rules.

The fourth reason that theory of teaching has eluded us can be attributed to the view that a conceptual dichotomy exists between theory and practice—a dichotomy which obscures issues that turn out to be central to understanding teaching. As it is typically cast, the theory/practice dichotomy has theory consisting of theoretical or "abstract" statements that describe regularities in classroom phenomena or give a "pedagogic" organization to subject matter. Practice, on the other hand, is taken to refer to "concrete" things teachers do. That is, *theory* of teaching consists of knowledge claims that may or may not be relevant to practice and the *practice* of teaching consists of "concrete" (that is, completely nontheoretic) things teachers actually do. The dichotomy leaves us with an unbridgeable crevasse between theory and practice. This chapter addresses the theory/practice problem by constructing

---

5. Ibid., p. 50.

6. Paul H. Hirst, "The Nature and Scope of Educational Theory: Reply to D. J. O'Connor," in *New Essays in Philosophy of Education*, p. 67 and passim.

theory of teaching as theory of practice.[7] If the program succeeds, the dichotomy will dissolve.

The fifth reason has two forms: one form is the belief that there logically cannot be evaluative criteria that cover all cases of teaching;[8] the other form is the belief that any general theory of teaching would be useless.[9] From the first it follows that insofar as theory of teaching would entail criteria to distinguish quality in all cases of teaching, theory of teaching is logically impossible. From the second one would have to conclude that any attempt to construct a general theory of teaching would be an exercise in futility. The argument goes as follows: (a) there are different types of subject matter that can be taught[10] or different kinds of methods by which one can teach;[11] (b) what counts as good teaching depends upon which type of subject matter is being taught (or which kind of method is being used); (c) therefore, there cannot be universally applicable evaluative criteria for teaching. As Martin has cogently argued, the conclusion of logical impossibility rests on the mistake of acknowledging differences, but denying commonalities in cases of teaching.[12] The conclusion of futility entails the error of ascribing a priori status to an empirical claim. To the contrary, this chapter will demonstrate that what general theory of teaching we adopt affects what we think constitutes teaching competence or excellence, on what bases we believe teaching ought to be evaluated, what research we believe to be relevant to teaching, and what we think ought to constitute

---

7. Though they call it the relationship between theory and practice in a "socio-practical field," rather than theory of practice, Suzanne de Castell and Helen Freeman in effect make notable conceptual headway toward developing the notion of theory of practice in their paper, "Education as a Socio-Practical Field: The Theory/Practice Question Reformulated," *Journal of Philosophy of Education* 12 (July 1978): 13-28.

8. For an extended development of this view, see G. H. Bantock, "Educational Research: A Criticism," *Harvard Educational Review* 31 (Summer 1961): 264-80.

9. Gage, "Theories of Teaching," p. 281.

10. Bantock, "Educational Research: A Criticism."

11. Gage, "Theories of Teaching."

12. Jane Roland Martin, "Can There Be Universally Applicable Criteria of Good Teaching?" *Harvard Educational Review* 33 (Fall 1963): 484-91.

the professional education of teachers. And that, I submit, is useful.

Having noted the importance of theory of teaching and having reviewed the reasons why we still lack adequate theory of teaching, we are now ready to turn to the constructive task of the chapter—to develop a general theory of teaching. En route to that theory, we must answer a question regarding the language in which theory of teaching ought to be cast. Then we will turn to the task of generating the theory proper, which, as we shall see, consists of a theoretical description of teaching and an identification of the structure of quality in teaching. And finally, we will apply our theory of teaching to some specific concerns of educators and educational researchers. Perhaps the action-minded will wish that the last section (regarding teaching competence, evaluation, relevant research, and professional education) could be presented without the sections that precede it. The fact is that without such contemplative care, our claims, recommendations, and actions would be without warrant. In other words, we have no choice but to do some philosophy.

A Question en Route to Theory of Teaching

Whether we regard theories as essays to describe "how things really are" or merely (*sic*) as useful ways of regarding particular phenomena or actions, theories are at least descriptions. To construct a theory of teaching we must, then, face difficulties inherent in any attempt to *describe* teaching. Initially the task may seem rather straightforward: all we need is to look at an instance of teaching and just say what we see. But the matter is not so simple. Consider the following three descriptions of the same event: (a) the shortstop threw Reggie out at first; (b) a man standing at the grass's edge between two bags leaned forward from the waist while shifting from one foot to the other, then quickly skipped to his left, grimmaced, caught the speeding ball, and hurled it to another man (who was standing ever so awkwardly with his left leg extended behind him so that his foot touched a third bag), immediately after which yet another man ran across the third bag; (c) in a fraction of a moment the sphere shifted direction by thirty or forty degrees, almost without slowing down, even though it moved from glove to bare hand in the directional shift; then it abruptly came to rest in a second leather-gloved hand. While all three may be correct, only the first description depicts the event *as a baseball event*. Likewise, there is an indefinitely large number of descriptions of teaching events, only some of which portray the event *as a teaching event*. Even if a person had independent reasons to believe that he was observing a teaching event and even if his belief were true, whether he could describe the event as a teaching event would depend not on "raw" perception, but on the adequacy of his conception of what counts as teaching. To put the matter another way, we cannot give even a simple description of a single, specific event as a teaching event unless we already have in mind a general or theoretical description of teaching.

Just how, then, might we go about developing a general description of teaching? At first, an approach that might seem useful would be to observe many instances of what we suspect to be teaching events or a series of teaching events to note what categories of activities seem common. For example, if we were to observe that explaining, questioning, testing, and cajoling are common to the purported teaching events, then we might have reason to say that an observed activity that seems to fall under any of these general descriptions can be described as a teaching event. And, correlatively, to describe an event as a teaching event, we must depict a case of explaining, questioning, and so forth, much as one must depict a play that is part of the lexicon of baseball in order to describe an event as a baseball event.

But while such a search for commonalities might be useful for some purposes, it does not help us with the essentially conceptual task of describing teaching. Note that while some instances of explaining, questioning, testing, cajoling, and so forth *may* count as teaching, they do not always count. One might do any of these things and not be teaching. Often we explain, question, and the like as part of activities other than teaching. As well, virtually any activity (from winking or telling a joke to scaring someone) could count as a teaching event.[13] That is, our search for common activ-

---

13. See Gilbert Ryle, "Thinking and Language," in *Proceedings of the Aristotelian Society for the Systematic Study of Philosophy*, Supplement, vol. 25 (1951), pp. 65-82, on the polymorphous character of some activities.

ities can (logically) neither distinguish when those activities do and do not count as teaching nor show us the full range of activities that can so count, much less under what conditions.

Let us proceed, then, to describe teaching by appealing not to empirically derivable commonalities, but to the concept of teaching. But proceed in what language? I refer here not to natural languages such as English, Swahili, and Chinese, but rather to three sorts of conceptual sets or frameworks that are, I believe, commonly purported to have prevailed in talk about teaching. I shall call these metaphorical language, behavioral language, and action language. In that such languages are not expressively equivalent, it is pertinent to ask whether teaching as teaching can be described in each. Further, of those that *can* describe events as teaching events, we should ask whether they provide an appropriate basis on which to develop theory of teaching.

Historically and popularly, perhaps the most common vehicle for talking about teaching has been the metaphor: teaching as the midwife's delivery of ideas that have already come to full term in the mind of the pupil; teaching as pouring knowledge into the heads of students; teaching as employing learning traps; teaching as healing; teaching as gardening; teaching as sculpting; and teaching as many, many other things. If, for example, we understand teaching as the employment of learning traps, then when observing particular events we have a way to "see" and so to describe them as teaching events. In observing goings on in a classroom, if we can "see" that some activities "bait the trap" and that others "set the trap," and so forth, then we have a way of describing those events as teaching events. That is, if an event is in some way describable as a "baiting" or as another action that is part of deploying traps, then it counts. So quite apart from whether we like any given metaphor, it does seem that teaching can be described as teaching in metaphorical language. But should we use metaphor if our interest is in describing teaching in a way that will contribute to theory of teaching? This is not a question of whether metaphor can be useful. Metaphorical talk offers a way to begin, especially when we grope to form initial understandings, when poets try to extend the bounds of the expressible, when one does not yet understand. Or, at least it offers ways to misunderstand

and that is sometimes better than having no understanding whatsoever. But metaphor, by its essentially parasitic, gestalt-evoking nature, cannot substitute for the crisp, analytic thinking that can help us know when a particular metaphor should be abandoned—when analogical inference has reached its valid bounds. For example, if we treat teaching as sculpting, would seeking only the best stones or "seeing the figure in the stone" have a defensible analogue in teaching? Such questions we cannot answer until we have a nonmetaphorical description of teaching. We should not, then, adopt metaphorical language in our attempt to develop a description of teaching that is to serve as the core for theory of teaching.

Having opted for nonmetaphorical language, we face another choice. Should we attempt to describe teaching in behavioral or action language? With behavioral language we would be able to talk of observable happenings only (for example, physical movement and utterances). With action language we could talk of mental events that may not lend themselves to sense perception (for example, thinking, planning, deciding on the basis of reasons), as well as of intended events that have behavioral manifestations (responses to students, explanations, and so forth). To get a sense of what is at issue, it would be helpful to review examples of both languages in attempts to describe teaching. To follow common belief, it would seem that the most likely place to find behavioral descriptions of teaching would be B. F. Skinner's work on teaching. But we look in vain.[14] In describing learning as change in behavior through conditioned happenings, Skinner describes learning in "behaviorese." When he talks of teaching, his account has the teacher "shaping" behavior or "managing" contingencies of reinforcement. Now shaping and managing are not things that simply happen, as does the motion of an electron or the twitch of a muscle.[15] Instead, they are intentional, purposive doings. That is,

14. B. F. Skinner, *The Technology of Teaching* (New York: Appleton-Century Crofts, 1968). The one possible exception comes in chapter 11, "The Behavior of the Establishment," where Skinner writes about contingencies that reinforce teaching. But here his behavioral language appears to be only metaphorical. His concern instead seems to be with what he might encourage or persuade persons to choose to teach.

15. To be sure, there is a behavioral or phenomenal component, "shaping" or "managing," but there is more.

while Skinner employs *behavioral* language to describe *learning*, he uses *action* language to describe *teaching*. Indeed, Skinner exhorts teachers to choose to do these actions.[16] I make this observation about Skinner's language not to point out any logical inconsistency in Skinner's two descriptions. There is no such inconsistency: behavioral descriptions of learning neither imply nor presuppose behavioral descriptions of teaching (nor is the converse true), so the two are not logically incompatible.[17] Rather, I wish to point to the possibility that, contrary to common belief, we may have no ready examples of behavioral descriptions of teaching. (That Skinner's treatment of teaching is commonly cited as a paradigmatic case of behavioral description can be attributed, I submit, to the failure to distinguish between descriptions of learning and descriptions of teaching.)

But could one describe teaching in behaviorese? To try to give a running behaviorese account, one might offer the following sort of description: "Evidently having received sufficient reinforcement from the pupil's nod, Smith's lecturing behavior continues," and so on. Just what in such a description could correctly be labeled "teaching"? Those activities that Smith intends to help someone learn something? No, for intention is not expressible in behavioral language. The contingencies of Smith's behavior? No, for pointing to a cause of a behavior only accounts for the occurrence of the behavior; it cannot tell us whether the behavior would count as teaching. Could, then, the teacher's response (for example, the behavior of continuing to lecture) be correctly labeled "teaching"? Only arbitrarily so, for there is nothing in the behavior itself that would qualify it for teaching status. Instead, if anything could reasonably be named "teaching" it would be any behavior that under "normal conditions" might be part of a causal chain that in fact has led to someone's learning something. The result appears a bit bizarre, for while a behavior that under "normal conditions" might be part of a causal chain that leads to learning, such natural

---

16. Skinner, *The Technology of Teaching*.

17. Some argue on normative rather than logical (conceptual) grounds that teaching, properly understood, entails intended learnings that cannot be expressed in behaviorese. This point reappears in the section on the structure of quality in teaching.

hiatuses as the pupil's having hiccups, a stomach ache, or an ill-timed lapse of memory could disqualify the "manager's behavior" from counting as a teaching behavior. Moreover, the "teaching" that behavioral language is capable of describing can be predicated only of behaviors and not of persons as agents. Thus, while the teaching label might arbitrarily be applied in behavioral language, behaviorese cannot describe teaching as something that persons, as agents, do. To accept this arbitrariness in the use of the label "teaching" and its application to behavior only, would be to conclude that teaching can be described in behaviorese. To deny such a construal of the term would be to deny that it can.[18]

Even if we are inclined to tolerate the violence that behaviorese does to our ordinary concept of teaching as a purposive undertaking, on other grounds we still might disallow behavioral language as the basis for theory of teaching.[19] In a behavioral description there is only one way in which an event may fail as a teaching event. Namely, it can fail to be causally efficacious. If there is another language that will allow us to develop a theory of teaching that has greater discriminatory power, then the alternative would seem preferable. Action language allows just that, as we shall see in the next sections.

Theory of Teaching as Theory of Practice

DESCRIPTION OF TEACHING AS ACTION[20]

Ordinarily we do seem to talk of teaching in action language.

---

18. For one paper that argues that teaching cannot be understood if we regard it merely as behavior, see Thomas F. Green, "Teaching, Acting, and Behaving," *Harvard Educational Review* 34 (Fall 1964): 507-24.

19. This is *not* to say that behavioral language is inappropriate in empirical research on teaching behaviors. But even there pure behaviorese is employed less frequently than is perhaps believed. For example, observation categories such as "gives suggestions," "shows negative feelings," and "asks for information" (W. W. Lewis, John M. Newell and John Withall, "An Analysis of Classroom Patterns of Communication," *Psychological Reports* 9 [October 1961]: 211-19) are something more than behavior. For example, whether an utterance counts as giving a suggestion depends upon the context and the intent of the speaker, as well as upon the utterance (the behavior) itself.

20. For a review of issues regarding the description of teaching that have been treated in the philosophy of education literature, see my "Analyses of 'Teaching'," *Educational Philosophy and Theory* 6 (March 1974): 59-67.

What is one doing when one is teaching? One is "engaging in activities intended to help someone learn something" or "doing things purposely to facilitate learning." In that action language countenances intentionality and purposiveness, it enables us to label events as teaching events if they are in some way part of what someone is doing to the end of helping someone learn something. But that we can and commonly do describe teaching in action language is not reason enough for doing so in an attempt to develop theory of teaching. Adequate reason is to be found in an analytic point: if our interest is in theory of teaching as theory of practice, then only action language is appropriate, for practices are themselves species of action. They are things we do with intents and purposes, rather than things that merely happen.

But just what are those doings (undertaken with the intent to help someone learn something) that count as teaching? Some things one might do with the intent of helping someone learn something (for example, the action of taking one's child to a piano lesson) do not count as teaching. To begin our response, let us step back to ask a more general question: what does one do when one does anything? Or, more precisely, what must be true to say that someone m does action a? To avoid the lengthy task of ourselves establishing a set of conditions, it is helpful to assume the defensibility of an analysis that has some currency in the literature of theory of action. As a result of developing an analysis of action as a modified analogue of the standard analysis of knowledge, Danto answers as follows: m does a, only if (a) m intends a; (b) a happens; (c) m does b; (d) b is adequate for a; (e) m believes that b is adequate for a; (f) m does b because m intends a.[21] For example, m may be said to light the lamp only if (a) m intends to light the lamp; (b) the lamp in fact is lighted; (c) m flips the switch; (d) flipping the switch is adequate for lighting the lamp; (e) m be-

21. Arthur C. Danto develops this analysis of action in his *Analytical Philosophy of Action* (Cambridge: Cambridge University Press, 1973), pp. 1-28. For those familiar with recent literature on theory of action, it may be worth noting that borrowing Danto's general description of how actions are embedded in other actions (in the same way that knowings are embedded in other knowings) does *not* commit us to Danto's view of the nature of basic actions. For purposes of this discussion, b does not stand for an action that must be on the bottom rung of the action order.

lieves that flipping the switch is adequate for lighting the lamp; and (f) *m* flips the switch because *m* intends to light the lamp. Should any of these conditions not obtain, then it is not the case that *m* does the action "lighting the lamp." (Of course, *b* might be something other than flipping the switch, for example, screwing in the bulb.)

When one is teaching, for what does *a* stand? Is there more than one action that counts as a teaching action? What distinguishes teaching actions from other actions? If we return to our ordinary language notion of teaching, we might say that the *a* that *m* does is "engages in activities the point of which is to facilitate learning." The move suggests that *a* may have more than one part, that it may be compound. As any purposive, goal-directed doing, teaching might be "factored" into three components: one that regards a choice of goal, one that concerns a choice of means or plan, and another that regards acting on the plan. In a case of teaching, an action would fall under the teaching description if it counts as choosing a learning to encourage (a'), as designing a plan to encourage that learning (a''), or as acting on that plan to encourage said learning (a''').[22] Explaining, questioning, testing, or cajoling would, then, count as a teaching action only if it is part of any one of the three component actions; a particular case of planning would count only if its intent were to encourage the learning, and so on.

Now if we treat teaching as consisting of three component actions, to do any one of those actions would be to teach; to do all three would be to do a complete case of teaching. Much as a sentence can be incomplete, so a case of teaching can cease *in medias res*. And, much as persons can correctly be said to be speaking English, even though they may make false starts and leave phrases dangling in air, so persons can correctly be said to be teaching, even though they might abandon a "teaching sentence" midway. That is, if "*m* does *a*" is given the value "*m* teaches" or

---

22. Some would object to my inclusion of curricular considerations in an analysis of teaching. If we are interested in understanding the dimension of quality in teaching, however, we have no choice but to acknowledge the requirements that curricular issues set for instructional actions.

"*m* is teaching," it may be rewritten as *m* chooses a learning to encourage, *m* designs a plan to encourage the selected learning,[23] and *m* acts on that plan to encourage the selected learning. This is *not* to say that the three actions have no connection one with another. One can (logically) hardly act on a plan to encourage a selected learning until one has selected a learning to encourage (or at least selected a category of learning to encourage, for example, learnings regarding Plato's conception of knowledge or social learnings that might be promoted within a small group of seven-year-olds) *and* made a plan, however sketchy. Nor can one design a plan to encourage a selected learning until one has selected a learning or learnings to encourage.[24] So while each of the three actions can independently be considered part of teaching, they are connected by logical priority and so stand as a logically ordered series which, if completed, might be said to constitute a complete case of teaching.[25]

THE STRUCTURE OF QUALITY IN TEACHING

With our description of a complete case of teaching as consisting of the three ordered actions, we meet the requirement that a theory *describe*. What beyond description should be expected of theory of some practice, as contrasted with a theory of natural

---

23. Some maintain that a plan to encourage learning can count as part of teaching only if it specifies that the pupil be given corrective feedback whenever the teacher judges that such correction makes learning more likely. See, for example, James F. Andris, "'Person X is Teaching,'" in *Philosophy of Education 1971*, Proceedings of the Twenty-seventh Annual Meeting of the Philosophy of Education Society, ed. Robert D. Heslep (Edwardsville, Ill.: Studies in Philosophy and Education, Southern Illinois University), pp. 234-46.

24. Of course, one might in a sense vary the temporal order of the series. For example, one might have a general instructional design that requires that one await pupil responses to specify more fully the learning goal; but still the fuller specification of the design is dependent on settling on the learning goal. The logical point stands.

25. For a paper that argues on ordinary-language grounds for the necessity (to a complete case of teaching) of three similar actions, see Donna H. Kerr and Jonas F. Soltis, "Locating Teacher Competency: An Action Description of Teaching," *Educational Theory* 24 (Winter 1974): 3-16. For those familiar with that article, it might be noted that the main advance of this paper over that one is the explicit treatment of the component actions (*a*) as having embedded actions (*b*).

phenomena? As noted in the introduction, the primary points of theories of the two sorts differ: the point of theories of phenomena is to improve our understanding of those phenomena for purposes of prediction; the point of theory of practice (or a practical activity) is to augment our understanding of that practice for purposes of improving the actions that constitute the practice. While the central test of theory of phenomena might be writ narrow as a standard of predictive efficacy (though some believe it to include much more[26]), the base-line test of theory of practice must be cast as a standard of quality, where the criteria of quality in some way include but are not limited to considerations of efficacy. From theory of practice, then, we should await a framework for identifying the ways in which teaching actions can succeed (or fail).

Let us return to Danto's analysis of action for guidance in identifying the quality structure of teaching as part of theory of practice. Recall that m does not "simply" do a; rather, m does a by, through, or in doing b. In a case of teaching, m does not simply choose a learning to encourage or design a plan to encourage the selected learning or act on that plan. Instead, m does a teaching action (a) by, through, or in doing other things (b). There are, for example, many ways that one might go about choosing a learning to encourage. One might garner two possibilities from a friend and flip a coin, one might consult "the textbook," or one might choose merely by asking the pupils what they would like to learn. Clearly, some things one might do (b) to choose a learning (a) would be better than others. It would appear, then, that it is action b, when considered in relation to action a, that admits of quality.

Before proceeding, it may be important to acknowledge and deal with a potential puzzlement. Why, one might wonder, should we complicate the task by talking about doing b, when our con-

---

26. For example, it might include a consideration of the status of those hypotheses in the theory that suffer from predictive failures, that is, whether they are part of the "hard core" or part of the protective belt of "auxiliary hypotheses." See Imre Lakatos, "Falsification and the Methodology of Scientific Research Programmes," in *Criticism and the Growth of Knowledge*, ed. Imre Lakatos and Alan Musgrave (Cambridge: Cambridge University Press, 1970), pp. 91-196.

cern is with doing *a* and, anyhow, is not '*b*' just another name for *a*? Let us first address the second point. Actions, taking place within a hierarchy of intentions and meanings, can be described on as many different levels. Plato sees Socrates and asks him what he is doing. "Talking," responds Socrates. Plato: "I see that, but what are you doing?" Socrates: "Replying to Meno's question." Plato: "I know that; what are you *doing*?" Socrates: "Explicating the paradox of learning." And so on. The description on any level is not interchangeable with that on another; the criteria for judging a reply to Meno in particular are not necessarily the same as those for judging an explication of the learning paradox. But if we wish to judge a particular explication of the paradox (*a*) *and* if that explication is achieved through replying to Meno (*b*), then we could ask whether the particular reply to Meno is adequate as an explication of the paradox. Put otherwise, by utilizing both descriptive layers (*a* and *b*), we generate a way to judge action *a*. Namely, we can ask whether what *m* does under one description (*b*) is adequate for what he wants to do under the more general description (*a*). Thus we can evaluate *m*'s doing of *a*. Or, in terms of our earlier example, we can ask whether *m*'s flipping a coin or consulting the textbook (*b*) is adequate for choosing a learning to encourage (*a*).

The structure of quality in teaching shows itself when we ask for each teaching action (*a*) whether there might be more than one type of adequacy of what *m* does (*b*). That is, can actions succeed or fail in more than one way? There are two general tests of adequacy for any teaching action (and, presumably, for actions that constitute other practices as well). The first, the test of *subjective adequacy*, queries whether *m*'s action *b* fits *m*'s relevant beliefs and values. As an illustration, if *m* were to fail to bring to bear his beliefs about the nature of historical inquiry when selecting learnings to encourage as part of his teaching history, or if *m* were to choose learnings to encourage merely by "following the textbook" when *m*'s beliefs regarding the nature of historical inquiry are at variance with those beliefs on which the textbook is structured, *m*'s teaching action would fail the test of subjective adequacy. The second test features *objective adequacy*. While *m* might believe that what he is doing (b) is adequate for choosing a learning to encourage, for designing a plan, or for acting on that plan (a), what he is doing may not be adequate for a on standards either of the knowledge community or of the moral and political context, or of both. To continue the example of the logically first teaching action (choosing a learning to encourage), let us regard a case in which m bases his choice of learnings in a science course on beliefs about the nature of doing science that the knowledge community does not accept. While m's doing may be subjectively adequate, it would fail to be objectively adequate.[27]

To identify these two tests of quality may be suggestive, but it is not sufficiently specific to be helpful when testing teaching actions in particular. That is, these standards properly apply to actions that constitute any practices or practical activities and so do not provide enough specificity to distinguish quality when applied to teaching actions. The key to practice-specificity is the relevance consideration that is part of the general definition of both adequacy tests. The subjective adequacy of b for a requires that m's relevant beliefs and values neither be violated nor ignored in doing b. And if b is objectively adequate for a, it is consonant with the relevant beliefs and values of the knowledge community and of the political and moral context. To qualify the adequacy tests so that they will apply to teaching in particular, we must specify what beliefs and values are relevant to teaching. Only then will we have in hand the quality criteria for teaching and so have fulfilled the second expectation of theory of teaching.

27. To clear up a possible conflation, it is helpful to return to Danto's analysis of action to note that the locus of the quality structure is Condition 4, "b is adequate for a." Condition 5 ("m believes that b is adequate for a") does *not*, as it may first seem, express the test of subjective adequacy. That is, quite apart from m's beliefs regarding the adequacy of b for a, what m does (b) may not fit his relevant beliefs regarding a. For example, m may *believe* that what he is doing (employing particular diagnostic tools to collect relevant information, etc.) is adequate for choosing a learning to encourage and yet he may either unwittingly base his choosing on premises and values he does not believe and cherish or he may fail to bring his relevant beliefs and values to bear or both. Were Danto's analysis to be rewritten to display the quality structure of action, Condition 4 would read: "b is subjectively and objectively adequate for a." Condition 5 would stand as is.

Just what are, then, the relevant considerations of teaching actions? Or, more generally, what is relevant to the component actions of any particular practice? A reasoned answer can be found by regarding (a) the generic point of the particular practice (here, teaching), (b) the contextual point of the practice, and (c) the immediate context of the particular actions. First, from our understanding of teaching as actions intended to encourage *persons* to *learn* things, we see that the nature of the subject matter to be learned, the nature of learning, the nature of the particular learner or learners, and the nature of available means and resources for encouraging persons to learn particular things constitute part of the relevant considerations of teaching actions. Second, since to encourage persons to learn particular things is to "intervene" in the lives of others and to promote particular values, understandings, appreciations, and so forth, that are supportive of particular ways of living and interacting, teaching actions are inexorably political and moral in nature. Thus, the political and moral contexts are also relevant considerations of teaching actions. And third, any one component teaching action (whether choosing a learning to encourage, designing a plan to encourage that learning, or acting on that plan) takes place within the context of the two other component teaching actions. Inasmuch as what is appropriate in the case of any one teaching action relies at least in part upon the actuality or possibilities of the other teaching actions, the other teaching actions are relevant considerations. For example, in teaching we choose a learning to encourage in the context of our beliefs, values, and understandings of the sorts of plans on which we might reasonably expect ourselves to act. Only if one believes that one can come up with at least some plan for how to teach someone a particular something does it make sense to choose that something as a learning to encourage.

In sum, then, doing b is subjectively and objectively adequate for any component teaching action a, only if the natures of (a) the subject matter, (b) learning, (c) the particular learner, (d) the available means and resources, (e) the political and moral contexts, and (f) the other component teaching actions are taken into account. That just some beliefs and values regarding these contextual factors of teaching be brought to bear may suffice for the subjective adequacy of a teaching action. But objective adequacy (the quality standard that seems appropriate for public practices such as teaching) presents a stricter requirement: those relevant beliefs and values brought to bear in any teaching action must be judged on the standards of the knowledge community and the standards of the moral and political context.[28]

To display the numerous ways in which teaching can succeed or fail, it is useful to inquire just what considerations would be brought to bear in a subjectively and objectively adequate case of teaching. The task here is to exemplify the sorts of considerations that would be brought to bear in each of the three component teaching actions (a', a'', and a'''), if their doing (b', b'', and b''', respectively) were *ideal*. Thus, I intend the discussion to be suggestive of the kinds of considerations that are part of super competence in teaching, rather than to describe what considerations teachers generally do in fact bring to bear in teaching (an empirical matter).[29] Though the latter would be pertinent to assessing the state of educational practice, to be useful it would presuppose an answer to the question at hand, namely, What *should* (given our understandings, knowledge, and values) be brought to bear in teaching?

For economy of exposition, I shall indicate the kinds of issues that are inherent in excellent teaching by surveying the sorts of questions for which each of the six relevant considerations requires answers in choosing a learning to encourage (a') and in designing a plan to encourage that learning (a''). After having worked through the six categories of relevant considerations with the first two component teaching actions, I will turn to the third component action, acting on the plan (a''').

---

28. In the case in which the conservative and the revolutionary disagree over which moral and political contexts are appropriately invoked, the quality of the particular case of teaching will be in dispute. My thanks to James E. McClellan for reminding me, in his inimitable way, that it may be important to make this point explicit.

29. In his *Scientific Basis of the Art of Teaching* (New York: Teachers College Press, 1978), N. L. Gage proposes just such an empirical study (p. 80).

Nature of subject matter. Just what particular learnings might be appropriate choices depends at least in part on the nature of the subject matter. If one's concern is to teach physics, history, mathematics, how to play the violin, or any other such general subject, selection of appropriate particular learnings to encourage calls for an analytic understanding of the general subject. Whatever their form (propositional knowledge, appreciations, skills, attitudes, understandings, or dispositions), subjects and subject matters cannot be acquired whole, in the way a snake devours a rat. For a physics teacher to select appropriate learnings, he must know the epistemic parts into which physics might defensibly be factored. The quality of his choice of learning can be no better than his understanding of the nature of scientific explanation, the nature of scientific inquiry,[30] standards of adequacy of evidence in physics, and so forth, as well as his knowledge of particular hypotheses to which empirical tests lend support. And even once one has selected (or, by default, has had selected for him, for example, by unthinkingly following a prescribed syllabus), one cannot ignore the nature of subject matter. If one wanted to teach someone "merely" that the statement "force is the product of mass and acceleration" is true, just what sorts of possible plans of action one ought seriously to consider should, again, depend upon the nature of the subject matter. Unless, for example, the student understands the language of quantification and the nature of empirical knowledge and has acquired some of the central concepts of Newtonian physics (and much, much more), he cannot (logically) learn that the statement $f = ma$ is true. So no matter how skillful one might be in "getting students to learn things," the quality of one's teaching depends in important part upon one's understanding the subject well enough both to choose appropriate learnings and to design plans that do not violate the nature of the subject matter.

Nature of learning. The literature of psychology and philosophy presents two purportedly distinct types of views regarding

---

30. For those whose particular concern is science education, D. C. Phillips's chapter in this volume will be of special interest. It summarizes positions in the recent debate over the nature of scientific inquiry.

the nature of learning.[31] The first treats learning as the acquisition of behaviors via conditioning and the second describes learning as the ordering and reordering of beliefs. Variations on the behaviorist view range from strict behaviorism, which disallows all mental terms (for example, 'belief' and 'reason'),[32] to empirical "behaviorism," which countenances mental terms as hypothetical constructs.[33] The cognitive view ranges from Locke's *tabula rasa* on which simple impressions of experience are accumulated, associated, then generalized to the view that one learns by experiencing *with* innate or acquired cognitive patterns (deep structures,[34] operational structures,[35] or paradigms[36]). The point here is not to provide even a cursory review of learning theories, but to indicate enough diversity to show that the perceived appropriateness (subjective adequacy) of any choice of learning and any plan depends in part upon one's beliefs about the nature of learning. And one's choices of learning and plan can, of course, be no more defensible (objectively adequate) than one's beliefs about the nature of learning. For example, the strict-behaviorist fad (one might hope) of requiring that even cognitive objectives be expressed as behavioral objectives in effect severely and mistakenly limits the selection range of admissible learnings. Likewise, misunderstanding the span of applicability of a given view of learning can result in inappro-

31. For a paper that briefly discusses the recent shift in psychological-research emphasis from the behaviorist to cognitive view and proceeds to survey cognitive research, see M. C. Wittrock and Arthur A. Lumsdaine, "Instructional Psychology," *Annual Review of Psychology*, ed. Mark R. Rosenzweig and Lyman W. Porter, vol. 28 (1977): 417-59.

32. For a critique of strict-behaviorist learning theory, see Kenneth A. Strike, "On the Expressive Potential of Behaviorist Language," *American Educational Research Journal* 11 (Spring 1974): 103-20.

33. See, for example, R. M. Gagné, "The Acquisition of Knowledge," *Psychological Review* 69 (July 1962): 355-65.

34. See, for example, Noam Chomsky, *Studies on Semantics in Generative Grammar* (The Hague: Mouton, 1972).

35. Jean Piaget and Bärbel Inhelder, *The Growth of Logical Thinking from Childhood to Adolescence* (New York: Basic Books, 1958).

36. Thomas S. Kuhn's psychological claims in *The Structure of Scientific Revolutions*, 2d ed. (Chicago: University of Chicago Press, 1970) suggest this view of learning.

priate plans for encouraging particular learnings as, for example, when a parent tries to reason with a young child to change the child's behavior before the necessary structures for comprehending the reasoning have been acquired by the child.

Nature of the particular learner. While it seems fairly obvious that learner differences suggest that what specifically is appropriate subject matter and what sorts of instructional plans are appropriate varies with the learner, the multiplicity of relevant considerations may elude the cursory glance. For convenience, these may be grouped in four general categories. One regards our physiological and psychological beliefs about the stage of maturation or development of the learner. For example, if Piaget and company are right, some subject matters and institutional plans are clearly more appropriate than others prior to the pupil's development of logical reasoning proper. Another category includes learner traits or characteristics that are believed to affect the likelihood that a given student might learn a particular subject matter and do so in the ways presumed by the considered instructional plans. Such characteristics, given present research, range from habitual patterns of information processing to proneness to anxiety and the individual's "style" of motivation.[37] The third category subsumes considerations of the learner's beliefs, values, and personality traits *relative to those of the teacher*. Minimally, this category addresses questions of what choice of prior learnings (including acquisition of particular attitudes, values, and so forth) would assist the student in learning the selected subject matter and what nature of instructional plans would at least not hinder the student's learning.[38] Here it is worth noting that although we collectively know less about all these matters than we would like, such does not detract from the fact that subjectively adequate teaching brings to bear the teacher's beliefs and values regarding such matters and that in objectively adequate teaching those beliefs and values are not at odds with what is defensible within the knowledge community and the

37. For a review of research on these and other topics under the rubric "aptitude x treatment interaction," see Lee J. Cronbach and Richard E. Snow, *Aptitudes and Instructional Methods* (New York: Wiley, 1977).

38. Ibid., pp. 478-80.

moral and political context. Fourth, what beliefs, attitudes, appreciations, and so forth regarding the prospective subject matter the student has and has not yet acquired is relevant to a choice of any particular subject matter. To choose subject matter that the student has already acquired is to err pedagogically—an obvious point, perhaps, but one that our institutionalization of teaching into required course offerings tends to obscure.

Available means and resources. Techniques, technologies, and resources are commonly the focus of popular beliefs about what good teaching takes into account and so likely loom obviously relevant to devising instructional plans. And the appropriateness of plans does, at least in part, turn on the availability of "tools" and the feasibility of particular arrangements of the student's environment. It is also apparent that available resources are pertinent to selecting learnings to encourage. For example, the choice of encouraging someone to acquire an appreciation for the music of Sibelius makes sense only if there exist resources to avail the student of particular musical performances or if some technology is available for providing good reproductions of those performances. Perhaps less obvious is that the repertory of tested techniques also bears on the quality of subject matter choice. As that repertory of techniques (for example, algorithms for helping the severely mentally retarded learn to tie shoe laces) expands, so grows the list of subject matters that might be appropriate choices.

The moral and political context. To appreciate the relevance of moral and political considerations to teaching quality, it is helpful to note the point of teaching beyond encouraging someone to learn just something in just any way. Placed in its moral and political context, the purpose of teaching is to encourage (in morally acceptable ways) some learnings in particular.[39] In an ideal case of choosing a learning one would take into account the moral context, so that the choice of subject matter might be at least com-

---

39. Some argue that it is the cultural context that ought to guide choice of subject matter, on the view that to educate is to initiate others into the worthwhile activities of the culture. See R. S. Peters, *Ethics and Education* (Palo Alto, Calif.: Scott, Foresman and Co., 1967), especially chap. 4, "Worthwhile Activities," and idem, "Education as Initiation," in *Authority, Responsibility, and Education*, 3d ed. (London: George Allen and Unwin, 1973).

patible with a morally defensible conception of what it is to be a person and how persons ought to conduct themselves.[40] And, insofar as learnings enable persons to act in the world, the choice of subject matter must be evaluated for compatibility with a morally justifiable political order, whether that of the status quo or of the revolutionaries. Further, one would have to ask whether the political economy can, at the time in question, afford to encourage learning of the particular subject matter, for any political order possesses limited resources (for example, persons acting as teachers) and so can supply only a limited amount of learning assistance. Choices of subject matter are, therefore, unavoidably political in the sense that they concern the allocation of scarce resources. And finally, whether in any given case teachers should base their decisions about what learning to promote on their own judgment or on that of the potential learner can be determined only by appeal to moral and political considerations.[41]

Not only one's choice of subject matter, but also one's instructional-plan design can succeed or fail morally and politically. This quality consideration includes but goes beyond the immorality of wasting students' time and energies with instructional designs that are known to be ineffective. Consider the hypothetical case of teacher Smith who (for economy of the example) does not understand the structure of the subject matter and who wants to teach Jones that $f = ma$ is a true statement. Smith regards his task as being either to help Jones respond "true" whenever Jones is asked whether the statement $f = ma$ is true or help Jones acquire the knowledge and skills that would provide him grounds for deciding whether in fact $f = ma$. Now to be sure, if Smith's interest is to teach Jones physics, then the former approach misconceives Smith's task. But quite apart from that matter, that approach might fail also when the moral context is taken into account. If, for example, central to our view of what it is to treat students as persons is offering reasoned grounds for beliefs, then to regard the case as

---

40. Cf. T. F. Daveney, "Education—A Moral Concept," in *New Essays in Philosophy of Education*, ed. Langford and O'Connor, pp. 79-95.

41. For a paper that also argues for understanding curricular decisions as normative, see Jane R. Martin's chapter in this volume.

appropriate for the application of behavioral learning theory could constitute a moral howler.[42] Moreover, in some moral contexts, it might be argued that to be acceptable as a means for helping Jones learn something, Jones must have the option not to learn it. Some means, such as classical conditioning, can deny that choice, unless the potential learner chooses to undergo the conditioning with full knowledge of the likely consequences.

As usual, the moral and political issues are not easily untangled. Today's political agenda features one consideration that can make a profound difference when one is designing a plan to help someone learn something: How much help is appropriate? Or, is the same kind and amount of help appropriate for everyone?[43] Generally, the more elaborate and thorough the design, the greater the resources it requires. Should those who, for whatever reason, tend not to learn things of a particular nature with "usual" sorts of help be given more intensive assistance? It cuts a second way: When does assistance become coercion?[44] Answers to such questions generally do not follow easily from political ideologies.[45] Nonetheless, in an objectively adequate case of teaching, one would have to work out (or already have worked out) and bring to bear morally defensible answers to such questions.

The immediate action context. In an ideal case of teaching one would neither select a learning to encourage nor devise a plan without consideration of the other teaching actions. In selecting a

42. Especially Israel Scheffler has championed the view that the point of education (thus, teaching) is to help persons come to hold reasoned beliefs. For a brief and most readable presentation of this view, see "Moral Education and the Democratic Ideal," in his *Reason and Teaching* (Indianapolis: Bobbs-Merrill, 1973).

43. For a paper that identifies some of the complexities in determining when any two educational opportunities are equal, see Robert H. Ennis, "Equality of Educational Opportunity," in *Ethics and Educational Policy*, ed. Kenneth A. Strike and Kieran Egan (London: Routledge and Kegan Paul, 1978), pp. 168-90. Reprinted in *Educational Theory* 26 (Winter 1976): 3-18.

44. For a lucid analytic study that distinguishes such notions as offers and threats, see Robert Nozick, "Coercion," in *Philosophy, Science, and Method*, ed. Sidney Morgenbesser, Patrick Suppes, and Morton White (New York: St. Martin's Press, 1969), pp. 440-72.

45. For one example of an attempt to map a political ideology onto decisions regarding education, see Kenneth A. Strike's paper in this volume.

learning one would have to bring to bear one's beliefs about whether one could devise an appropriate instructional plan and implement that plan. In devising a plan one would have to bear in mind not only the selected learning, but also one's assessment of the nature of a plan that one could implement (or could become able to implement within an acceptable period of time). Commonly we label "unrealistic" those cases of teaching either in which the instructors fail to take into account what they perceive as reasonable (subjective inadequacy) or in which the instructors misjudge the requirements and possibilities for the other teaching actions in view (objective inadequacy). Consider, for example, the instructor who decides to encourage someone to learn to appreciate the fine arts and whose range of instructional plans is, for whatever reason, limited to didactic lecturing. Though that action of selecting a learning to encourage might be subjectively adequate, it would likely fail to be objectively adequate. This is not to say that the instructor could not learn how to encourage acquisition of particular appreciations. My hunch is that the greater problem in fact lies in teachers' beliefs that they must instructionally pound on the world with whatever the hammers they have in hand, rather than in believing that they could become capable of reasonably selecting a much broader range of learnings to encourage and of reasonably designing far more widely ranging instructional plans.

Acting on the plan. At first glance, just what might be entailed by "acting on the plan" in an ideal case of teaching may seem so obvious as not to merit remark: ideally, one would do exactly what the plan calls for. Or would one? This way of regarding what ideal teaching involves casts teaching as consisting of a period of careful thinking followed by totally unreflective doings, as if the teacher were functioning as a robot that programs itself and then, willy nilly, just lets the program run its course. Even if one conceives of a period of evaluation as following the program's run, I submit that it is just this sort of picture of rational action that has unjustly tarnished the image of systematic planning and rationality in teaching.

Contrary to this think-then-act program, in the ideal case of teaching one may in fact not execute the plan as conceived. Intelligent teaching entails averting the *idée fixe*, knowing when to proceed and when to change course, and taking into account information and insights that one has acquired since the initial conception of what should be done. If we intend our actions to help someone learn something, then we must know how to decide whether we should hold to our plans. Merely waiting around to see whether the learning takes place will not do for two reasons. First, one can learn something in spite of someone else's efforts to help. Second, one can learn whatever another is helping one learn and yet the teaching might be inappropriate. My point is this: the quality of acting on any plan to help someone learn can be judged not by whether the learning takes place, but only by what is established in the knowledge community regarding the relevant considerations of teaching.

In short, to act intelligently on any plan may be to abandon the plan, to forebear. Of the three component actions of teaching, the third may well be the most difficult, for it requires an unabating, virtually continuous, critical reassessment of all considerations of the other two teaching actions, in addition to requiring often the employment of intervention techniques and technologies. Arriving at a more sophisticated understanding of the subject matter or learning, noticing something new about the learner, coming to fresh insights about the moral and political context, or realizing that one is not as skillful as one had thought in the use of particular methods and media could be grounds for a change of plan. (Here a parenthetical note: in the extent to which our institutional requirements [for example, submission of "lesson plans," publication of course notes, standardization of curriculum and methods, and other practices that tend to discourage perpetual critical reassessment] impede the very flexibility that intelligent action on plans requires, they hamper quality in teaching.)

To recap, this theoretical description of a complete case of teaching treats teaching as consisting of three component actions: choosing a something to help someone learn, designing a plan to carry through that intention, and acting on that plan. The quality of each teaching action is dependent upon what regarding the relevant context is taken into account and brought to bear when doing each of the three teaching actions, where the relevant context includes the nature of the subject matter, the nature of learning, the nature of the learner, the nature of available means and resources, pertinent moral and political considerations, and the other component teaching actions. Subjectively adequate teaching brings to bear relevant beliefs, values, and understandings; objectively adequate teaching requires that those beliefs, values, and understandings be consistent with those of the knowledge community and with the moral and political context.

Practical Applications

There are four practical points to be derived from this theoretical description of teaching and its quality structure. The first regards teaching competence. How well one teaches in any given case is a function of the quality of one's beliefs and how well one brings to bear what one believes. Excellence in teaching can hardly be expected of someone who has substantively anemic understandings of the nature of the subject matter, the nature of learning, the nature of the particular learner, the available means and resources, the moral and political context, and the immediate action context. But even sophisticated understandings and defensible commitments cannot ensure excellent teaching. One must bring to bear what one believes and cherishes. The former defines the scope of pertinent beliefs and values in competent teaching; the latter suggests that those beliefs and values must be so organized as to make them readily available in making judgments and in performances.[46]

The second and related point with considerable practical ramifications regards the evaluation of teaching. If our theory of teaching is adequate to its task, then one cannot evaluate the quality of a case of teaching by looking at whether the student learns whatever the teacher intends that the student learn. In a proper and thorough evaluation of a case of teaching, one would have to assess

46. Some work that begins to address the organization of beliefs and values can be found under the label "competence," as distinguished from "performance." For a brief discussion of competence theories, see Nel Noddings, "Competence Theories and the Science of Education," *Educational Theory* 24 (Fall 1974): 356-64. Though Noddings applies competence to learning rather than teaching, her paper can be read with the organization of the *teacher's* beliefs and values suggestively in mind.

the beliefs and commitments that the instructor brings to bear in choosing the subject matter, in designing a plan, and in acting on that plan. The pertinent standards of assessment would be: what in the research community is believed about the nature of the subject matter, the characteristics of learners and how one learns different things; the moral and political context of the case of teaching; and what is believed in the research community about the range of appropriateness and efficacy of available techniques and technologies. A case of teaching cannot, then, qualify as excellent just because in it the instructor brings to bear relevant beliefs, values, and understandings. It must be evaluated on the substance of the epistemological, psychological, moral, and political premises that are brought to bear. Under this view, to call mere classroom observation "evaluation" would be to err grossly; and to suggest that the evaluation of teaching can be apolitical would be to misunderstand the nature of teaching.

The third point of practical application regards what research is pertinent to teaching. The existing base of directly relevant research ranges more widely than I think is commonly recognized. This narrowness of view might be attributed to the mistaken assumption that the rubric "research on teaching" covers all considerations that must be brought to bear if one is to teach well.[47] By understanding as immediately relevant to teaching the work that illuminates the contextual considerations that distinguish excellent from poor teaching, we find the first categories of research that pertain. While there is always more to be done, the insights into the nature of some subject matters are seminal in the literature

---

47. For a sample of the sorts of considerations that are typically treated under the rubric "research on teaching" see two AERA-sponsored volumes: *Handbook of Research on Teaching*, ed. N. L. Gage (Chicago: Rand McNally, 1963) and *Second Handbook of Research on Teaching*, ed. Robert M. W. Travers (Chicago: Rand McNally, 1973).

Under this "research on teaching" rubric, Gage distinguishes two approaches: one that generalizes across subject matters and the other that is curriculum specific. See N. L. Gage, "The Generality of Dimensions of Teaching," in *Research on Teaching: Concepts, Findings, and Implications* (Berkeley: McCutchan Publishing Corp., 1979), pp. 264-88. But that distinction does not widen the view. My point here is that much more research is relevant to teaching than can be found under the label "research on teaching," *regardless of its ilk.*

of philosophy of language, philosophy of logic, philosophy of history, philosophy of art, philosophy of mathematics, philosophy of the natural sciences, philosophy of the social sciences, and other subareas of philosophy. Although systematic inquiry into the nature of subject matter in the knowledge disciplines has a richer history than that into the nature of other sorts of learnings (from physical skills to attitudes), research on the nature of any "learnables" would be pertinent to teaching. A second category of relevant research focuses on the elaboration of theories of learning for the purpose of identifying the defensible ranges of applicability, repectively, of those theories. The third and fourth categories can be separated only analytically, for one probes our learning-relevant characteristics and the other queries how those characteristics interact with various "treatments" constituted from available means and resources. The fifth category inquires into the nature of moral and political orders and into the substance of particular moral and political systems, such as Western liberal democracy. Especially pertinent would be work that attempts to map particular moral and political values onto considerations in any fully articulated case of teaching. The sixth category derives from the basic requirement for excellence in teaching—the requirement that we actually bring to bear in our teaching what we know and cherish. Unfortunately, we still understand the problem only in a crude way. Some have suggested that what is needed is research to reduce the gap between our "knowledge that" and "knowledge how."[48] The theory of teaching presented in this chapter suggests a somewhat more refined formulation: instead, we need research to help us reduce the gap between our knowledge and commitments on one hand and what we do when we teach on the other—the gap between the best that we could bring to bear and what considerations we actually bring to bear in our teaching. One suspects that how instructors conceive of teaching (that is, their theoretical descriptions of teaching and their understandings of what constitutes quality in teaching) and the "connectedness" of their pertinent beliefs and commitments would be key. We shall have to await the research.

48. Gage, *Scientific Basis of the Art of Teaching*, p. 81.

The fourth practical application regards the professional education of teachers. If we believe that the purpose of professional teacher education ought to be to help persons learn to teach well, then it follows that the central program for teacher education ought to address the nature of the subject matter, the characteristics of learners and how people learn different things, the uses and limits of the various techniques and technologies, the moral and political context, and the nature of teaching as action. While we await definitive research on how to reduce the gap between what we know and value and our actions, teacher education could productively be reconsidered with the problem in mind. For example, we might refine and enrich our notions of what counts as practicing teaching. To practice anything, one must single out and work on the component parts that need improvement. To depict practicing teaching merely as something that can be done and observed in the classroom is to misunderstand teaching by ignoring the full and rich range of considerations that comprise quality in teaching.

Concluding Note

I have written this chapter both with a substantive agenda and with a demonstrative program in mind. On the side of the substantive agenda, I have tried to show that until we develop a proper theory of teaching, we will fail to understand what constitutes excellence in teaching. Until then, our attempts to evaluate teaching will be wide of the mark. Until then, our empirical research, presently focused on "teaching effectiveness," will fail to regard the quality of teaching. Until then, we shall not understand teaching well enough to practice it, much less to teach it. That is, until we attend to the quality of relevant beliefs and values brought to bear in teaching, we shall misunderstand the practice of teaching and so miscast our inquiries. Moreover, I have sketched the general outlines for the needed theory of teaching as practice.

At the same time, I have tried to demonstrate the practical potential of taking philosophical care in thinking about what we do as teachers and what questions we ask as scholars concerned with the study of teaching. Especially for those practitioners and researchers who generally are disinclined to read "theoretical" works because such works are removed from practice, I wanted in some way to show the profoundly practical import of *theory* of *practice*.

Epistemology

Theories about what constitutes knowledge and how we arrive at it have perennially been of central concern to both philosophers and educators. In the first half of this century, the rapid development of science lent credence to the progressive educator's and pragmatic philosopher's view of knowledge as "experimental" and "instrumental," but it did not totally overshadow the more conservative views of knowledge found in idealism, realism, or Thomism. The 1942 and 1955 yearbooks clearly reflected the fact that both philosophers and educators saw the philosophical dimension of knowledge tied tightly to some metaphysical world view. However, the curriculum reforms of the 1960s, which were based on the idea of each subject having a basic structure, were accompanied by a shift in the philosophical discussions of the nature of knowledge in terms of multiple "realms of meaning" (Philip H. Phenix) and distinct "forms of knowledge" (Paul H. Hirst). At about the same time, Piaget's views on "genetic epistemology" and knowledge as "construction" were finding their way into educational theory and another quite different philosophical treatment of the concept of knowledge surfaced in Israel Scheffler's unmetaphysical analysis of skillful (knowing how) and propositional (knowing that) types in the *Conditions of Knowledge* (Chicago: Scott Foresman, 1965). This chapter reflects broadly on a number of different contemporary views of knowledge and how they might affect our views on educating. (Editor)

CHAPTER V

Education and the Concept of Knowledge

JONAS F. SOLTIS

Educators and Knowledge

Human beings know and they are also *conscious* that they know.[1] Being conscious that we know opens up a vast territory for human exploration not otherwise available to us. It allows us to ask such questions as: By what processes do we come to know things? (the psychological question); How can we be sure what we claim to know is true? (the philosophical question); Of what use is this or that particular knowledge? (the practical question); and What knowledge is of most worth? (the traditional curriculum question). These and a host of other questions become possible because we know that we know. Moreover, and most important to educators, being conscious that we know also allows us as human beings to try *consciously* to help others come to know what we know. Because we can stand apart from our knowledge, we can think of how best to impart that knowledge. We call this most distinctive human enterprise of intentionally imparting knowledge "teaching" in its individuated sense and "education" in its collective social sense. In this fundamental way the concept of knowledge is inextricably intertwined with the concept of education and the answers we give to the host of possible questions about knowledge and knowing will have an important bearing on how we think and act as educators.

Through the centuries, philosophers and educators have had and have operated with various conceptions of knowledge and

1. This is a paraphrase of the first sentence in Stephen Toulmin, *Human Understanding*, vol. 1 (London: Oxford University Press, 1972), p. 1. His observation provided me with the theme for my inaugural lecture at Teachers College, Columbia University in 1979. This chapter is a revised version of that lecture.

knowing which have underwritten many diverse forms of educational emphasis and practice. I will not rehearse them here, but what educator has not heard of Plato's "forms," Herbart's "apperceptive mass," or Locke's "tabula rasa," that blank slate on which perhaps even some of us have tried to write? Clearly, how we think of knowledge does influence to a considerable extent how we think of educating. By way of a simple example, if we take knowledge primarily to be captured in words, then we give lectures and books to our students and ask them to give us back test booklets filled with words. Or, as a fabled critic of the traditional recitation method put it, we send messages into the ears of our students which come out their mouths frequently without ever passing through their minds. It was this view of knowledge that William Heard Kilpatrick called "Alexandrian," with reference to the ancient library at Alexandria in which all of the knowledge of the world supposedly was stored, and throughout his career as an educator, he fought against this static and narrow view of "book knowledge" and the idea of education as mindlessly transmitting it.

Such a simplistic view of knowledge is hardly possible today, when we have a number of serious attempts to investigate and understand human knowledge from the vantage point of many academic specializations. For instance, we have cognitive psychologists who describe the acquisition and use of knowledge in the language of systems theory, cybernetics, and information processing; behaviorists who take knowledge to be behavioral repertoires built through the effects of contingencies of reinforcement operating in the environment; and neurophysiologists who search for the chemical, biological, and physiological basis of knowledge. There are also linguists and developmental psychologists exploring the avenues opened up by the study of language development and by Piaget's extensive research program in genetic epistemology. There are epistemologists in the philosophy of science who argue over the nature of scientific knowledge and conceptual change in terms of the evolution or revolution of scientific paradigms. And there are anthropologists and scholars in the sociology of knowledge who seek to understand the social construction of reality while struggling with the fundamental problem of transcending their own premises of knowledge as culture-bound.

In fact, as we approach the end of the century, I believe that we are on the verge of formulating and adopting a view of knowledge, mind, and learning quite unlike the dominant view with which the century began. From a Cartesian view of mind, an associationist view of learning, and an absolutist view of knowledge, I believe we have been moving toward what might be called an "organic" view of mind, a "transactional" view of learning, and a "contructionist" view of knowledge. This shift is important for educators to understand because a different view of knowledge ultimately will underwrite different views of educating.

The Sociocentric Perspective

While the final shape of this emerging view has yet to be set, the essential nature of the shift can be captured by analogy with the change from a geocentric to a heliocentric view of the earth's place in the universe. The earlier dominant philosophical view of mind, learning, and knowledge was "egocentric," focusing on the individual and how one acquired true knowledge of the world external to oneself. The newer view is "sociocentric," still considering the individual and the world but also taking into account the cultural nature of knowledge as a communal human construction that is both formed by and forms human beings. Just as the earlier view of a geocentric universe put the earth and human life at its center, so the "egocentric" view of knowledge put the individual there and focused attention on such epistemological problems as the privacy of sensations, illusion and the veridical perception of the external world, skepticism, and solipsism. From this perspective the paramount philosophical problem was making sense of the single knowledge relation between the individual and all else in the universe. But by conceptually moving the earth and individual off-center, whether by means of adopting a heliocentric (astronomical) or sociocentric (epistemological) view, a new and more complex set of relations enriches the possibilities for a fuller and more accurate description that brings with it new problems as well as new perspectives.[2] From a sociocentric perspective knowledge

2. I would like to make it clear that there is by no means contemporary agreement on a singular formulation of what I here am calling a sociocentric view of mind, knowledge, and learning, nor is such a perspective without its

must be viewed as both individual and social, personal and public constructions designed to make sense of and provide for effective action in a reactive, malleable yet independently existing reality. Thus knowledge claims, epistemological inquiry, and theories of education and human development need to take into account the complex reciprocal relations between an individual and his or her biological, social, and cultural inheritance, between individuals and groups, between public knowledge systems and the structure of both the natural and social worlds, and between any relevant mix of these in multiple combination.

Central to the development of the sociocentric perspective in this century has been an increasing recognition that knowledge cannot be separated from knowers, that human beings construct different knowledge systems, and that all knowledge is imbedded in the fabric of social life. Some have taken such ideas and used them as premises in radical arguments that call into question a number of our other assumptions about the nature of knowledge. Thus we hear arguments like these: If it is impossible to eliminate the subjective element completely from knowledge seeking, then no really objective knowledge is possible. If knowledge is a social product that differs from culture to culture, then there is no escape from complete relativism. If two theories are really totally different ways of seeing the world, then there is no way to compare them and judge which is correct. If knowledge serves as a regulative mechanism in social life, then knowledge is an oppressive tool in the hands of the establishment.

Arguments like these not only force educators back on their heels with respect to their view of knowledge, but also raise serious questions about the morality of educating. We are forced to ask

---

own set of seemingly unreconcilable positions and problems. In fact, among those who have adopted some version of this perspective in the twentieth century, we find many different and sometimes conflicting theories advanced to explain one or more of the complex relations between individuals, society, the world, and all types of human knowledge. To use the geocentric-heliocentric analogy again, just as the shift to the heliocentric view did not immediately solve all the problems of explaining the movement of the heavens or the nature of the universe, so shifting to a sociocentric perspective has not solved the old problems as much as it has recast them in a different frame of reference and created a number of new problems in need of solution if we are to make sense of a broader concept of human knowledge. In this chapter I am disregarding important basic differences among twentieth century sociocentrically oriented theorists in order to be able to stress some commonalities of the emerging perspective.

such questions as: Are we as educators the unwitting agents of the status quo, or worse, of some oppressive bureaucracy or invidious ideology? Do we deserve the implicit trust our students place in us not to dupe them? Can we ever honestly say *"We know"* to our students? Can we ever claim to know what is good and right for them to know? These are serious questions but to what extent must educators accept the arguments that give rise to them? And to what extent does a sociocentric view of knowledge help us to understand and answer them?

I believe the key to not being taken in by simplistic forms of these arguments and thereby led into morally impossible educational postures lies primarily in our capacity to be reflective about knowledge and also in our ability to recognize that these arguments gain much of their force from assumptions built into an egocentric concept of knowledge and would be moderated considerably if a sociocentric perspective were consciously adopted. In this essay I will use some often cited contemporary scholarly work to try to show that problems like subjectivity, relativism, incommensurability, and uncontrollable invisible social forces are not what they first seem to be, nor are they morally impossible to deal with if viewed from the newer perspective. I will argue that while such problems still remain, they do so in a less virulent form, and that the gain from consciously adopting this newer perspective on the concept of knowledge makes possible more reflective control over one of education's most fundamental social and cultural responsibilities, to transmit and assure continuity in the development of human knowledge.

Language and Human Knowledge

Consider the provocative thesis developed by Berger and Luckmann in their popular description of *The Social Construction of Reality*.[3] They argue that knowledge is the result of human activity and thus an artifact, and yet its claim to capture and represent reality makes it the basis for education into the only world available to us, that provided by the society into which we are born. The idea that this socially constructed world is the only one available to us is an important one in many ways, and in one sense it

---

3. Peter L. Berger and Thomas Luckmann, *The Social Construction of Reality* (Garden City, N. J.: Doubleday and Co., 1966), passim.

could not be otherwise, unless at birth we are left to fend for ourselves in a world devoid of any human contact.

I am reminded of the story of Frederick Barbarossa, who tried to settle once and for all the scholars' debates over which was the natural language of humankind: French, German, Spanish, Italian, Latin, or Greek. He separated a child from its mother at birth and gave instructions that no one speak to it so that it might be seen which language it developed on its own. Needless to say, the child never spoke a word. No doubt we learn a language in which certain metaphysical assumptions about the world are imbedded in Whorfian fashion and we learn to participate in a social system that defines roles, manners, morals, institutions, and even develops formal fields of knowledge. While this is the way it has to be, in the very nature of things, to what extent is this socially constructed world the only world available to us? To what extent are we locked into it and to what extent are we free to go beyond it or contrary to it? To what degree does formal education make us more of a prisoner of that social world or on the other hand provide us with the means to achieve some measure of freedom to transcend it?

Notice I used terms like "in one sense," "to what extent," and "to what degree." By doing so, I am trying to convey the idea that this is not an all-or-nothing affair. We need to recognize the dynamic and reciprocal quality of the relationships between the world, individuals, collectives, and the culture as a whole. At different times and under different conditions, we should expect the influence of individuals on collectives, collectives on culture, culture on individuals, and the world on all of these, to vary. To illustrate these relationships and to demonstrate the educational power that can be achieved by becoming consciously aware of aspects of what we mean by knowledge, let me suggest some of the limits and freedoms inherent in such human constructs as language, theories, skills, roles, and formal knowledge.

Language is an enormously versatile human instrument. Unlike immediate experience it can reach into both the past and the future, describe the real and the imaginary, and be used to state truths as well as falsities. Using the flexibility of language we can put forward widely different views about religion, morals, and art as well as argue about scientific claims and educational aims. No matter how restrictive we may claim any particular language to be, it is still necessarily an extremely viable system for human communication and for the symbolic formulation of multiple views.

Does the language of our society lock us into a way of viewing the world? Not if we mean thereby that our language permits only a particular theory, because obviously it is always possible to construct any number of different theories in any given human language. To be sure, we may be uncritical of a particular view of the world or not even conscious that we are operating with it, but the very possibility of making such a view conscious and explicit also allows it to be examined critically. When or why one reflects on a theory of the world is an empirical psychological problem, but that it can be reflected upon is an important philosophical datum. In fact, regarding theory Michael Polanyi has argued that we have the idea of objectivity all wrong.[4] It is not one's immediate perceptions of things that are the most objective and theory an abstract subjective entity once removed from reality. Rather it is theory that we hold up for public inspection, argue over, and accept or reject on reasonable grounds, while a person's immediate perceptions are just that—immediate, private, and subjective. Language and theory are the wherewithal to make knowledge claims public and debatable in a shared real world.

Sometimes, however, the claim that a language locks us into a way of viewing the world is asserted about the very categories imbedded in the language itself and not about some particular theory expressed in it. For instance, it may be argued that Cartesian dualism, a world view based on the belief in the existence of both mental things and physical things, is written into the language spoken in the Western world. To a degree, this is so. There are words for mental things and other words for physical things, and through those words we see the world. But that does not mean that we can not stand apart from those categories and ask if they make the best sense of the world we experience. Gilbert Ryle's celebrated philosophical work at mid-century, *The Concept of Mind*, did just that.[5] He argued that we make a philosophical

4. Michael Polanyi, *Personal Knowledge* (New York: Harper and Row, Torchbooks, 1964), p. 4.
5. Gilbert Ryle, *The Concept of Mind* (London: Hutchinson and Co., 1949).

blunder—he called it a category mistake—with regard to the concepts of mental and physical things. He said that this Cartesian way of dealing with the world misleads us badly in our ability to deal sensibly with ideas like knowledge and intelligence. He recommended that we rid ourselves of the "ghost in the machine" by recognizing that our mental language does not refer to the inner workings of some mysterious mind-stuff, but rather to the ways in which we judge the performances of people as witty, intelligent, dull, stupid, and so forth. B. F. Skinner also has argued against the mental/physical dualism of our ordinary language and has recommended that we translate our misleading ways of speaking of human mental functioning into a scientific language that reflects only the physical and the observable. A major program in educational psychology has been built on this possibility of using more functional concepts than the supposedly binding basic categories built into the very structure of our language.

This is not to argue that Ryle and Skinner are right. Rather it is to point out by example that our basic linguistic categories do not necessarily negate our ability to think along certain lines nor do they make it impossible for a particular individual to create new categories. Moreover, while the Cartesian world view ultimately may be wrong-headed, transcending it as Skinner or Ryle do might deliver us into greater evils. But we can come to know that only over time as we debate, use, and test such views for their fruitfulness and adequacy in our search for ways to understand human beings.

Being made aware of the possibility that basic concepts or categories may distort or limit certain ways of thinking, however, does encourage us to seek ways to overcome this perceived deficiency. Thus, it would seem reasonable to hold that we are neither totally free nor totally restricted by the language we inherit from our primary social group. On the conceptual and theoretical levels, language is constantly being reshaped by individuals and collectives within the group. Each person has the potential to engage in such activity in order to make more sense of the world, and educators have the obligation to make people aware of this fact.

But of course, individuals must begin somewhere and the somewhere to begin is with a grasp of what we think we now know before we can intelligently alter basic concepts or theories. While it is possible for an individual to invent *de novo* a unique way to think of the world, the advance of knowledge more ordinarily comes from refining or moving beyond what we now collectively claim to know. Thus knowledge making from the sociocentric perspective is more a communal rather than a private enterprise and educators play an essential role in insuring its continuity and success. Its development requires not only public expression and testing of knowledge claims by an individual or by a group, but also serious consideration of the knowledge claims of others. According to this view, education has the obligation not only to transmit current knowledge and methods of inquiry but also to develop in individuals and groups the disposition to be willing to hear and test critically new claims in the future and to seek ways to improve upon methodology and instrumentation.

Besides learning the language, theories, and knowledge claims of our social group, we also learn recipes and skills for effective action, and roles and mores that dictate "appropriate" conduct. The human capacity to do, to invent, to create, to make, to develop skills, arts, crafts, and dispositions in the service of "humanness" is part and parcel of human knowledge. From the sociocentric perspective, knowledge is not just what is contained in heads and books but also in hands and actions as we take part in social living. Knowledge viewed singularly as truth about the world is too narrow a view. A sociocentric perspective invites our attention to those forms of human knowledge imbedded in human activities that embody the techniques and institutions we have developed to provide for our needs, satisfy our wants, and regulate our social lives. The mastery of skills and techniques, and of institutional and role-specific behavior is too vast an area of human knowledge acquisition, development, and use to be overlooked by educators or scorned by philosophers. Knowing how to do something and how things are done are every bit as important as forms of knowledge as is knowing that something is true or false. Without treating these important matters in detail here, I point to them primarily to underscore the fact that our concept of knowledge has been broadened beyond what can be stated in words so as to include such legitimate categories as proper action and human skill.

But again, it might be useful to note by way of example before leaving this aspect of human knowledge that our awareness of something can give us some control over its actual affect. If we take skills and techniques to be knowledge, then we know that paper and pencil tests will be inadequate in the evaluation of all but paper and pencil skills. Or if we judge the unconscious transmission of appropriate sex-role behavior to be detrimental to what we also judge to be an important emerging social concern (for example, women's rights), then we can act to eliminate, modify, or equalize the sex-role information received by individuals in certain circumstances, as indeed we have tried to do in contemporary textbook publishing. While it is quite possible to be guided by the invisible hand of unconsciously transmitted and received social-role definition, it is equally possible to reflect on the appropriateness, justice, or reasonableness of it. The point, again, is to see that the more adequate our grasp of what we understand as "knowledge," the more we can consciously, responsibly, and morally play the role of educator.

Forms of Human Knowledge

At the heart of formal education is the narrower but also highly important conception of knowledge as organized fields of inquiry and study. Here we have represented the organized efforts of collections of human beings through time to make sense of some aspect of experience. While we learn a common language quite easily and naturally as young children interacting with others, formal education in effect also includes the learning of special languages and special symbol systems for dealing with different kinds of experience. R. S. Peters, the British philosopher of education, and his colleague, Paul Hirst, have made interesting use of the idea of education as initiation into the various public forms of knowledge developed by human beings to bring order to the several realms of human experience and to induct the learner into these various perspectives.[6] For example, the appreciation of art

---

6. Much of their individual and joint work is permeated with this theme. One of the earliest statements of it was provided by Peters in his inaugural lecture at the University of London in December, 1963. See R. S. Peters, *Education as Initiation* (London: Evans Brothers Ltd., 1964). Hirst's cumulative treatment of the "forms of knowledge" idea is fully displayed in Paul H. Hirst, *Knowledge and the Curriculum* (London: Routledge and Kegan Paul, 1974). My colleague, Philip H. Phenix, published his own independently developed version of this view of knowledge under the title *Realms of Meaning* (New York: McGraw-Hill, 1964).

calls into play a set of concepts, relations, and standards of judgment different from that employed in the appreciation of a logical argument or the development of an empirical claim. The concept of beauty is essential to art, the concept of truth to logic, and the concept of evidence to factual assertions. Different domains of human experience call for different ways to justify a claim to know something.

Hirst has argued that the concept of a liberal education has as its central tenet the development of mind and that to have a rational mind requires experience structured under some conceptual scheme, some publicly developed form of knowledge that allows one to see the world with others as they see it.[7] Thus, liberal education for Hirst becomes an education in the seven or eight distinctive "forms" of knowledge that he claims humankind has created to order and deal meaningfully with experience. His most recent list includes mathematics, physical science, knowledge of persons, of literature, and of fine arts, morals, religion, and philosophy.

In Hirst's view, the justification for teaching the forms of knowledge becomes analytic and/or self-justifying just as the Peters-like question "Why be rational?" presupposes being rational in the very asking of the question. Why develop the mind *via* the forms of knowledge? Because that is what we mean by developing a rational mind—acquiring a mastery of the fundamental rational structures of knowledge, meaning, logical relations, and criteria for judging truth claims that human beings have developed over the centuries. Each of these "forms of knowledge" are "distinct worlds of discourse" that provide different "modes of structuring experience" and as such must therefore be the ultimate and fundamental components of any education. According to Hirst, they fully embody what it *means* to be rational and to know. Without them we are cut off from basic human perspectives on some essential part of our shared world.

As broad and as radical as is Hirst's view of knowledge with its inclusion of the arts, religion, and morals on a plane equal to mathematics and science, I still must join Jane Martin in her assessment that this is too narrow a view of mind, knowledge, and lib-

7. Hirst, *Knowledge and the Curriculum*, passim. The summary of his views contained in this paragraph and the next one is drawn from this source.

eral education with its omission of concern for skills, attitudes, and the emotions.[8] Nevertheless, within Hirst's framework, the idea that there are different worlds to see *is* an educationally powerful idea. We can view education as helping others to see the world from a new perspective in two ways. One way is to think of it as actually providing students with a particular world view or interpretation of experience. The other way is to provide them with lenses to be able to see it, that is, with concepts, relational systems, and standards of judging whatever aspect of human experience is brought into focus by using that particular set of ideas.

As an analogy, think of different conceptual systems as different sorts of optical instruments that allow us to see, explore, and make sense of different visual phenomena. The telescope and microscope point at and help us visually resolve very different things, just as do aesthetic language and scientific language, for instance. Both open up new worlds invisible to us before. But to become a skilled user of a telescope or miscroscope is not necessarily to be committed to a "big bang" theory of the universe nor to a DNA theory of genetic transmission nor to any other particular theory (although we do need a theory to see some things). Content and form in human knowledge are at one and the same time independent while also being interdependent in important ways. As educators, we need to deal with both form and content and the more consciously we do so, the more effective will be our educating.[9] To transmit the content is only part of the job. To also provide a knowledge of and sensitivity to the concepts and standards of judgment in a domain of experience is to equip a person with the ability to use form to add to or after content and even to refine or change the form itself and to act reasonably in future encounters within that realm of experience.

But this may be more easily said than done. We know form and content are intimately intertwined. Dewey reminds us that only in abstraction can we separate subject matter from method.[10] Polanyi

8. See chapter 3 in this volume.

9. See my critique of Hirst on this point in Jonas F. Soltis, "*Knowledge and the Curriculum:* A Review," *Teachers College Record* 80 (May 1979): 777-79.

10. John Dewey, *Democracy and Education* (New York: Macmillan Co., 1916), chap. 13.

puts the matter in a slightly different way: in acting on the world we use knowledge "tacitly," [11] that is, we do not focus our attention on the knowledge we are using to interpret the world or on the standards we are using to make judgments about the world. Our focal attention is on the objects being interpreted and judged, not on what we are doing that *with* (our knowledge). Similarly, we focus on the *meaning* of what we are reading. In fact, we have to be able to see the letters not as simple discrete things, which is probably the way a child learning the alphabet sees them. We must be able to look through or past or beyond the letters and words to "see" the meaning that they convey. Being initiated into a "form" of knowledge, therefore, must be more than acquiring some sense of its form and some part of its content. It must include being able to use both form and content tacitly to deal meaningfully and reasonably with phenomena appropriate to that form of knowledge.

Thus, while education in an important sense is the initiation of the neophyte into the public forms and content of socially constructed knowledge, it need not be an indoctrination into a closed system, but it can be invitation to enter, participate in, enjoy, use, and even be creative in a dynamically developing human knowledge system. This is most especially true if we are consciously aware of what we are doing and what the constraints and freedoms allowed by the social and individual dimensions of knowledge and inquiry are. Knowledge *is* in one sense an artifact of collective social construction, but it is also intimately related to the everyday world we experience as human beings. At any one time, it represents the best individual and collective judgment of sensible and reasonable ways meaningfully to capture, represent, and deal effectively with some aspect of human experience in a world that exists to some degree independently of our shaping and knowing of it.

The educator, being aware of this, should seek to use subject matter to help students make more sense of their experience and ways of acting on the world, and students should not be content with less. From a sociocentric perspective, sense-making and being able to act effectively are the social and individual purposes of knowledge. To achieve these ends, educators should help students

---

11. Polanyi, *Personal Knowledge*, chap. 5. See also, idem, *The Tacit Dimension* (Garden City, N. J.: Doubleday and Co., 1966).

see, appreciate, and gain skill in using the standards of reasonable judgment appropriate to the particular forms of knowledge being taught and learned.

Dynamics of Knowing

But what if there is a radical alteration in world view or form of representing and dealing with experience as occurred, for instance, with nineteenth century impressionist art, or Darwin's theory of evolution? What burdens does the phenomenon of conceptual change put on the educator?

Relevant to this question are the recent debates in philosophy of science sparked by Kuhn's seminal work, *The Structure of Scientific Revolutions*.[12] While he and his critics have many differences, they generally share the view that scientists construct elaborate conceptual frameworks for ordering what can be claimed as knowledge about the natural world and that these frameworks or "paradigms" change, sometimes quite radically, in the course of scientific investigation and theory building. Phillips deals more fully with these ideas in his chapter in this volume.[13]

For our purposes, it will be sufficient to note that Kuhn originally argued that a newly created conceptual framework is such a totally different view of the world and set of rules for ordering experience of it that the new view is completely incommensurable with the old one. They are so different that reasons for accepting the new view cannot be seen by one standing within the old. The key difference between Kuhn's original view and the views of "evolutionist" critics like Lakatos[14] and Toulmin,[15] is that they see each change of a scientific paradigm (like the adoption of Einstein's theory of relativity or the acceptance of a behaviorist program in psychology) less as a radical and complete overthrow of

---

12. Thomas S. Kuhn, *The Structure of Scientific Revolutions* (Chicago: University of Chicago Press, 1962).

13. See chapter 10.

14. Imre Lakatos, "Falsification and the Methodology of Scientific Research Programmes," in *Criticism and the Growth of Knowledge*, ed. Imre Lakatos and Alan Musgrave (London: Cambridge University Press, 1970), pp. 91-196.

15. Toulmin, *Human Understanding*. See also, idem, "Does the Distinction between Normal and Revolutionary Science Hold Water?" in *Criticism and the Growth of Knowledge*, ed. Lakatos and Musgrave, pp. 39-48.

all aspects of the previous view and more as being based, at least in part, on certain fundamental beliefs in reasonableness and on a hard core of assumptions about the nature of the phenomena in question, the nature of science in general, and on the assessment of progress or retrogression in a research program over time. This latter modified evolutionary view avoids unbridled relativism by pointing to the self-regulatory nature of collective knowledge seeking, and I believe we have much to learn from it just as we do from developmental theories of conceptual changes in individuals, who do not start afresh even when radical shifts occur in their reasoning processes or world views.

Piaget's work on human cognitive development brilliantly illuminates the phenomenon of conceptual change in individuals.[16] One could describe human cognitive development by pointing to the key characteristics that define a way of knowing the world at each particular stage of development or one could describe the mechanisms and processes that provide for the individual's development and use of knowledge in the world over time. Piaget does both. His descriptions of the sensory motor, preoperational, concrete operational, and formal stages of human cognitive development clearly indicate the different ways in which one's experience of the world is shaped by the different categories, concepts, and modes of thinking about it available at any particular stage in one's growth. First to be born without the concept of object permanence, then to achieve it without having the idea of conservation, and finally to know that changes in form do not alter quantity is to live and act differently in different worlds while occupying the same one. But it is also important to recognize that one is the same person with one biography and not many different ones. With conceptual change, even radical change, there is always some basic continuity of many dimensions of a person or of a group. Thus, while Piaget's description of stages of development has helped educators to see the child's world not just as quantitatively short on knowledge but as qualitatively different from ours, so too can we see that even radical shifts in our ability to think about the

---

16. Much of Piaget's work is available in translation. One of the most thorough explications of his theory is Hans G. Furth, *Piaget and Knowledge* (Englewood Cliffs, N.J.: Prentice-Hall, 1969), which also includes selections from Piaget's writings.

world and act on it do not necessarily commit us to complete discontinuities in the process.

Piaget's theory also deals with more than just the conceptual and operational differences between stages. His organismic biological model posits "assimilation," "accommodation," and "equilibration" as the mechanisms of adaptive human behavior. In this way, he helps us to see development in another sense—not as the static description of stage characteristics, but as the continual acquisition, use, and modification of our knowledge of the world by means of our transactions with the world. This recognition of the intimate reciprocal relationship between knowing and doing, conceptualization and operation, having a world view and acting in terms of it gives us yet another way to broaden the concept of knowledge to include knowledge-in-use. Using schemata developed by engaging the world, the individual acts, and these schemata are continually modified and made more useful in the very act of taking on the world. Schemes in Piaget's theory are acquired patterns of assimilations and accommodations. The process of assimilation is sometimes described as the taking in by the organism of those aspects of the environment that are "capturable" by or "fit" the schemes it has acquired to deal with the world. For example, letters of the alphabet are but marks on paper for children who cannot yet recognize them, while light specks on a reflective mirror are galaxies and nebulae for the trained astronomer. And every assimilation is also an accommodation, the adjustment of the scheme so as to fit the assimilated input better. Thus, the child learning the alphabet soon learns there are variations in the depictions of each letter.

This is a slightly passive way to view the mechanism Piaget depends upon to show how our knowledge of the world is modified by experience. One could also view assimilation and accommodation in more active terms, as Elkind does. He describes accommodation as "changing one's action to fit the environment" and assimilation as "changing the environment to fit the action."[17] In this way, knowledge can be seen as part of the adaptive mechanism

17. David Elkind, *Child Development and Education: A Piagetian Perspective* (New York: Oxford University Press, 1976), p. 65 and passim. He draws this view from his reading of Jean Piaget, *The Origins of Intelligence in Children* (New York: W. W. Norton and Co., 1963).

of the organism and this provides us with an active sense of knowledge-in-use to counter the dominant view of knowledge as a passive thing both in its acquisition and use. It is also important to note that conceiving of knowledge in this way provides a much needed link of knowledge to reality by continually forcing a fit of what we believe we know about the world with our intimate contacts and dealings with it. Thus, even when major conceptual-developmental shifts occur, one would expect them to be readily acceptable to the individual for whom they represent effective adaptiveness.

Recognizing that conceptual shifts do actually occur for both individuals and collectives, we educators can no longer safely view the curriculum and school learning as a simple linear and cumulative affair, and must recognize that there are points in the learning and developmental career of an individual and, indeed, of society and fields of inquiry, when whole new and different worlds open to view. Kuhn likens such events to a gestalt switch, while Piaget's demarcation of stages of development is more evolutionary, building on an earlier core of concepts and operations in the development of more refined, reversible, and second-order modes of thinking that permit reflection on thinking itself.

The nature of such conceptual changes needs to be understood more fully by educators since so many come to us to learn who, by reason of ethnic group, social class, developmental stage, genetic endowment, or even idiosyncratic accident, live in worlds to some degree different from the one we, as teachers, are trying to get them to see, understand, and participate in. If others cannot see the world as we do, or if we cannot enter their world to begin to help them to see ours, then we cannot share experiences in a meaningful way. To recognize that understanding different worlds is possible is to be in a position to do something about it. While *not* to recognize that possibility *may* be to be caught in incommensurable worlds forever apart, *to* recognize it is to be in a position to seek ways to understand empathetically and work within another's world to build bridges of reasonableness between the two. In many respects this is the key pedagogical problem of the educator in a pluralistic society.

Conclusion

I have tried in this essay to point to some theories that are forcing a reconsideration of our contemporary epistemological beliefs and assumptions. There are many more. What they all have in common and offer us as educators is heightened reflectiveness on some aspect of the concept of knowledge from a sociocentric perspective that in turn should cause us to reflect more fully on what we do as educators. I have also tried to treat the concept of knowledge in a broader way than it is usually treated by either philosophers or educators.

Philosophically, the epistemological tradition generally has tended to view knowing "egocentrically," from the perspective of the individual knower. Too often this has led to a spectator or contemplative view of knowledge. But even where the knower has been taken by epistemologists to be quite active in acquiring knowledge, their concern with truth and certainty has seldom allowed for the richer exploration of an individual's acquisition and use of social knowledge, skills, and standards of judgment in the various domains of human experience.

Educationally, on the other hand, we have tended to focus on the formal collective forms of knowledge imbedded in the traditional subjects and to treat them as highly organized static collections rather than as dynamically growing and changing systems. In doing so, we have too often ignored the function of knowledge in service to our collective and individual human needs to make good sense of the world and to be able to act effectively in it and on it. While we have not totally ignored the broader dimensions of knowledge, which include skills imbedded in all forms of human activity and values imbedded in ethical standards, institutions, arts, and ways of life, we have tended to treat such things peripherally. But they are also a central part of human knowledge.

Knowledge thus broadly conceived at any single moment in the dynamic nexus between individual, collective, and the world provides both the individual and the group with initial modes of communication, interpretation, and understanding as well as with a basis for judgment and for skilled action, but never without the possibility of critical reflection, modification, development, and change. Such social and individual knowledge not only enriches, and gives meaning to our experiences, but also provides the wherewithal, however tentative, to act effectively in the world and to seek more effective ways to conceive of it and act on it. Polanyi has likened our use of knowledge to the blind man's cane, literally as an extension of ourselves reaching out into the darkness and used to help us perceive and get about in the world.[18] In every immediate life situation in which we act as individuals or as collectives, we draw upon our reservoir of developed knowledge, skills, beliefs, and values and tacitly use them to diagnose and understand the situation, to choose appropriate ways to act, and to assess the consequences of our actions. In these many ways, we see that knowledge ultimately gets its sense, effect, and value in use and develops or changes as we test its fit in our common world.

To what do such broad and basic reflections about the nature of knowledge from the emerging sociocentric perspective commit us as educators? Certainly to the view that knowledge seeking and using is both an individual and collective affair of trying to make sense of, appreciate, and operate effectively in the world. But that has always been so. It is only now as we become more aware of this fact that we are also becoming more aware of both the problems and opportunities that are part of this conception of knowledge.

I began this chapter by remarking that because we are aware that we know, we can "consciously" educate. I argued that our conception of knowledge will determine to a great extent how we think and act as educators. As we come to recognize and develop more fully a concept of knowledge from the sociocentric perspective, we will become more sophisticated about such ideas as objectivity, relativism, learning, mind, science, art, judgment, and the like. Then we will be better able to invent educational strategies and practices that will help us fulfill our obligation to pass on human knowledge and to provide for its continual development in all its forms.

I note again that having the power to reflect on knowledge gives us the power to educate intentionally. I end with the plea that we use those powers wisely.

18. Polanyi, *Personal Knowledge*, pp. 55-56.

Aesthetics

Recognizing the basic capacity of all human beings for aesthetic experience, both Dewey and Whitehead more than fifty years ago addressed the idea of aesthetic education. Since that time a number of other philosophers of education have been intrigued by the educational possibilities of the aesthetic domain. Many will recall Harold Rugg's urgings to push forward the "esthetic frontiers" of education and Robert Ulich's sincere hope to ground general education in the arts and in the shared, equal human capacities for emotional feeling and communication. The more recent and sustained work of Ralph Smith, editor of the *Journal of Aesthetic Education,* and others like Donald Arnstine, Harry S. Broudy, and David W. Ecker speaks to the continuing interest of the philosopher of education in the relation between the aesthetic domain and schooling. Maxine Greene, author of the following chapter, also has devoted much of her scholarship and teaching to aesthetics. Here she sketches a philosophical perspective that is basic to her work with teachers at the Lincoln Center in New York City. (Editor)

CHAPTER VI

Aesthetic Literacy in General Education

MAXINE GREENE

Neglect of the Arts by Educators

In many schools and colleges today, the arts are dealt with as if they were of little social or pedagogical significance. And yet, in the culture at large, the arts are enjoying a remarkable apotheosis. People stand in long lines for tickets to the classical ballet. They crowd into museums to see masterpieces borrowed from the great European art centers; they gather in wonder before the paintings of Rothko and Rauschenberg, not to speak of Rembrandt, Cézanne, and Monet. Virtuoso pianists and violinists are treated as popular heroes and heroines wherever they perform; orchestra conductors and chamber music players are attended to with curiosity and awe. There are audiences for an unprecedented range of theatrical productions: Greek tragedy may compete with a Pinter play or *Porgy and Bess* for attention, while popular works like *A Chorus Line* and *Sweeney Todd* continue to win applause. Theatergoers, operagoers, gallery habitués, film enthusiasts understand themselves to be pursuing a unique kind of pleasure as they seek out more and more experiences with the art forms that interest them the most. Certain ones are able to say that the encounters they are having are valuable because they provide moments of imaginatively enriched perception: they are hearing new sounds, seeing colors more vividly, discovering a fuller and more adequate experience of what it signifies to be human and to inhabit a multifaceted world. Other people, however, are either unwilling or unable to give the reasons for their enjoyment; often, they are not even sure precisely *what* they enjoy. They find something immediately appealing, sometimes exalting in the flashing shapes on the ballet stage, the colors of Matisse's paintings, the sounds of the "Ode to Joy"; but they cannot articulate what they have experienced nor find words for what they have heard or seen. Then, of course, there are those who attend performances and visit galleries because they feel it gives them a certain *cachet*, the mark of being members of an elite community; and there are those who remain at the fringes, glancing at the paintings in gallery windows as they pass, listening to classical music on the radio, watching public television for glimpses of Nureyev, Liv Ullmann, or Laurence Olivier.

There are numerous qualitative differences in responses to the arts; but, for all the differences, for all the range of sensitivity and sophistication, audiences are growing constantly more open and more curious. Communities are investing in exhibitions and performances. The federal government is paying increasing attention. The arts, some say, are an important industry; others make the point that they are the health of our society, a means of countering materialism. Yet the same arts continue to be treated cavalierly or suspiciously in educational institutions, at least outside the studios and music rooms and the few school theaters that exist.

It is rare to find an educator willing to entertain the thought that the students presently in the classroom will one day compose the audiences for the exhibitions and performances proliferating throughout the culture. It seldom occurs to the classroom teacher that something might be done to empower those students to approach such art forms with understanding and awareness, to make informed choices among them, to "cherish" what they encounter in an enlightened way.[1] Few teachers even consider the possibility that the capacities needed for grasping and enjoying works of art may be as basic as those required for verbal and numerical literacy.

If included in the curriculum at all, the arts tend to be relegated to the "creative" domains. Literature, of course, is an exception; but literature is not ordinarily categorized as art. Art teachers are thought of mainly as persons committed to making paint, clay, papier-mâché, and other media available for self-expression. Music teachers, drama teachers, dance teachers are similarly conceived as people concerned about playing, performing, improvising; they are not expected to engage students with the complexities of

---

1. Harry S. Broudy, "Preparing Teachers of Aesthetic Education," in *Teacher Education for Aesthetic Education: A Progress Report* (St. Louis, Mo.: CEMREL, 1972).

finished works of art. The Matisse painting, the Mozart quintet, and the Balanchine ballet are treated as the property of the world outside the institution, an adult world of quite a different order than the one constructed by colleges and schools. There is some acknowledgement of the cultural importance of visiting museums, attending dramatic and orchestral performances and the like; but these are dealt with as extracurricular entertainments, in no way integrally related to classroom life. There is little effort to talk about such experiences in advance. No one thinks about introducing students to the modes of attending that a particular performance requires, to the qualities that distinguish the work of art they are about to hear or see, to matters having to do with expressiveness and style. And after students have had museum experiences or theatrical experiences, their art and drama teachers are seldom inclined to explore the connections between what happened outside the school and what they are trying to bring into being in the art rooms and studios within.

When asked to justify their lack of attention, classroom teachers will argue that their classrooms are intended for cognitive instruction or for the teaching of "competencies." They view the arts as largely noncognitive modes of communication, or vehicles for the expression of feeling. This being so, there is no way of measuring the outcomes of teaching aesthetic awareness; nor is there any way of translating what is to be learned into visible behaviors or quantifiable competencies. Conventional wisdom suggests, in any case, that all that is needed for aesthetic enjoyment is some affectivity, an emotional readiness that cannot be taught. It may be said, in fact, that sensitivity to form and color and sound is probably inborn, a type of genetic inheritance. It follows that educators can do little to make it possible if it does not already exist. Many will admit that aesthetic experiences are pleasant, fulfilling, and undoubtedly valuable; but efforts to cultivate them seem too difficult to undertake, even in the rare cases when such cultivation is thought warranted. Few are convinced that encounters with the arts have anything to do with the pursuit of meanings. For many, aesthetic experiences occur apart from the "realms of meaning,"[2] in quite another domain. This partly ex-

2. Philip H. Phenix, *Realms of Meaning: A Philosophy of the Curriculum for General Education* (New York: McGraw-Hill, 1964), pp. 139-85.

plains why the artistic-aesthetic is so often spoken of as being ornamental or therapeutic, why the arts are so easily disposed of as "frills."

Similar fragmentations can be found in higher education. Art history, criticism, and aesthetics are recognized as integral to the study of the humanities or liberal education generally; but teaching in these areas is conducted without the live presence of works of art (again, with the exception of literature) and, frequently, without specific reference to individual works. In the university too, spaces may be set aside for painting, sculpting, composing, film making; but they are at a figurative distance from the locations where inquiry and research take place. Little is done, on this or any other level of education, to nurture the aesthetic impulse in an ambience of aesthetic objects, or to relate creative explorations to the cultivation of aesthetic attitudes. Little is done to empower students to perceive aesthetically, to become discriminating in their encounters with the arts, to develop vocabularies for articulating what such encounters permit them to see or to hear or to feel.

It is as if there were two mutually exclusive worlds: one reserved for mastery of the structures of knowledge; the other, for the qualitative dimension of life, for the play of emotion, for the exploration of imaginary realities. Not only does this falsify the nature of the arts and obscure their significance for human experience. Cognitive learning is depersonalized and technicized in the absence of aesthetic concerns. The split widens between "unfeeling knowledge and mindless arousal";[3] it becomes difficult to hold in mind the variety of ways there are for making sense of the world. This persistent dualism may explain why the subject called "English" (commonly assumed to be pedagogically serious) is so infrequently dealt with as one of the arts. If it were thought of as the study of the *art* of literature, it could no longer be compartmentalized as the mastery of the skills of verbal literacy. Connections between the cognitive and the perceptual, the emotive and the imaginative, would come clear; and the barrier between the two worlds might be breached, at least in this instance. But

3. Israel Scheffler, "In Praise of the Cognitive Emotions," *Teachers College Record* 79 (December 1977): 171.

English continues to be relegated to the domain of the mainly cognitive; the rifts and the fragmentations remain.

There are various ways of accounting for the separation of realms. Educational history and sociology have made clear the dominance of moralism over the years and the preoccupation with utility in the educational sphere.[4] The prevailing ethos has been hostile to whatever has appeared to be playful, expressive, or impractical, except in those cases where particular created works (pious tales, hymns, caricatures) could be used didactically in schools. It is one thing, however, for educators to accumulate information with respect to the treatment of the arts. It is another thing to look critically at what has been learned, to inquire into preconceptions, to try to construct "networks of relationship"[5] instead of acceding to either/ors. Something more than an acquaintance with historical phenomena and social facts is demanded if educators are to become sensitive to the role of the artistic-aesthetic—sensitive enough to recognize its place in the interpretation and symbolizing of experience, in the effort to make sense of the common world.

Art Education, Art Appreciation, and Beyond

The argument in this chapter is threefold: that aesthetic experiences should be given a central place in general education; that such experiences require a distinctive mode of literacy; and that classroom teachers and general educators, working in cooperation with art teachers and practicing artists, are potentially capable of enabling students to learn how to learn to be literate in this way. The focus of the chapter is on aesthetic education, or on ways of teaching intended to make aesthetic literacy possible. To use the term "literacy" in this context is to suggest that there are certain decoding or interpretive skills, certain modes of "knowing how"[6]

---

4. See Michael B. Katz, *The Irony of Early School Reform: Educational Innovation in Mid-Nineteenth Century Massachusetts* (Cambridge: Harvard University Press, 1968), pp. 115-60, and David B. Tyack, *The One Best System: A History of American Urban Education* (Cambridge: Harvard University Press, 1974).

5. Paul H. Hirst, "Liberal Education and the Nature of Knowledge," in *Education and Reason*, Part 3, or "Education and the Development of Reason," ed. R. F. Dearden, Paul H. Hirst, and R. S. Peters (London: Routledge and Kegan Paul, 1975), p. 23.

6. Gilbert Ryle, *The Concept of Mind* (New York: Barnes and Noble, 1949), pp. 25-61.

involved in fully realized encounters with the arts. It is also to suggest that the discrimination, sensitivity, and responsiveness associated with such literacy contribute to an understanding of the world around. No form of literacy, of course, is taught for its own sake. Like verbal and numerical literacy, aesthetic literacy provides acquaintance with specifiable languages, as it does with particular ways of perceiving and imagining. Not only may this lead to heightened awareness of actual works; it may bring about an enriched acquaintance with the appearances of things (and the feel, and the sound), even as it enlarges the symbolic repertoires needed for thinking about the world and expressing what is thought.

Aesthetic education differs considerably from what has been traditionally known as art education, crucial as art education is for the development of the young. It is assumed that art teachers (drama teachers, dance teachers, music teachers, film teachers) and practicing artists will be present in schools and colleges seriously committed to the arts. Such persons create opportunities for exploration of the raw materials of art; they make it possible for students to pose questions having to do with shape and texture and imagery. They free those who are interested to make things out of paint, clay, sound, language, even the body in motion—to bring into the world new objects and enactments and events, each an embodiment of feeling, each a rendering of the "real." Experiences like this help provide a foundation for aesthetic literacy, for learning "what it feels like to live in music, move over and about in a painting, travel round and in between the masses of a sculpture, dwell in a poem."[7] They are likely to do so, however, only when classroom teachers are willing to open themselves to what transpires in the studio settings, theaters, and music rooms. What happens there must be incorporated in a live context of aesthetic concern, of articulated attention to the arts.

Aesthetic education, however, is not to be identified with art appreciation any more than it is with art education in any given school. In its simplest and most familiar form, art appreciation has entailed diverse efforts to acquaint students with the structures of particular art forms, their languages, their history, their styles. Too often, especially in junior high schools and high schools, the works

7. Louis Arnaud Reid, *Meaning in the Arts* (London: Allen and Unwin, 1969), p. 302.

of art under study have been introduced as "givens," objectively existent in the world. Chopin's piano music, French nineteenth-century opera, neoclassical painting: all such works have been presented as types of inspired creation, there to be admired and properly named. Little attention has been paid to the stance or the responsiveness of the percipients—the beholders or the listeners. Little has been done to enhance their awareness of the elements of perception peculiar to the music or the opera or the painting, of the qualities aware percipients may summon into existence by the intensity of their noticing, the manner in which they attend.

Art appreciation has, of course, taken a variety of forms. At its best, the teaching of literature may provide a sophisticated example of what art appreciation might mean, especially in those rare cases when literature is treated as an art. The forms and structures of literary works are studied; attention is paid to the analytical and critical phases of interpretation. On occasion, a process is undertaken that evokes and grounds a noticing (and cherishing) of the expressive, sensual, and formal qualities of novels, stories, poems. Sometimes, novels and stories are considered within historical contexts or social schemes, or in connection with contemporary works of art in other domains. No matter what the focus, an effective teacher functions as a good critic functions; and this is true—or ought to be true—wherever efforts are made to illuminate and make accessible particular works of art.

Criticism is a way of talking about specific works (novels, poems, short stories, films, paintings, plays, musical pieces) for the sake of elucidating them and helping others encounter them discriminatingly. It has been said with regard to literary criticism that it is a "normal prolongation of intelligent reading." In comparing what is disclosed by a book with what one has experienced, or in comparing one book with another, one begins to be a critic. Criticism always begins with actual and personal engagements, after a number of which "there arises the need to question, to analyse, to set in order, to compare." [8] The same can be said with regard to criticism of other art forms. The primary task is to disclose, to illuminate, to enable other people to see. There follows the activity of interpretation or explanation; and, after that, there

8. Graham Hough, *An Essay on Criticism* (New York: W. W. Norton and Co., 1966), pp. 25-61.

is the task of delivering verdicts, making judgments, offering recommendations.

The critic as teacher, one writer says, is a person "who affords *new* perceptions and with them new values." [9] The teacher as critic (the teacher of literature or art appreciation) must be someone perceptive enough to bring the qualities of particular works into view. Students, for example, may have a vague feeling about the vividness of a landscape described in a short story, the delicacy of a line in a painting, the frenzy of a dance movement, the exhilaration of a musical theme. The idea is for the teacher to point to and make visible (or audible) such qualities. Like the critic, the teacher endeavors to orient the perceiver, to direct perception in such a way that the individual student becomes better able to discriminate details and discern emerging forms. Not only is attentiveness heightened if this occurs. A ground is created for the making of judgments, since works of art can only be praised or condemned with reference to the qualities they possess.

Since the focus of criticism is ordinarily on the work in its specificity, questions having to do with the nature of the aesthetic object are ordinarily set aside. Little is said about what it signifies to break with habitual modes of seeing and sense making and move into imaginary or fictive worlds. Little is said about the distinctiveness of the symbol systems, the languages of the various arts.[10] The poem or the play or the painting makes so many demands in its concrete presentness that teachers scarcely think about such matters as illusion and representation, or the relation between the reality of the work and what people in the street or scientists call "real." They are unlikely to wonder about the status of a Faulkner story or an Ives sonata or a Martha Graham dance in the general framework of things. Nor are they inclined to ponder what it might signify to locate such created things in an art world, a space where questions might arise with respect to each of them as an aesthetic object, susceptible to realization as a work of art. Questions relating to aesthetic experiences are seldom raised; nor are questions having to do with the place of the artistic-aesthetic

9. Arnold Isenberg, "Critical Communication," in *Philosophy Looks at the Arts*, ed. Joseph Margolis (Philadelphia: Temple University Press, 1977), p. 411.

10. See Nelson Goodman, *Languages of Art: An Approach to a Theory of Symbols* (Indianapolis: Hackett Publishing Co., 1976).

in human lives. And, for all their dependence upon criticism, teachers are not prone to inquire into the meanings of criticism nor into the ways in which different critical approaches are influenced by different conceptions of the arts.

The opening up of particular works of art is a necessary foundation for the achievement of aesthetic literacy. It is in the course of reflecting upon actual experiences with works of art that the crucial questions arise. They can be responded to when the specific understandings gained through the aid of criticism or courses in art appreciation are placed in a larger context. The classroom teacher or the general educator may well develop the capacity to create that context, given a degree of familiarity with certain concepts in aesthetic philosophy. There might then be opportunities to place particular works within an art world large enough to include the range of artistic genres and forms, rich enough to provoke a distinctive conversation centering on the kinds of apprehension the realm of the artistic-aesthetic requires. In such a context, the undertakings of teachers of art, of literature, of drama, of music, and the rest may be brought together. The initiative, however, can best be taken by the general classroom teacher (who, of course, may also be an English teacher or a teacher in one of the other disciplines), if that person can be opened to aesthetics and the multiple questions respecting the arts.

Philosophy and the Art World

Teachers willing to take such an initiative require acquaintance with the "doing" of philosophy. They ought also to be familiar with what it means to explore at least one art medium; and they should have at hand a range of reflected-on experiences with works of art. Philosophic concepts and modes of inquiry become meaningful when they can be applied to actual encounters, and when they appear to clarify or resolve questions posed at moments of significant involvement. To "do" philosophy in the domains of the artistic-aesthetic is to think about one's thinking with regard to the ways in which engagements with the arts contribute to ongoing pursuits of meaning, efforts to make sense of the world. It is to reflect upon perceived realities as well as those that have been conceptualized, and to ponder the phases of remembered experiences with the arts. It is, moreover, to examine the possibilities of making available the kinds of insights, the ways of proceeding that might enable students to develop a discriminating and aware apprehension of created things, objects and events like sculptures and sonnets and sonatas offered for enjoyment, for an intensified and more vivid life. And it is to ponder ways of acquainting students with the meaning of aesthetic qualities and enabling them to become conscious of them when they appear. As John Dewey saw it, the doing of philosophy may well help "indicate what to look for and what to find in concrete aesthetic objects"; but it ought also to make persons aware of the function of the arts in relation to other experiences and to suggest the conditions under which "the full realization of that function" might be achieved.[11] Some mastery of aesthetics by practicing teachers may not only illuminate "what to look for" but also empower them to devise a pedagogy founded in "making" and informed "attending." It ought to be a pedagogy that links art to understanding, even as it liberates students to look through alternative perspectives and take new vantage points on the world.

More than a perception of individual art forms is involved, fundamental as that perception is. Taking one philosophic standpoint, teachers may choose to see aesthetic experience as a form of understanding, as "cognitive experience distinguished by the dominance of certain symbolic characteristics and judged by standards of cognitive efficacy."[12] This is Nelson Goodman's view; and it is elaborated by a conception of the different arts as distinctive symbol systems. They range from the nonverbal to the verbal; they differ in the sense that some are "autographic" and others "allographic." An autographic art form, like a painting, cannot be forged or duplicated without losing its quality of genuineness; while an allographic art form, like music or dance, depends upon notation and is realized at a second stage, when it is performed. Literature is a one-stage form, because it does not have to be performed to be realized; but it is not autographic, because there can be many accurate copies of a given text. These differences (involving scripts, texts, scores, and notational systems) are what interest Goodman, not the question of whether any particular art form

---

11. John Dewey, *Art as Experience* (New York: Minton, Balch and Co., 1934), p. 12.

12. Goodman, *Languages of Art*, p. 252.

represents external reality better than any other or brings us closer to a "truth." He has written that "the world is as many ways as it can be truly described, seen, pictured, etc. . . . and there is no such thing as *the* way the world is." [13] Teachers who turn to this approach as a mode of aesthetic education would concentrate on enabling students to make discriminations and identify symbol systems. They would emphasize the importance of interpreting specific works and "reorganizing the world in terms of works and works in terms of the world." As Goodman sees it, "Much of our experience and many of our skills are brought to bear and may be transformed by the encounter. The aesthetic 'attitude' is restless, searching, testing—is less attitude than action: creation and re-creation." [14] Satisfaction is the primary aim of the activity demanded. This makes the arts different from the sciences, the aim of which is an increase in knowledge. There is often pleasure connected with scientific inquiry, as there is a great deal of satisfaction; but, again, the end-in-view of scientific inquiry is not satisfaction but knowledge. The point is that the states of mind in the arts and sciences are not inherently at odds. It is important to discover modes of fostering aesthetic abilities and, at once, to discover how the skills associated with the arts and sciences sustain or inhibit one another. Distinctive though they are, they do not inhabit separate worlds.

Another standpoint that might be taken is that associated with phenomenological ways of thinking. Here, the artistic-aesthetic constitutes an identifiable "province of meaning," one of several provinces that offer human beings perspectives on experience.[15] Reality, according to this view, can be understood to be interpreted experience; and since there are multiple ways of interpreting experience, human beings live in multiple realities. Central is the world of everyday life each person lives along with others and interprets by means of standard cultural constructs, interpretations that are taken for granted most of the time. Taking them for granted, most people do not realize that even ordinary social reality derives its meaning from the ways the members of some in-

13. Ibid., p. 6.
14. Ibid., pp. 241-42.
15. Alfred Schutz, *Collected Papers I, The Problem of Social Reality* (The Hague: Martinus Nijhoff, 1967), p. 231 ff.

group learn to think and talk about it. Individuals are dominated, in their everyday existence, by what is called the "natural attitude," an unquestioning way of addressing a world conceived to be given, predetermined, resistant to redefinition or to change.

There are, however, interpretations of reality that differ from commonsense interpretations. They have been called "provinces of meaning," each one of which is characterized by a definable "cognitive style" and mode of directing attention. According to Alfred Schutz, "all these worlds—the world of dreams, of imageries and phantasms, especially the world of art, the world of scientific contemplation, the play world of the child . . . —are finite provinces of meaning." [16] Each province, each "subuniverse," includes sets of experiences that are compatible with one another in attitude taken, degree of distance from the lived world, symbolism used to schematize what is selected out for attention. This is why people experience "jolts" or "shocks" when they move from the movie theater to the street, when they are aroused from dreams, when they go from the church to the scientific laboratory. It is not that they are moving into disparate worlds; it is simply that they have to accommodate to different ways of sense making, of interpreting what they find around them at a particular moment of time. Much the same thing may be said about the academic disciplines such as history, sociology, geology, physics, mathematics. Each may be considered a distinctive province of meaning; each one offers a distinctive perspective on the world.

Identifying the artistic-aesthetic with a province of meaning, as Schutz does, suggests that certain recognizable kinds of apprehension are included within it, each one marked by a specifiable cognitive style—a style that marks them all artistic-aesthetic in character. These modes of awareness all involve a break with the "natural attitude," for one thing, with ordinary ways of looking upon and making sense of the world. Art works select out certain dimensions of experience, frame them, set them apart; and, by so doing, they make available new possibilities of perception and cognition. Because so much depends upon the live, attending consciousness of a percipient, this is a domain that depends upon subjective awareness (and the contribution of such awareness) more than, for example, mathematics or history. The percipient's

16. Ibid., p. 232.

personal history and distinctive perspective cannot be excluded or "bracketed out," as they have to be when something approximating "objectivity" is sought. The arts, therefore, offer new standpoints on the taken for granted by requiring that those who engage with them break with the conventional and routine, hear with their own ears, see through their own eyes. The world disclosed through such engagements is different from the determined world of purely rational apprehension; it may be what Jean-Paul Sartre called "a magical world" [17] apprehended in horror or wonder or delight, always apprehended anew.

Again, there are identifiable and compatible experiences included within the artistic-aesthetic subuniverse. To experience an Auden poem as if it were an expression the readers have made their own is compatible with listening to a Schubert song as if it were the listener's own emotional expression, and with perceiving the scene within a painting as if the beholder were inside it, looking from the artist's vantage point at the mist rising over the Seine or the child behind the metronome or the destruction of the Basque town.[18] This "style" of paying attention allows the percipient to apprehend feelings embodied in the work at hand. It is a distinctive mode of noticing, not for case histories or historical records, but for art forms alone. The alternative (as when one hears a cry on the street or notices some one gesturing in welcome or alarm) is to assume that a personal emotion is being expressed and to look *behind* the work to the maker's biography in the incorrect assumption that what is being apprehended through the work is the artist's own bitterness or longing or awe or outrage. To do this is to misconceive the function of art.

There is, it happens, another equally valid mode of attending that has to do with experiencing an art form from without. This, too, is distinctive of the artistic-aesthetic province of meaning; and experiences of this sort may occur throughout the range of art. They involve a clear perceiving of a work as a created artifact, of content embodied in form, of subject matter transfigured through such embodiment. *The Adventures of Huckleberry Finn,*

17. Jean-Paul Sartre, *The Emotions: Outline of a Theory* (New York: Philosophical Library, 1948), p. 85.

18. See R. K. Elliott, "Aesthetic Theory and the Experience of Art," in *Philosophy Looks at the Arts*, ed. Margolis, pp. 45-57.

viewed as an artifact, reveals a type of content—a journey on a raft on the Mississippi, a contest between innocence on the river and corruption on the river banks—that cannot be separated from its form, anymore than it can be conceived apart from the invented vernacular through which it is expressed. At once, the subject matter (rural life in the antebellum South, the predicaments of a fatherless boy and a runaway slave) has its own effect on how the form of the journey is apprehended, even as it gives rise to the particular form and is transformed and transfigured by it. So it is with Monet's river paintings and Matisse's domestic scenes, which—when viewed from without—reveal content transfigured, fundamentally altered by composition as well as the colors and the treatment of light. So it is with most art forms when they are attended to in a manner that allows patterns and relationships to come clear, when perceiving and feeling and understanding come together to make the transformations possible. But, again, this can never happen unless the percipient is actively and personally engaged.

If teachers can begin to view the artistic-aesthetic as a province characterized by such experiences and become conscious of the cognitive style that allows them to occur, they are on the way to identifying the insights and awarenesses that must be fostered if people are to engage themselves fully with the arts. If they can view this as one of a range of provinces of meaning (or view the arts as distinctive symbol systems), they may realize the place of the arts in relation to other modes of interpreting experience, the modes with which they have been normally concerned. It is a matter of choosing to expand perspective and discovering a more inclusive view of what it signifies to educate persons, not simply to equip technicians with skills.

Perspectives on the Aesthetic

To speak of the requisite cognitive style and of the experiences that define the province of the arts is not to provide a definition of art. There is considerable doubt, in fact, whether "art" can ever be finally or conclusively defined. Every day new forms appear: minimal art; aleatory art; plotless stories; constructivist sculpture; pieces intended to shock and to surprise. None of the existing theories can account for all such phenomena, although people continue to devise theories of art, even as they work out theories of beauty, harmony, organic unity. Certain theories in the past have focused on the relation of works of art to the universe or the forms of nature; others have explained art forms by their relation to particular artists, who have been thought to embody their personal feelings or perceptions of reality in poetry, painting, song.

Oedipus Rex, *Hamlet*, and Michelangelo's *David*, for example, have been partly accounted for by the ways in which they "imitate" or represent cosmic rhythms, forces, patterns, forms. Men and women have always been moved or ennobled or instructed by them, it is said, because they bring living beings in touch with something ultimate, with the "really real." Lyric poems, according to the expressive theories, exemplify something quite different: they bring readers in touch with the artist's emotions (recollected or present); they communicate in the dimension of sentiency. Expressiveness, in whatever art form, is presumed to impart efficacy and power to the aesthetic experience. Directly or indirectly, percipients are brought in touch with artists' emotive lives; or they come to understand "the form of feeling" [19] by attending to their works.

There are other theories as well, alternative definitions: those that explain art in terms of the responses it evokes; those that center on the self-enclosed poem or painting or piece of music, upon its autonomy, its "significant form." [20] Still others direct attention to the hidden meaning in each work of art, something to be uncovered by a grasping consciousness; still others, to the ways in which a work presents itself to perception and is brought into existence as a work of art. There is today, however, a general agreement that no one of the theories mentioned can do more than disclose certain dimensions of or perspectives on the artistic-aesthetic. They function to draw attention to aspects of what is involved.[21]

The philosopher of criticism, Morris Weitz, believes that none of the theories succeeds in defining "art" once and for all, espe-

19. Susanne K. Langer, *Problems of Art* (New York: Charles Scribner's Sons, 1957), p. 88.

20. Clive Bell, *Art* (London: Chatto and Windus, 1914).

21. Morris H. Abrams, *The Mirror and the Lamp* (New York: W. W. Norton and Co., 1958), pp. 3-8.

cially in the face of the fact that new forms are constantly challenging what we have "known" and taken for granted about aesthetic phenomena. He proposes, therefore, that "art" be treated as an "open concept" and that we think about *how* the concept should be used rather than expecting an answer to the question, "What, finally, is art?" And, indeed, there would seem to be a value in consideration of aesthetic theories, because they teach us "what to look for and how to look at it in art." Weitz goes on to say: "To understand the role of aesthetic theory is not to conceive it as definition, logically doomed to failure, but to read it as summaries of seriously made recommendations to attend in certain ways to certain features of art."[22] This is how teachers ought to read it—not for the sake of becoming aestheticians but for the sake of discovering the modes of attending they can associate with aesthetic literacy.

Most philosophers of art agree that one perspective is not enough. They presume that understanding is enriched when various, overlapping perspectives are used for examining the artistic-aesthetic domain. This does not exclude the necessity for locating specific modes of awareness in the artistic-aesthetic province of meaning. Nor does it diminish the importance of urging persons "to attend in certain ways" so as to bring aesthetic objects into existence as works of art. There is little question but that such attending enables people to see more, to take more into account. Art, as Herbert Marcuse has said, "breaks open a dimension inaccessible to other experience."[23] Doing so, it provides a vantage point on other experience, a standpoint from which to attend to patterns and nuances, to see what is ordinarily obscured. Joseph Conrad was exemplary when he wrote: "My task which I am trying to achieve is by the power of the written word to make you hear, to make you feel—it is, before all, to make you see. That—and no more, and it is everything."[24] Writing about Paul Cézanne, Maurice Merleau-Ponty said: "Cézanne, in his own words, 'wrote

22. Morris Weitz, "The Role of Theory in Aesthetics," in *Problems in Aesthetics*, ed. Morris Weitz (New York: Macmillan, 1959), p. 155.

23. Herbert Marcuse, *The Aesthetic Dimension* (Boston: Beacon Press, 1978), p. 72.

24. Joseph Conrad, Preface to "The Nigger of the 'Narcissus'," in *Three Great Tales* (New York: Modern Library Paperbacks, n.d.), p. ix.

in painting what had never yet been painted, and turned it into painting once and for all.' ... The painter recaptures and converts into visible objects what would, without him, remain walled up in the separate life of each consciousness."[25] He, too, makes the world visible; he, too, enables human beings to see. Meyer Schapiro, discussing modern painting, speaks of multiple new orders being created before our eyes, permitting us, if we are perceptive enough and free enough, to see forms we have never imagined before. And he goes on: "Only a mind opened to the qualities of things, with a habit of discrimination, sensitized by experience, and responsive to new forms and ideas, will be prepared for enjoyment of this art."[26]

"Will be prepared," says Schapiro. It appears to be the obligation of the classroom teacher to open minds in the way Schapiro describes, to empower young persons to discriminate and to respond. The point is that none of the arts makes itself naturally available for understanding and enjoyment. The visions so many critics describe, the dimension the artistic-aesthetic promises to "break open," can only be made accessible through some mode of aesthetic education, some stimulation of aesthetic literacy.

Teachers and students require a minimal cognitive familiarity with the symbol systems and with the cognitive style involved. Such familiarity may feed into the reflectiveness that deepens and extends experiences with art forms. Also, it enables persons to encounter works of art in their own spaces, on their own aesthetic terms. A painting is more likely to be enjoyed for what it enacts upon the canvas rather than as a representation of something outside in the world—a bather, say, or a viaduct, or a cafe scene; and it will not be seen as a mere illustration of something that can be better said in words. Understanding of this kind may enable persons to distinguish between the text of a poem and the notation required if a musical work is to be performed and therefore heard. Perceptual and imaginative awareness must be deliberately cultivated against the background of this understanding if Melville's

25. Maurice Merleau-Ponty, "Cézanne's Doubt," in Maurice Merleau-Ponty, *Sense and Non-Sense*, trans. Hubert L. Dreyfus and Patricia A. Dreyfus (Evanston, Ill.: Northwestern University Press, 1964), pp. 17-18.

26. Meyer Schapiro, *Modern Art: 19th and 20th Centuries, Selected Papers* (New York: George Braziller, 1978), p. 232.

"Bartleby the Scrivener" is to emerge as a fiction rather than as a case history, if Othello's passion is to be responded to in *Othello*'s dramatic space.

Such concepts as the concept of psychic distance or disinterestedness[27] ought to become familiar to those who come to witness a play like *Othello*, an opera like *Tosca*, or even *A Chorus Line*, so that audiences will become able to watch the enactments on the stage as enactments taking place, not in the ordinary, commonplace world, but in an alternate world, an aesthetic space. Without some acquaintance with the notion of "uncoupling" from the familiar and the inescapably personal, spectators cannot establish themselves in the special psychic relationship required for the achievement of *Othello*, *Tosca*, or any other enacted work as a work of art. Those who come to see a classical ballet or to hear a symphonic poem must know enough to break with ordinary expectations and affairs if the dance piece or the music is to enter their consciousness as art. This is not to be taken to mean that spectators must take an impersonal or detached view, that they must not be present as persons with a history. It simply means that mundane and practical interests ought not to be allowed to overcome the imaginative engagement with the works at hand. A memory of a jealous relative or a prejudice against Moors ought to be set aside if *Othello* is to be realized; so ought a resentment of kings and princes, or of aggressive women, be set aside if *Tosca* is to exist for the spectator as a work of art.

No one can be "trained" into this sort of awareness or what we are calling aesthetic literacy. It is not the kind of attainment that can be separated out into discrete "competencies." A kind of aesthetic education must be invented, therefore, that provides certain fundamental insights, certain ways of proceeding; but its emphasis must be on releasing learners to attend in such a fashion that they are moved to go further on their own initiative, to begin teaching themselves as they uncover (through repeated readings, viewings, hearings) particular works, and as they move more and more deeply into the province of the arts.

27. See Edward Bullough, "Psychical Distance as a Factor in Art and an Aesthetic Principle," in *The Problems of Aesthetics*, ed. Eliseo Vivas and Murray Krieger (New York: Holt, Rinehart and Winston, 1965), pp. 393-405.

Aesthetic Educating

A teacher who attempts to educate with such ends in view ought to be perceptually and imaginatively involved with several of the arts and have experience with shaping the raw materials of at least one into something approximating an expressive form. It would help to experiment with writing short poems or paragraphs of imaginative prose, to experiment with the sounds emitted by a recorder. It would certainly help if teachers were familiar enough with their own physical beings to experience some degree of body response when attending to a ballet they wish to make accessible to students. To say all this, however, is equivalent to saying that all practicing teachers ought to feel alive and in the world, excited about their subject matter, even in love with some of it. To say this is equivalent to saying that teachers need to keep their own questions open, continually to break with "created structures," striving to move beyond.[28]

What, then, can such a teacher do to enhance students' opportunities to achieve aesthetic literacy? It is important, first of all, to realize that the domain of the aesthetic is more far-reaching than the world in which works of art exist. Everyone has some memory of sunsets, moon-flecked woods, snowy streets, children's hands. An awareness of certain aesthetic concepts (distancing, let us say, shape, timbre, form) may move an individual teacher to uncouple certain phenomena from the context of ordinariness and to perceive them aesthetically: a black tree shape on a winter day; the texture of a flower petal; the wind moving the leaves. In the effort to enhance perceptual acuity among students, the teacher might urge them to attend to the appearances of things around in unaccustomed ways. If teachers can enable the students to detach what they see and hear from its use value for a time, from its mundane significance, the students may be brought in touch with shapes, masses, shadings, tonalities of which they are hardly likely to have been aware.

The weight of the flagstones making up a wall, the deepening green on the playing field, the wail of a railway whistle: these are the kinds of qualities a teacher might bring into the field of attention. They are the attributes of actual objects and events that may

---

28. Maurice Merleau-Ponty, *The Structure of Behavior* (Boston: Beacon Press, 1967), pp. 160-66.

be made to appear intrinsically interesting and expressive when heeded in a certain way. Not only may this provoke certain persons to heightened attentiveness. It may introduce them to the idea of the qualitative, an idea focal to aesthetic literacy. It may, in some cases, permit a return to some original landscape, what William James called "the world of living realities" that he identified with "that sense of our own life which we at every moment possess." He said that that world (that landscape) is "the hook from which the rest dangles, the absolute support."[29] It is the world in which human beings are aware of the qualities that underlie and ground the logical properties they devise, the scientific judgments they make. They come in touch with these, it well may be, when certain suggestive notions direct their retinal viewing, when they are enabled to uncover their qualitative worlds.

This mode of attending, of qualitative perceiving, is fundamental to aesthetic literacy. No matter how the concept "art" is understood, the notion of perception always has a central role to play. For a long time, it was believed that perceiving entailed a passive taking in of images and shapes and sounds that later would be conceptually ordered into a pattern. According to this view, a person might see a dancer's body flashing through space, circles of light, the curve of an arm, the lift of a leg. Then one would work mentally to organize the disparate sense data in order to give them meaning, to interpret what had been sensed as dance. Or, contemplating an oil painting, a beholder might single out a red apple, a fold of drapery, a china vase, and only later pattern the disparate parts into an organized whole. It is now known that perceiving must be understood as an active mode of grasping the structures of the world of appearances, or what is otherwise called the "phenomenal" world.

We grasp the painting or the dance as a whole, fused with whatever meaning is imparted to it, depending upon our past experiences and the expectations those experiences have raised. It is our "subsidiary awareness," writes Michael Polanyi, that endows an object or an event with meaning.[30] In the case of an oil paint-

29. William James, *The Principles of Psychology*, vol. 2 (New York: Dover Publications, 1950), p. 297.

30. Michael Polanyi, "Sense-Giving and Sense-Reading," in *Knowing and Being*, ed. Marjorie Grene (Chicago: University of Chicago Press, 1969), p. 184.

ing, we have a subsidiary, almost an unconscious awareness of colors, lines, contours to use as visual clues. We attend *from* those clues *to* the forms of apples, folds of drapery, wallpaper patterns that make up the picture before us, the painting of which we are focally aware. We would be unable to endow it with meaning as a painting were it not for our tacit awareness of colors, lines, contours, and the rest.

More is required, however, if we are to perceive the painting as a work of art. It might be said that the painting as a work of art was created for precisely the kind of perceiving described above: the perceiving of the qualitative, of the appearances of things. In that respect the work (like all other works of art) is what we have called a privileged object when compared to the flagstone wall or the green playing field or the whistle of a train. It is an object or event that can be brought into being as a work of art if those who attend to it are capable of a special sort of noticing, of apprehending, of personal grasping. The object or event is a selection from the world as perceived, the shaped and colored and sounding world in which we live our lives. It is the kind of selection that must be located in what we have called aesthetic space, in part created by the intensity of the qualities of the medium involved.

The painting may, of course, be examined for its chemical composition, its weight in pounds, its worth in dollars, the history of its ownership. If it is to be achieved as a work of art, however, it must be treated as an object made for a certain *kind* of perceiving. Unlike the chalkboard or the office wallpaper or the flagstone wall, it offers itself in a distinctive way to the body and mind of the person who is interested in it sufficiently to make it the object of his or her own perspective. Also, unlike the chalkboard and the wallpaper and the flagstone wall, the painting is likely to disclose more and more of its qualities or its perceptual attributes the more often and the more attentively it is viewed. The range of visual clues may be extended; the teacher (or the students) may point out colors, contours that were not visible at the beginning, that cannot be seen from a single perspective. The more clues, the richer the subsidiary awareness; and the more opportunities exist for attending from visual details to forms, folds, patterns, nuances, shadows, glimmers of light.

Even if one chooses to apprehend a painting or a dance piece as an emotional communication through the medium of color and movement, or as an imitation of something large and representative in the surrounding world, one is still required consciously to attend if the painting or the dance or the poem is to be realized as a work of art, no matter how "art" is defined. Dewey has written about the "work to be done on the part of the percipient" with respect to all aesthetic forms. "The one who is too lazy, idle, or indurated in convention to perform this work will not see or hear. His 'appreciation' will be a mixture of scraps of learning with conformity to norms of conventional admiration and with a confused, even if genuine emotional excitation."[31] Like many other students of aesthetic experience, Dewey was suggesting that an appropriate stance must be taken and that persons must live up to certain norms of perceiving if works are to exist for them as aesthetic objects.

Ernst Gombrich has also laid stress upon the mind's constitutive acts and upon the importance of "mental sets."[32] For him, there can be no such phenomenon as the "innocent eye," either on the part of an artist or a person who succeeds in realizing an object as a work of art. All art, he writes, must be understood as illusion; it always involves image making and transformation. The transformation takes place through the use of certain "cryptograms," largely to be understood in terms of other symbols used in other works. We come to works of art, he writes, "with our receivers already attuned. We expect to be presented with a certain notation . . . and make ready to cope with it."[33] Our expectations are set up by previous experiences or by acquaintance with certain styles; and there are occasions when we are prevented from either seeing or interpreting because our expectations interfere.

The implications for aesthetic education are considerable. Not only ought young persons (in association with their teachers) be provided a range of experiences in perceiving and noticing. They ought to have opportunities, in every classroom, to pay heed to color and glimmer and sound, to attend to the appearances of

---

31. Dewey, *Art as Experience*, p. 54.

32. E. H. Gombrich, *Art and Illusion* (New York: Pantheon Books, 1965), p. 60.

33. Ibid., pp. 39-41.

things from an aesthetic point of view. If not, they are unlikely to be in a position to be challenged by what they see or hear; and one of the great powers associated with the arts is the power to challenge expectations, to break stereotypes, to change the ways in which persons apprehend the world. George Steiner has written that "Rembrandt altered the Western perception of shadow spaces and the weight of darkness. Since Van Gogh we notice the twist of flame in a poplar."[34] We can say the same about alterations in our vision due to the work of writers ranging from Shakespeare to Sartre, alterations in our hearing due to composers from Bach to Schoenberg and John Cage. The point is that such perspectives do not open up spontaneously. The capacity to perceive, to attend, must be learned.

There is also the capacity to imagine. There is the whole matter of imaginative awareness, an awareness that is also required if works of art are to be achieved. Imagination has long been conceived as a mode of effecting relationships, bringing (as Virginia Woolf once put it) "severed parts together,"[35] making metaphors, creating new integrations and unities. Perceiving affects the patterns, the configurations of what we see; but imagination transforms what is perceived. Gombrich gives an example of the work of imagination in one of his discussions of impressionist painting when he explains how "the beholder must mobilize his memory of the visible world and project it into the mosaic of strokes and dabs on the canvas" when he sees a Monet painting. And he points out that "the willing beholder responds to the artist's suggestion because he enjoys the transformation that occurs in front of his eyes."[36] Without imagination, there could be no image creation on the part of the beholder; nor could there be the transformations that any art form allows.

The same thing happens when imagination goes to work on the language of poetry: on Robert Frost's "woods on a snowy evening," T. S. Eliot's "dry brain in a dry season." There is Melville's white whale to conjure up; there are the derelicts in Beckett's *Waiting for Godot*, Willy Loman in *Death of a Sales-*

34. George Steiner, "The Kingdom of Appearances," *New Yorker*, April 4, 1977, p. 132.
35. Virginia Woolf, *Moments of Being*, ed. Jeanne Schulkind (New York: Harcourt Brace Jovanovich, 1972), p. 72.
36. Gombrich, *Art and Illusion*, p. 202.

man, Blanche DuBois in *A Streetcar Named Desire*. Any of these ought to evoke the capacity to transform, to build imaginary worlds in the course of doing so, worlds alternative to the worlds of everyday. Doing so, we may recognize the sense in which we all stand against a world of possible forms. It is imagination that puts us in relation to such possibilities, when imagination is stimulated by engagement with the arts. Dorothy Walsh has said that works of art, confronting us as physical things and as cultural products, are at the same time "imaginative vistas out of the actual." She went on: "To enter into the contemplation of a work of art is to pass through the context of the actual to the appreciation of a unique, discontinuous possibility." [37] The poet Wallace Stevens has made all this dramatically clear in his poetry: in, for example, "Thirteen Ways of Looking at a Blackbird" and "The Latest Freed Man." In the latter poem, he writes of a man who is wearied of familiar and old descriptions of the world and who suddenly finds a banal landscape becoming meaningful to him because he sees it so differently when it is imaginatively described.

> It was how he was free. It was how his
>   freedom came.
> It was being without description, being an ox.
> It was the importance of the trees outdoors,
> The freshness of the oak-leaves, as the way
>   they looked.
> It was everything being more real, himself
> At the center of reality, seeing it—
> It was everything bulging and blazing and big
>   in itself.[38]

Not only does the poem illuminate the transformations of reality provoked by imaginative activity. It makes clear the idea that aesthetic perception is a mode of viewing that can only be *personally* undertaken, by an individual present to himself or herself. To be "at the center of reality, seeing it" is to grasp what surrounds from one's own center and, in so grasping, to be conscious of one's con-

---

37. Dorothy Walsh, "The Cognitive Content of Art," in *Contemporary Studies in Aesthetics*, ed. Francis J. Coleman (New York: McGraw-Hill, 1967), p. 297.

38. Wallace Stevens, "The Latest Freed Man," *The Collected Poems* (New York: Alfred A. Knopf, 1964), p. 204. © Alfred A. Knopf. Reprinted with permission.

sciousness. It is in this sense that the artistic-aesthetic domain brings us in touch with our authentic visions, allows us—as unique individuals—to be.

Again, this can only happen if a person is interested in an aesthetic object or event, if one can become absorbed in its qualities for a time for their own sakes. Melvin Rader, discussing the transforming effect of imagination, has made the point that one phase of the imaginative mode of awareness is "attentional." He meant that imagination (in one of its phases) permits us to focus disinterestedly on an object, to distance it, and, by distancing, to grasp the painting or the poem or the sonata "in its full qualitative richness and imaginative fecundity." [39] In another phase, the "elaborative" phase, we elaborate the experience made possible by our focusing. This elaboration is a "moody and imaginative mode of vision for the enrichment of the intrinsic perceptual value of the object." [40] It is at this point that the object or event is in some fashion incarnated. But there would be no such significant personal experience if it were not for the capacity to focus, to attend; and we have made the point that that capacity can be learned.

There is among certain educators the view that children are naturally imaginative, and that oppressive social structures serve to tamp down and frustrate their creative energies. Recent research indicates that young children tend to be literalists, and that young adolescents show themselves to be even less imaginative than when they were in the early grades.[41] Persons are clearly born with the capacity to see and hear, taste and feel; but they do not, simply through maturation, develop the ability to use such capacities. Whether this is because our culture discourages this development, or because the kinds of social conditioning provided results in its deflection, the fact is that attention needs to be paid in all kinds of classrooms if children are to effect the connections and make the transformations associated with imagining. Situations must be devised to make possible the recognition and invention of metaphors. Storytelling, the writing and reading of poetry must be

39. Melvin Rader, "The Imaginative Mode of Awareness," *Journal of Aesthetics and Art Criticism* 33 (Winter 1974): 136.

40. Ibid.

41. See Howard Gardner, "Promising Paths towards Artistic Knowledge: A Report from Harvard Project Zero," *Journal of Aesthetic Education* 10 (July-October 1976): 201-7.

encouraged, even as young students are learning how to look and how to see. The ability to categorize in various ways and to transfer schemata between realms is as revelant to scientific thinking as it is to the appreciation of art.[42] Art works and art activities, it appears, may be useful and illuminating in many kinds of learning.

The artistic-aesthetic cannot, therefore, be identified only with the emotive or the intuitive. There is no question but that informed engagement with the several arts enables persons to explore experiential possibilities they never imagined before. To perceive, to imagine new possibilities of being and action is to enlarge the scope of freedom for the individual; and, when people work to open new perspectives together, they may even discover ways of transforming their lived worlds. Students may become increasingly familiar with the symbolic characteristics of the several arts without finding the arts wholly reduced to the cognitive. They may be freed to apprehend works of art through their feelings without finding them reduced to noncognitive forms. Emotion may be a means of discovering the properties and qualities of many kinds of art; but, without some acquaintance with their languages, people may become incapable of interpretation, of making sense of art *qua* art. Moreover, it might be difficult for them to make appropriate distinctions among the arts. To identify a painting with a written text and to attempt to "read" the painting as if it were a poem would be to falsify. But once students and their teachers are enabled to recognize the languages of both painting and poetry, once they understand that Rembrandt's or Rothko's cryptograms cannot be translated into Baudelaire's or Debussy's or Beckett's, they must bracket out or put aside certain of their formal understandings. Only then can they respond to the summons of particular works, narrow their attention, permit them to inhabit their consciousness. Only then are they likely to value them as created realities made for their appreciation and to hear, to disclose, to see.

Herbert Marcuse, exploring such experiences, writes that the languages and images found in works of art make perceptible, visible, and audible that which is no longer or not yet "perceived, said, and heard in everyday life. Art makes the petrified world

---

42. Howard Gardner, "Sifting the Special from the Shared: Notes toward an Agenda for Research in Arts Education," in *Arts and Aesthetics: An Agenda for the Future*, ed. Stanley S. Madeja (St. Louis, Mo.: CEMREL, 1977), pp. 267-78.

speak, sing, perhaps dance."[43] To be petrified is to be granite-like, susceptible neither to learning nor to change. If the artistic-aesthetic can open up the petrified world, provide new standpoints on what is taken for granted, those who are empowered by their teachers to engage with the arts may find themselves posing questions never thought of before. They may find themselves posing questions from their own locations in the world and in the light of what they themselves are living, what they themselves are discovering to be warranted, to be true. This is because engagements with works of art—aware, informed engagements—make individuals present to what is given to them, personally present, no longer lulled by the natural attitude. And it is those who can ask their own questions, ask them in person, who are the ones most ready to learn how to learn.

The classroom teacher and the general educator are challenged to open up a new province of meaning for those they teach, a province that may be opened to them through the doing of philosophy with respect to the several arts. They are asked to make possible the enlargement of experience that can only derive from informed engagements. At a technological moment, when so many forces are working to thrust persons into passivity and stereotyped thinking, the open-mindedness and the sense of exploration fostered by aesthetic involvements may well move diverse individuals to break with "the cotton wool of daily life."[44] To break with ordinariness and stock response is, at any age, to achieve a new readiness, a new ripeness. Not only will there be an awareness of things in their particularity, of beauty and variety and form. There will be a fresh orientation to the search for meaning in the many spheres of life. And this, fundamentally, is the point of aesthetic literacy. People may be brought to watch and to listen with increasing wide-awakeness, attentiveness, and care. And they may be brought to discover multiple ways of looking at blackbirds and whales and riverbanks and city streets, looking at things as if they might be otherwise than they are. If this occurs, they will have learned how to move into the artistic-aesthetic domain; and they may have come closer to discovering how to be free.

43. Marcuse, *The Aesthetic Dimension*, p. 73.
44. Woolf, *Moments of Being*, p. 70.

Logic

Teaching people to think effectively has been an important theme in twentieth century educational theory and practice. Early on, John Dewey's description of reflective thinking as "problem solving" in *Democracy and Education* (New York: Macmillan, 1916) and in *How We Think* (Boston: D. C. Heath and Co., 1933) provided many progressive educators with a formula for getting students to think rather than memorize. The influential "Harvard Report" entitled *General Education in a Free Society* (Cambridge, Mass.: Harvard University Press, 1945) stressed the need to help students develop their abilities "to think effectively, to communicate thoughts, to make relevant judgments, and to discriminate among values." In the *Improvement of Practical Intelligence* (New York: Harper, 1950), R. Bruce Raup, Kenneth D. Benne, George E. Axtelle, and B. Othanel Smith provided a blueprint for educators to develop a democratic community of reflective thinkers who could handle social problems intelligently despite initial disagreements on values. One of the major aims of the post-Sputnik curriculum reform of the 1960s was that of getting students to think like scientists, mathematicians, historians, and so forth. During this same period H. Gordon Hullfish and Philip G. Smith continued the pragmatic tradition with *Reflective Thinking: The Method of Education* (New York: Dodd, Mead and Co., 1961) and B. Othanel Smith's work on "critical thinking" became the basis for a continuous project on that topic at the University of Illinois in which the work of Robert Ennis has played a central part. (Editor)

CHAPTER VII

Rational Thinking and Educational Practice

ROBERT H. ENNIS

Introduction

What should we believe? Why? What should we do? How can we find out? What should we say? These important questions permeate educational practice in many ways. By considering several examples and looking to informal logic for general advice I intend to show in this chapter some of the ways to deal with such questions.

My first example is a situation faced by Mr. Paulo, a third-grade teacher, who was offered a pamphlet entitled *Four Factors That Affect Your Child's Teeth* for distribution to his students' parents. This pamphlet, provided by the Procter & Gamble Company, contains the following statement: "Your best guide is to check the label on the box to see whether the brand you are considering has received the official statement relating to effectiveness issued by the Council on Dental Therapeutics of the American Dental Association." Should Mr. Paulo have distributed this pamphlet to his students? And suppose one of his students (or a student's parent) had asked him, "Should I believe that? Is that the best guide in choosing a toothpaste?" What should he have done and said?

My second example is one reconstructed from a dialogue in a ninth-grade social studies class. How would you have handled the following situation, if you had been the teacher?

Jim, giving an analysis of the content of the previous evening's edition of the local newspaper: The thing that I want to prove is that the contents of this newspaper are all propaganda. Look at the back page—a full-page advertisement. That's propaganda. Look at the next page. Half of it's advertisements. The other half looks like straight reporting, but it's not. This story on the rehearsals of the Community

Players is really an ingenious attempt to make us to go their show. This article on the left is trying to make us believe that within five years the sewage plant will be inadequate for this community.

Sally, interrupting: Wait a minute. That last thing isn't propaganda. According to my father, that article is a true and balanced account. It just so happens that the evidence shows that we need a new sewage plant.

Jim: That may be, but I guess you don't know what "propaganda" means. Let me quote from *Webster's New Collegiate Dictionary:* "A doctrine or ideas, spread through . . . any organized or concerted group, effort, movement. . . ." There are a few other meanings here, but they are even farther away from what you think "propaganda" means. The point is that propaganda consists of any doctrines or ideas that are deliberately spread. So this article is propaganda. In a deliberate, organized way the newspaper is spreading the idea that we need a new plant.

Sally: You must have misinterpreted the dictionary, because that's not what "propaganda" means. That's only part of the meaning. The article on the sewage system used reason and fact in a balanced presentation. So it's not propaganda.

Jim: You're just wrong about the meaning of "propaganda." Look in the dictionary and see if you can find a definition for "propaganda" that is anything like yours. If you won't believe the dictionary, what will you believe?

Sally, after looking at the dictionary: Ms. Norko, who is right?

What should Ms. Norko have done and said? Before examining these problems I should like to sketch out my program for this chapter on logic, rational thinking, and educational practice. It is my intention to speak to a diverse audience because I believe there is a widespread and increasing belief among educators and the public that schools at all levels should promote high quality thinking, and that the study and discussion of educational theory and practice would profit from higher quality thinking. I hope to provide here some of the guidance needed as a consequence. My plan is to present a conception of rational thinking and to illustrate aspects of that conception in a set of examples, two of which have already been given. This conception is comprehensive and sufficiently detailed to give guidance by providing criteria for making judgments. Throughout the chapter I will try to help the reader develop sound thinking skills by pointing out how I have used aspects of this conception to direct careful thinking. While I have framed the conception in terms of characteristics of rational thinkers for those who would view it as an educational aim, with minor adjustments it also can be viewed as a set of guides for someone who wants to think rationally.

An Outline of a Conception of Rational Thinking

A rational thinker has a variety of proficiencies, a set of tendencies, and good judgment as shown in figure 1. This conception

A. PROFICIENCIES:
1. Observing
2. Inferring explanations, points, meanings, and so forth
3. Generalizing
4. Conceiving and stating assumptions, alternatives, plans, implications, conclusions, predictions, and definitions
5. Offering well-organized and well-formulated lines of reasoning
6. Evaluating authoritative-sounding statements, deductive and inductive reasoning, explanations, value judgments, and definitions
7. Detecting standard problems and realizing appropriate action

PLUS

B. TENDENCIES TO:
1. Exercise these proficiencies
2. Take into account the total situation
3. Be well-informed
4. Demand as much precision as the subject permits
5. Deal with the parts of a complex situation in an orderly fashion
6. Consider seriously other points of view than one's own
7. Withhold judgment when the evidence and/or reasons are insufficient
8. Take a position (and change the position) when the evidence and reasons are sufficient to do so
9. Accept the necessity of exercising informed judgment

PLUS

C. THE EXERCISE OF GOOD JUDGMENT

→ THE RATIONAL THINKER

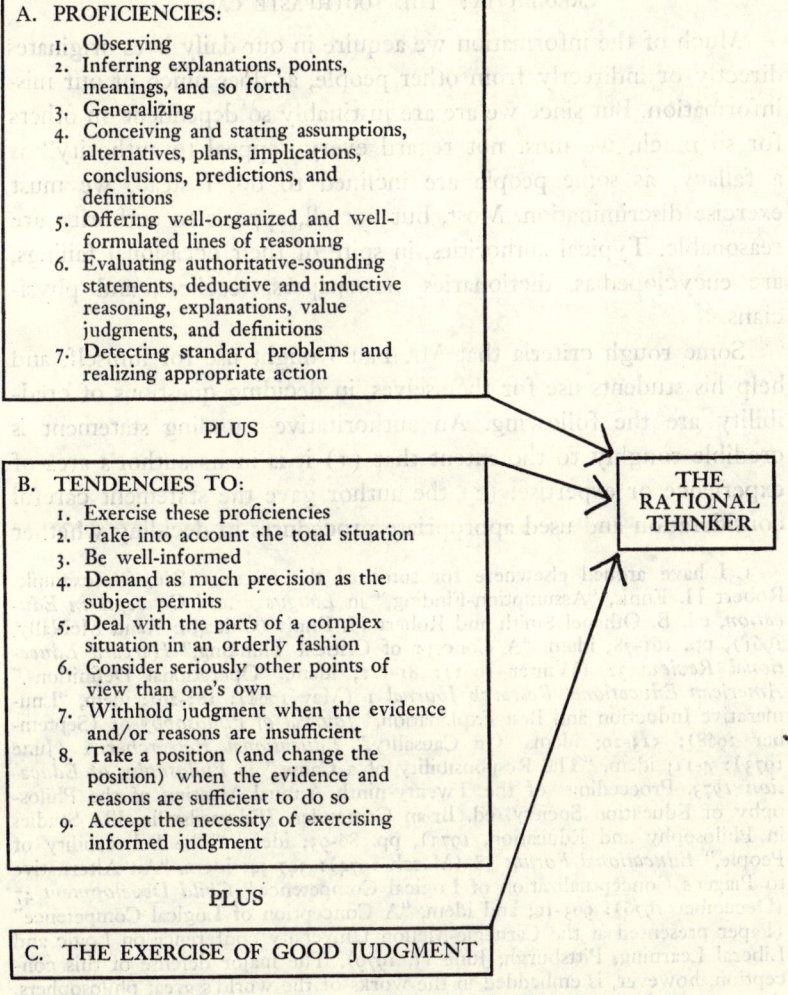

Fig. 1. Components of the rational thinker

combines creative thinking, critical thinking, and problem solving —all skills that are thoroughly interdependent in practice.

As I proceed I shall offer some commentary in defense of features of this conception, but for the most part I shall depend on what I believe to be the self-evident character of most of it when understood.[1]

Five Cases

CREDIBILITY: THE TOOTHPASTE CASE

Much of the information we acquire in our daily lives originates directly or indirectly from other people, as does much of our misinformation. But since we are are justifiably so dependent on others for so much, we must not regard every "appeal to authority" as a fallacy, as some people are inclined to do. Instead, we must exercise discrimination. Most, but not all, appeals to authority are reasonable. Typical authorities, in spite of their occasional failings, are encyclopedias, dictionaries, newspapers, teachers, and physicians.

Some rough criteria that Mr. Paulo might use for himself, and help his students use for themselves, in deciding questions of credibility are the following. An authoritative-sounding statement is credible roughly to the extent that (1) it is in its author's area of experience or expertise; (2) the author gave the statement careful consideration and used appropriate procedures in deciding whether

---

1. I have argued elsewhere for some of the features. See, for example, Robert H. Ennis, "Assumption-Finding," in *Language and Concepts in Education*, ed. B. Othanel Smith and Robert H. Ennis (Chicago: Rand McNally, 1961), pp. 161-78; idem, "A Concept of Critical Thinking," *Harvard Educational Review* 32 (Winter 1962): 81-111; idem, "Operational Definitions," *American Educational Research Journal* 1 (May 1964): 183-201; idem, "Enumerative Induction and Best Explanation," *Journal of Philosophy* 65 (September 1968): 523-29; idem, "On Causality," *Educational Researcher* 2 (June 1973): 4-11; idem, "The Responsibility of a Cause," in *Philosophy of Education 1973*, Proceedings of the Twenty-ninth Annual Meeting of the Philosophy of Education Society, ed. Brian Crittenden (Edwardsville, Ill.: Studies in Philosophy and Education, 1973), pp. 86-93; idem, "The Believability of People," *Educational Forum* 38 (March 1974): 347-54; idem, "An Alternative to Piaget's Conceptualization of Logical Competence," *Child Development* 47 (December 1976): 903-19; and idem, "A Conception of Logical Competence" (Paper presented at the Carnegie-Mellon University conference on Logic and Liberal Learning, Pittsburgh, June 13, 1979). The major defense of this conception, however, is embedded in the works of the world's great philosophers, the legal tradition, and the progressive development of the methodology of disciplines organized for the pursuit of knowledge.

to accept it; (3) the author was in full possession of his or her faculties; (4) the author had no conflict of interest when making the statement; (5) the author has a reputation for being honest and correct about the subject under consideration; (6) the author's reputation for being honest and correct could be affected by the statement; (7) in making the statement, the author is not in disagreement with others who satisfy this set of criteria; (8) the statement is not in conflict with what we otherwise have good reason to believe; and (9) the statement is close to being a statement of direct observation as opposed to being an inference.

These criteria fit under part of A, 6 in figure 1. In a fuller form they are included among the items in the more formal development of my conception of rational thinking that appears later in this chapter (pp. 167-82). Of course, good judgment (also part of the conception) is required in deciding how much weight to give to, and how to interpret, each criterion in a given situation.

In Mr. Paulo's judgment about credibility in the toothpaste case, the fourth and fifth criteria call for an adverse ruling about credibility in the making of the quoted statement. Procter & Gamble must accept its share of the reputation held by advertisers for being honest and correct—a low reputation, thus giving the statement a low score on the fifth criterion. Furthermore, when Procter & Gamble published the pamphlet in 1966, the only toothpaste I could find in the local pharmacy that had the Seal of Approval of the American Dental Association was one made by Procter & Gamble. Hence Procter & Gamble stood to profit from making the statement about the way to choose a toothpaste. That is what it means to have a conflict of interest.

In order to decide whether to use the Seal of Approval as a guide in choosing a toothpaste, Mr. Paulo must ignore the advice of Procter & Gamble on the matter. He probably should either seek the advice of experts who do not have a conflict of interest (whom he should then judge using the other criteria) or carefully investigate the processes of approval by the Council on Dental Therapeutics.

If he does neither, then he probably has no right to imply endorsement of the Procter & Gamble claim. Mr. Paulo, as a teacher, is likely to have his endorsements respected, so his implied endorsement becomes an implicit assertion that also is to be judged by the criteria for credibility. If he has done none of the things suggested, then he would not have credibility in such an implied assertion, since he has failed to satisfy the second criterion requiring the use of appropriate procedures.

But did his distribution of the pamphlet imply endorsement of the Procter & Gamble claim and involve him in making as an implicit assertion the one that I quoted? Without having the total context one cannot answer this question, although one might well think, "Probably so," on the basis of one's knowledge of the ways things generally go in our educational system. In the context (with its boundless details) I felt that his distribution of the pamphlet did constitute implied endorsement. If this endorsement came without the investigation I suggested—or something equally as good— then Mr. Paulo made a mistake in distributing the pamphlet.

Please be clear that again I am not challenging the worth of the product in question. I am only suggesting that we should not have used the Procter & Gamble statement as a ground for using the Seal of Approval as a guide to choosing a toothpaste. And I am saying that we should not have used Mr. Paulo's implied assertion as a ground either, if he had no other reasons to make the assertion.

How might a teacher so inclined attempt to teach students to be more discriminating in their judgments about the credibility of others? There is no simple formula; the teaching must fit the situation, and situations vary a great deal. I have found it useful to introduce the topic by mentioning the frequent appearance on the local television of the basketball coach of the University of Illinois encouraging us to buy a Chevrolet automobile. The coach, although he presumably has experience with automobiles, is not an expert in this area (and even if he were, this is an area where supposed experts disagree, giving his recommendation difficulties on the seventh criterion). But mainly, his expertise in basketball appears to be misleadingly exploited here. Furthermore he probably has a conflict of interest. That is, he was paid somehow for appearing in this testimonial.

When I judge the coach to lack credibility here, please be clear that I am not judging him to be wrong. All I am saying is that we should not let his testimony influence us in deciding, because he blatantly violates criterion one (or at least seven) and five: area of experience or expertise (or agreement with other "experts") and lack of conflict of interest.

Before leaving these examples, I should like to point out some important features of my commentary thus far because they will recur throughout this chapter. First, I have not provided a simple teaching formula. Second, in order to save space I have not referred to most of the criteria. One can probably infer how I would handle the others from what I have done with the criteria mentioned. If not, at least consider what you would do with them yourself, for this is what I seek most of all. Throughout the discussion I shall similarly omit reference to many of the criteria presented later in the conception of rational thinking.

Third, the list should be regarded as a loose set of criteria, most of which should ordinarily hold for a person to be credible in a given situation. It is not a list of necessary conditions. There is no mechanical formula for applying the list. Rather, it is a list of things that it is wise to consider in deciding whether to take someone else's word on something.

Fourth, you might have noticed how complex things became, and even then I have only scratched the surface. There is much more to say about these cases and the more one says, the more complex the situation seems to be. There is no easy road to rational thinking.

Last, note that the need for good judgment permeates every phase of the topic. In selecting certain criteria as overriding, and in deciding that these really are not satisfied, judgment is required. There is no mechanical way to make those decisions. Furthermore, since the list of criteria simply provides us with a set of things that often matter, good judgment is again required. Even conflict of interest does not always destroy a person's credibility. I once asked a colleague for a recommendation of a book on study skills. He had a conflict of interest since he had written a book on the topic, but I knew him to be scrupulously careful and honest. I decided in that situation to make little of his conflict of interest in evaluating his credibility on the question. *Good judgment is always required.*

THE "PROPAGANDA" CASE

When Jim said that propaganda consists of any doctrines or ideas that are deliberately spread he was offering a set of conditions that are, he implied, each necessary and jointly sufficient for something to be propaganda. That is, being deliberately spread was offered as a necessary condition for propaganda, as was being a doctrine or ideas. Jointly they are, he implied, sufficient for something to be propaganda. Sally did not deny their being necessary conditions when she said that he had given only part of the meaning. She was claiming that, even together, they were not sufficient. She was claiming this because she felt that the sewage article, although it satisfied Jim's definition, was a nonexample of propaganda.

In the previous paragraph I summarized the conflict and used certain logical words in so doing: "necessary" (roughly meaning *needed*), "sufficient" (roughly meaning *enough*), and "nonexample." These words represent ideas that are widely useful in rational thinking. Although the particular words are not essential for the expression of these ideas, I shall use them throughout this chapter because they are economical ways of expressing the ideas. However, I am not recommending their use in all circumstances; in some situations these terms are intimidating and unfamiliar to one's audience. Good judgment is again required.

What should Ms. Norko have done or said when faced with what some might derisively but unproductively call a "semantic dispute"? One move might have been to stipulate the acceptance of the definition in Jim's dictionary in order that the discussion proceed in an orderly manner (although as she might suspect in this case, dictionaries are in disagreement about this word). We need some kind of standard for word meanings in order to maintain efficiency of communication. She might justify this stipulation on the ground that dictionaries are a reliable standard, and that it is most convenient to adhere to the stipulated definition.

However, if someone produces another dictionary with a different meaning for "propaganda," then such a justification for stipulating Jim's meaning looks weak, because there would then be two conflicting meanings that would be endorsed by such an approach. But she could still stipulate Jim's meaning, and use a different justification. She might say that it is convenient and polite to let the speaker use a word in whatever way he likes, so long as he informs us of his meaning. This is a popular approach to definition, one that is frequently recommended for so-called "semantic disputes." Given really flexible people in the class, such a move by Ms. Norko could work at least for a while, but even so it would be wise to write the stipulated definition on the board so that the class does not forget that it is in accord with that particular meaning of the term that Jim has proved his thesis. This logical move, the arbitrary stipulation of a meaning for practical reasons, is often a dangerous one because it assumes that we are more flexible than we frequently are.

The danger is that Jim (or members of the audience), after he has proved his point using the given definition of the term, will interpret the term in its pejorative sense, and apply his conclusion using the term in that sense. (In its pejorative sense, "propaganda" means something like this: material intended to be used to persuade people of something, such persuasion being illegitimate in some way. In effect, I am offering an additional necessary condition, the *impropriety* of the persuasive techniques.) For Jim to make such a shift in meaning in the application of the conclusion would be to commit a fallacy called "equivocation." The fallacy of equivocation is a key concern in my treatment of this and the other examples in this chapter. I have picked these examples because I have so often found this fallacy to be a basic problem in issues that embroil people.

One way to have guarded against the equivocation would have been to write the definition on the board, but that would not have guaranteed protection against the fallacy. People might forget or ignore what is there.

To search out whether Jim is committing the fallacy, Ms. Norko might ask him the significance of his going to the trouble to prove his conclusion. If he says some things that show his intention to discredit the newspaper (such as "Do you want to get your information about the world from a propaganda organ?" or "I just want to show that we should be careful" or "We all should know how untrustworthy the media are"), then we have good reason to believe that he has committed the fallacy.

Actually in that example, Jim did not give such evidence in responding to Ms. Norko. Perhaps he was too quick-witted to get caught in that trap; or perhaps he just was not committing the fallacy. Even so, there is a danger that inflexible members of the class (this might be all of them) will get the impression that Jim has actually shown something bad about the local newspaper, and thus that they should regard it with suspicion. For a speaker or writer to invite such a mistake by using terms in a way that they are not likely to be interpreted is to commit the fallacy of *impact equivocation*. It is called this because the total impact is likely to be the same as that of equivocation. To call impact equivocation a fallacy is to assume that people are obligated to consider their audiences and to avoid saying things that are likely to mislead the audience. If you do not accept this assumption, then you are unlikely to endorse calling impact equivocation a fallacy.

However, it is quite possible that Jim was (perhaps unwittingly) talking out of both sides of his mouth when he avoided giving Ms. Norko such grounds for thinking that he had committed the fallacy. He might really have felt that something had been shown to be wrong with the newspaper, but he was smart enough to have avoided being caught in overtly committing the fallacy. This was probably so, if he had responded as indicated in the following dialogue:

Ms. Norko: Jim, last Saturday at the football game, you persuaded the referee that your opponent had stepped out of bounds by showing the referee your opponent's footprint and by getting testimony from people on the sidelines. Was that propoganda?
Jim: No, of course not.
Ms. Norko: Why?
Jim: Because the evidence was unbiased. There was no doubt about it. Everyone saw it.

Having suspected that Jim was consciously or unconsciously committing the equivocation fallacy, Ms. Norko used the strategy of asking him about a case very close to his basic interests and probing his response with the question, "Why?" People who consciously or unconsciously commit this fallacy tend to abandon their peculiar fallacy-inducing definitions on matters that are close to their hearts in their ordinary everyday experience. Their pseudo-intellectualization melts away in such circumstances.

Now I have tipped my hand about the definition that is in *Webster's New Collegiate Dictionary*, which in more recent editions incorporates the pejorative force of "propaganda" in its definition of the term. The definition read aloud by Jim is not a correct account of the current usage of the word. Current usage dictates defining the word as a pejorative term. That is, as a reported definition of the term for our culture, Jim's definition is mistaken because it omits a necessary condition. (A *reported definition* is one that attempts to depict actual usage. The function of a dictionary is to do this for large cultural groups.) I have found that people whom I encounter in everyday life think "propaganda" to be a pejorative term and furthermore are relatively inflexible on this matter. They have trouble accepting, or even operating with, the reported definition from Jim's dictionary. In our current culture, "propaganda" is a pejorative term; attempts to use it in Jim's stated way usually are at least cases of impact equivocation.

In order to avoid the impact equivocation and the possibility of ordinary equivocation, then, Ms. Norko could have suggested that Jim's definition was out of date and that the rest of the class would have trouble adhering to his definition. She could have then suggested (or drawn from the class) a definition that is more in accord with current usage and asked Jim whether he still wanted to make and defend a point, using the term in that sense.

It was important for Ms. Norko to have had a sense of where Jim was going with his line of reasoning and a feel for the flexibility of the class on the matter before she could work out a strategy. In general, one must have a grasp of the total situation in order to respond to a possible equivocation.

I do not mean to suggest that only the teacher can handle the threat of an equivocation fallacy. It is very important for students to learn how to handle this threat. Somewhere they should learn to do so. Perhaps Ms. Norko, instead of assuming responsibility for seeing that no fallacy was committed, might have tried to provide instruction about the dangers of equivocation and how to detect and respond to it.

There were many possibilities but they could not be pursued unless the teacher was cognizant of the equivocation problem. Hence I think that acquiring such cognizance should be part of the content of the study of pedagogy for teachers who will be in situations in which their students will try to prove things to each other or to their teachers. And it should be part of the content of general education. We all frequently find ourselves in positions like Sally's or Jim's.

In examining this "propaganda" example I have tried to do

several things. First, I introduced some technical and quasi-technical terms, on the assumption that the concepts attached to these terms are important ones for a rational thinker to have and to employ. The terms were "necessary condition," "sufficient condition," "nonexample," "reported definition," "stipulated definition," "equivocation," and "impact equivocation." These terms appear again in my treatment of other examples and in my later detailing of the proposed conception of rational thinking.

Second, I tried to show how these concepts can be useful in dealing with real teaching situations, particularly those where definitions and linguistic issues are concerned. These issues plague us more than most people suspect and are often at the root of a problem when attention is focused elsewhere.

Third, I advanced several hypotheses that are to be judged primarily by their ability to explain the evidence. One hypothesis is that "propaganda" is a pejorative term. Another is that people are relatively inflexible about the meaning of propaganda. A third is the hypothesis that Jim was using the term "propaganda" in one sense when he tried to establish his claim about the newspaper, and in a different sense when called upon to state the importance of his claim. A fourth is that Jim was intending to condemn the newspaper.

A new idea here for some is that interpretations and statements about meaning, intention, and human traits should be regarded as hypotheses to be tested by their ability to explain the data (unless they are too obvious to be regarded as hypotheses). An inference to such a hypothesis should then be looked upon and judged as an inference to the supposedly best explanation. Such inferring is listed as $A,2$ in figure 1 and criteria for judging the results will be offered under a later detailing of $A,6$ (pp. 174-75).

AN EDITORIAL ABOUT "SEGREGATION"

An editorial entitled "Jim Crow, Long Outlawed, Still Hangs On in Chicago" appeared in an Illinois newspaper. The editorial commenced with a reference to the decision of the United States Supreme Court in *Brown vs. Board of Education of Topeka*[2] and continued by challenging "segregated" schools in Chicago:

2. *Brown vs. Board of Education of Topeka*, 347 U.S. 483 (1954).

It's a long time since 1954 and the United States Supreme Court decision declaring state laws providing separate but equal schools unconstitutional.

Illinois children affected by school desegregation efforts, or the lack of them, today were not even alive at the time of that decision. . . .

If [Illinois Board of Education] members stand up to Chicago, they are justified in doing so, and would deserve the support of those who believe segregated schools are bad for children and bad for America. . . .

There are a whole set of reasons—some racist, others not—that have brought about this situation.

But it exists. And what it means is that nearly twenty-five years after the *Brown* decision, whatever the legality of the situation, white and black children in the Chicago area in effect are largely attending schools almost as segregated as when Jim Crow laws and practices prevailed over much of America.[3]

Has the equivocation fallacy been committed? This is a difficult question to answer because there are a number of things about which we cannot be certain and because of different ways of construing the evidence. We must operate on the basis of the best-established hypotheses we can find about what the writers involved mean and about the impact on the readers. We must then make a somewhat tentative judgment on these grounds. One thing is clear, however: it would be illegitimate for the editorial to base its conclusion on the decision of the Supreme Court if in the conclusion the term "segregation" is used in a different and less restrictive sense than it was used by the Court. To so shift the meaning would be in effect to apply a different judgment from that delivered by the Court and to commit the equivocation fallacy.

I shall advance three hypotheses about the meanings and inferences in the editorial and in the Court's opinion.

1. The first hypothesis is that the editorial intended to use the decision of the Court to support the contention that the Chicago situation is illegal. This hypothesis seems to be the best explanation of the title given to the editorial, "Jim Crow, Long Outlawed, Still Hangs On in Chicago." How else could we explain that title? There might be another explanation, but what could it be? Another piece of evidence (though weaker, I believe) in support of the

---

3. *Morning Courier*, Champaign, Ill., 10 December 1978, p. 38.

hypothesis is the last sentence in the last quoted paragraph. This sentence suggests that the situation in Chicago is inconsistent with the *Brown* decision. It also clearly declares the Chicago schools "segregated," segregation having been outlawed, as most people view things, in the *Brown* decision. The phrase that weakens this sentence as a piece of evidence for the first hypothesis is "whatever the legality of the situation." One might explain this phrase by suggesting that either the writer was too bright to get caught in an outright equivocation, or that the writer was just inconsistent. If neither of these explanations holds, then at least many readers will ignore this qualification and still be led to think that the *Brown* decision is being used against the situation in Chicago (indicating a danger of impact equivocation). In Chicago, and in other large cities, there were then and are still schools attended almost exclusively by children of a single race. These schools fit the racial housing patterns in this large city.

Now if the first hypothesis is correct, and if the Court actually used "segregation" in a different sense from that used by the editorial to justify labeling the Chicago situation as "segregation," then there is an equivocation problem. There are essentially two different senses of "segregation" in our contemporary culture. The first, because of its consistency with what is in dictionaries, is the basic meaning that people carry around with them, and about which they have formed some basic attitudes. The second is an extension of the English language of fifty years ago, an extension introduced by the phrase, *"de facto* segregation," the *"de facto"* part now having been dropped, as in the editorial quoted. The issue then becomes this: Did the Court prohibit segregation in the first sense, and did the editorial apply the term correctly to Chicago in the second sense?

The two senses of "segregation" I have in mind are roughly these: (a) the separation of a group with characteristic A from a group with characteristic B, the intention being to separate them because they have these different characteristics; (b) the separateness of a group with characteristic A from a group with characteristic B, whatever the reason for the separateness.

All cases of segregation in the first sense would also be cases of segregation in the second sense, but not vice versa. Satisfying the definition of "segregation" in the second sense is a necessary but not sufficient condition for satisfying the definition of "segregation" in the first sense. The first sense has an additional necessary condition, one concerning intention. I shall call the first sense the *intentional sense,* and the second sense the *statistical sense* of "segregation."

2. A second hypothesis is that the Court had the intentional sense in mind when it prohibited racial segregation in *Brown.* Otherwise I find it hard to explain the following passages from the Court's unanimous opinion in that case. The first passage states the problem and the second appears to give the primary reason in support of the decision.

We come then to the question presented: Does segregation of children in public schools solely on the basis of race, even though the physical facilities and other "tangible" factors may be equal, deprive the children of the minority group of equal educational opportunities? We believe that it does (p. 493).

To separate them [children in grade and high schools] from others of similar age and qualifications solely because of their race generates a feeling of inferiority as to their status in the community that may affect their hearts and minds in a way unlikely ever to be undone. The effect of this separation was well stated by a finding in the Kansas case: . . . "The policy of separating the races is usually interpreted as denoting the inferiority of the negro group. A sense of inferiority affects the motivation of the child to learn. Segregation with the sanction of law, therefore, has a tendency to [retard] the educational and mental development of negro children and to deprive them of some of the benefits they would receive in a racial[ly] integrated school system."

Whatever may have been the extent of psychological knowledge at the time of *Plessy vs. Ferguson,* this finding is amply supported by modern authority (p. 494).

The hypothesis that the Court meant to be prohibiting segregation in the intentional sense would explain why the problem was stated as it was, in particular by using the phrase "solely on the basis of race." If the Court had intended to prohibit segregation in the statistical sense, why would it have used the word "solely"?[4] The hypothesis is also supported by the kind of evidence that the Court appeared to think most relevant, as indicated in the second

4. James Conant made a similar point in his *Slums and Suburbs* (New York: McGraw-Hill, 1961), p. 28.

passage. That the Court meant to be prohibiting segregation in the intentional sense explains why it limited the indicated evidence to the consequences of separating individuals "solely because of their race" and of "the policy of separating the races," rather than including in the body of the opinion the consequences of just being in different places.

On the other hand, consider the following passage in the concluding paragraph of the Court's decision in *Brown*:

We conclude that in the field of public education the doctrine of "separate but equal" has no place. Separate educational facilities are inherently unequal (p. 495).

The key sentence here is, "Separate educational facilities are inherently unequal," suggesting that such facilities refer to segregation in the statistical sense. This sentence suggests a competitor to the second hypothesis, namely that the Court is using the term "segregation" in the statistical sense. A plausible way to handle this problem is to regard the sentence as oversimplified for rhetorical purposes and not indicative of the literal meaning of the Court. Now it is clear why detecting equivocation is difficult, if it was not already so. Here (as with the editorial's phrase, "whatever the legality of the situation") is some apparent counterevidence that must either count against this second hypothesis or be explained away. It seems more plausible to me (a) to explain away the key sentence by regarding it as not indicative of the literal meaning intended by the Court and accept the second hypothesis on the basis of its good fit with the previous quotations than (b) to accept this competitor to the second hypothesis, which would require us to try to explain away the first and second passages. This judgment is partly on the grounds of simplicity and partly on the grounds that lawyers take a more specific statement to be more indicative of intention than a less specific one. Note here the need to be informed about the area of concern.

Another challenge to the second hypothesis might be based upon the fact that the Court used "solely" in the first passage quoted. If the Court used "segregation" in the intentional sense, then it would be almost redundant to add "solely." But this possibility of redundance is not necessarily in conflict with the hypothesis, for it is very common for lawyers to be redundant as, for example, in the phrase "cease and desist." Note again the need for being informed about the area of concern.

3. Now if the editorial writer intended to lean on the opinion of the Supreme Court in *Brown* (the first hypothesis), and if the second hypothesis (that the Court had in mind segregation in the intentional sense) is correct, then the writer has committed the equivocation fallacy, if he or she has used the term "segregation" in the statistical sense (which is the third hypothesis).

The third hypothesis (that the editorial was referring to segregation in the statistical sense) is strongly supported by the situation in Chicago and by what is being said about it, in the editorial and elsewhere. The percentage of distribution of students explains why the writer would believe that there is segregation in the statistical sense, and the writer's use of the term in the statistical sense would explain why there is no complaining that the authorities have assigned students to existing schools on the basis of their race. Furthermore, the fact that people are currently focusing on segregation in the statistical sense makes it more likely that this is the concern of the editorial, for editorials generally express concern about what other people express concern about.

In sum, then, I have offered three hypotheses: one concerning the connection that the editorial claims to exist between the Court decision in *Brown* and the situation in Chicago; a second concerning the sense in which the Court used the term "segregation," and a third concerning the sense in which the editorial used the term "segregation" with reference to the situation in Chicago. If my conclusions regarding these hypotheses are correct, then an equivocation problem exists in the editorial line of reasoning.

I am not contending that the editorial is wrong or right in condemning the Chicago school system. I am only suggesting that the editorial line of reasoning here is weak because of an equivocal use of the term "segregation."

But it really is not my primary purpose to show that there is an equivocation here. To do that, if it can be done, would require much further treatment, for there are many avenues of exchange that I have left untouched concerning this particular editorial. I do hope to have exhibited what the fallacy could be like in this important situation, so that we all can guard against it in discussions of educational policy, limiting our reasons in condemnation and defense of the Chicago situation and other situations to good ones, and in particular making sure that equivocation is not a basis of decision making.

Suppose, however, that we decide that the first hypothesis is not acceptable. Then the fallacy of equivocation would not have been shown to have been committed. Has the writer been exonerated and should we take the writer's word on the alleged impropriety of the Chicago situation?

I am not ready to exonerate the writer. Even if the editorial did not mean to say that the *Brown* decision gives support to a claim of illegality in the Chicago segregation (statistical sense) situation, there is a real danger that people will take it that way. Very few people actually remember the language and details of the *Brown* decision and some, contrary to a reasonable application of the criteria for authoritative-sounding pronouncements, will accept the editorial writer's apparent opinion, as suggested especially in the headline ("Jim Crow, Long Outlawed, Still Hangs On in Chicago"), on the ground that editorial writers should know what they are talking about. Since editorial writers should know that some will in fact take their apparent word on this, I believe that this writer should have been more circumspect. (Or perhaps it was the fault of the headline writer, to introduce another complication.)

But beyond the possible authority problem there is another, the fallacy of impact equivocation. In this case "segregation" was implicitly stipulated or assumed by the writer to mean segregation in the statistical sense. If most people do in fact apply and (deep down) interpret the term "segregation" in the intentional sense, then the editorial at least commits the fallacy of impact equivocation.

It is important to notice in this case the employment of the following aspects of rational thinking (listed together with the classification number in the conception that is outlined on pages 167-82 of this chapter):

Inferring meaning, implicit reasons, and reported definitions (and thus inferring to putative best explanations) (A,2)
Conceiving and stating implications, assumptions, alternatives (A,4)
Thinking suppositionally (explained later) (A,4)
Offering a line of reasoning in writing (A,5)

Judging authoritative-sounding pronouncements (A,6,a)
Thinking in terms of necessary and sufficient conditions (A,6,b)
Evaluating inferences to putative best explanations (A,6,c)
Evaluating explanations (A,6,d)
Evaluating definitions (A,6,f)
Detecting and dealing with such standard problems as the equivocation fallacy (A,7,c), the impact equivocation fallacy (A,7,d), the existence of a plausible competing explanation (A,7,f), and an unclear term (A,7,g)

In dealing with this case I also attempted to:

Exercise whatever proficiency I possess (B,1)
Take into account the total situation (B,2)
Be well-informed (B,3)
Demand as much precision as the subject matter permits (B,4)
Deal with the parts of a complex situation in an orderly fashion (B,5)
Consider seriously other points of view than my own (B,6)
Withhold judgment when the evidence and/or reasons were insufficient (B,7)
Take a position and change the position when appropriate (B,8)
Accept the necessity of exercising informed judgment (B,9)
Exercise good judgment (C).

I invite you to reread the treatment of the "segregation" example and identify examples of each of these aspects. This is a long list. It suggests that in any real case one must exercise many aspects of rational thinking at one time. These aspects do not operate separately. A rational thinker must do many things at once.

TEST RELIABILITY

Evaluation instruments are employed for a variety of purposes, including teaching, administration, research, policy establishment, and curriculum planning and appraisal. A key concept in appraising evaluation instruments is *reliability*. But in its employment, there is often at least a likely impact equivocation, exacerbated by a frequently attached criterion for the determination of reliability.

In everyday use, reliable things are things on which we can depend to get things right. My Webster's dictionary gives the following as its definition of "reliable": "suitable or fit to be relied on; trustworthy." But in the technical terminology of testing, however, reliability simply means consistency. As Cronbach puts it, "reliability always refers to consistency throughout a series of measurements."[5] According to this concept of reliability, a gyrocompass that is initially set with an error of plus 90 degrees is quite reliable if it provides and continues to provide consistent directional information (for example, consistently reads north when pointed west, reads east when pointed north). In testing terminology, it would be reliable, but it would also be invalid (validity being the quality of testing for what a test is supposed to test). All that matters for reliability in the technical sense is consistency. Reliability in the technical sense is a necessary but not a sufficient condition for reliability in the ordinary sense.

The danger is that the public and unsophisticated professionals will misunderstand a claim that a test is reliable. A claim in accord with a correctly reported definition of the technical sense of "reliable" might be accepted and interpreted in accord with the dictionary's reported definition, and the test then receives acceptance that it does not deserve. That is, it might be a consistent measure of something other than what is indicated by its name, but an untrustworthy measure of the latter. Although test specialists are widely aware of this danger, the dissemination of facts about tests to the unsophisticated often neglects to mention this misleading tendency. This neglect is at least usually a sin of omission. Experts often unwittingly, although sometimes arrogantly, assume that their technical meanings are the correct meanings for terms, inviting impact equivocation.

Unfortunately, it is particularly inviting to specialists in testing to present information on reliability rather than information on validity, because it is generally much easier to gather data on reliability than on validity, and because the indexes that can be computed for reliability are higher than the indexes that can be computed for validity, if the latter can be secured at all. The higher the index the better the test looks. Test specialists are generally trying to build tests that will attract users, so they make decisions promoting reliability at the expense of validity. When I served as a consultant and item writer for the Educational Testing Service, a large testing organization, I found an overwhelming concern with reliability.

Test specialists and teachers in the employ of a school board will sometimes want to recommend tests, and if they recommend

---

5. Lee J. Cronbach, *Essentials of Psychological Testing*, 2d ed. (New York: Harper and Brothers, 1960), p. 126.

tests that do not appear to be good tests, the justification of their recommendations (and even the existence of the test specialists) will be questioned. So it is to their interest also to seek high indexes. Result: a temptation to overemphasize reliability all along the line, and thus a stronger invitation to some form of equivocation.

Note that I am here employing one of the criteria for authorities mentioned earlier—the desirability of lack of conflict of interest. I point this out here in order to reinforce my contention that the items in the conception of rational thinking that I present are interdependent and interactive.

But another and less widely realized problem with reliability is yet to come. It so happens that a frequently used index for estimating reliability is literally not an index of consistency of repeated measures, but rather an index of internal consistency. The widely used indexes of reliability, such as those obtained with the Kuder-Richardson formulas, are indexes of *the extent to which every item correlates with every other item* on a *single administration of the test*. The more homogeneous the items the higher this coefficient of internal consistency will be. Hence in choosing a test of, say, rational thinking, a heterogeneous trait, one is pressured by the use of Kuder-Richardson reliabilities to accept tests that have eliminated nonconformist items (which validly test for significant but disparate elements of rational thinking) in favor of items that are just like the rest. Thus a misleading criterion is frequently used to determine reliability (in its technical sense) and the problem is thereby compounded. Unfortunately, this aggravation of the problem usually goes unadvertised by test specialists.

When a line of reasoning in support of the use of a test gives as the reliability the result of the use of an item-conformist, internal-consistency Kuder-Richardson formula, there is at least a danger that, as a result of using this criterion, the pursuit of high reliability conflicts with the pursuit of test validity for heterogeneous traits. There also is the danger that the reliability so determined will be interpreted as reliability in the ordinary sense, that is, trustworthiness. The moral: beware of this impact equivocation.

In this discussion of reliability, I have exhibited another case of possible equivocation and impact equivocation, and have employed the concepts of necessary condition, sufficient condition, reported definition, and criteria attachment. I have also exhibited a concern with thinking about the broader context in which a claim (in this case about reliability) might be used. We often forget this broader context, and thus neglect the prospective consequences of our intellectual operations. If they are to act responsibly, teachers, researchers, and evaluators, as well as administrators (although administrators do not usually need this reminder) must consider the interpretations that the public—or less sophisticated professionals—will put upon their terminology.

DETERMINING EFFECTIVENESS OF INSTRUCTION IN RATIONAL THINKING WITHOUT A CONTROL GROUP

At the Rational Thinking Project at the University of Illinois (Urbana-Champaign) we have often been asked to supply one version or another of our *Cornell Critical Thinking Test*, the requester's intention being to use it as a pretest and a posttest in order to see whether a given course is effective in teaching rational thinking. Two problems stand out in this approach to determining instructional effectiveness. First, the improvement, if any, that is found might be the result, at least to some degree, of having given the pretest rather than the result of instruction (even if there were different, supposedly parallel, forms). Second, the improvement, if any, might be the result of maturation or it might be the result of some experience outside the course. Thus there are other competing explanatory hypotheses that indicate factors that could separately or jointly explain a statistically significant gain, if there is one. (*Significance*, by the way, is another concept that invites equivocation.)

An explanatory hypothesis is strong only to the extent that its competitors are inconsistent with the evidence.[6] The pretest-posttest research design is unlikely to result in the data needed to eliminate the competing hypotheses. This is the sort of consideration that argues for the use of a control group. A posttest-only, control-group design can rule out the maturation and effect of previous testing as competing explanations and reduce the number of possibly relevant outside influences.[7] Setting up a control is a

---

6. See criterion A,6,c,(1),(d) on p. 174 of this chapter.

7. $A_{,4}$,c in the conception calls for ability to design controlled experiments.

very efficient way of eliminating many competing hypotheses all at once. This is useful knowledge for students, teachers, researchers, administrators, policy makers, and the public and its representatives.

A REVIEW OF THE CASES

In reviewing these cases I shall not repeat the aspects of rational thinking involved in considering them, but I do want to note their diversity and interdependence in application. Furthermore, they directly exhibit the role of rational thinking in four areas of educational practice (teaching, policy making, research, and evaluation); and in part they comprise the sort of thing I am proposing as a goal of general education—rational thinking, the fourth R.

In the previous paragraph I was not assuming that only teachers would be concerned about teaching rationally, or that only official educational policy makers would be concerned with the rational making of educational policy. Rather, anyone concerned with education must have an interest in the rational conduct of all educational practice. For example, classroom teachers are also concerned with educational policy, partly because of its impact on their work, but also because of the part they play in making it in their day-to-day decisions about just what and how to teach and in their consultations with parents and other voters who through the ballot have a voice in policy making. Teachers are also concerned with evaluation and research and the communication of results. I could similarly show a desirable comprehensive concern for rational thinking on the part of administrators, evaluators, researchers, parents, and others. My point is that rational thinking should be of interest in a variety of ways to all people interested in education.

Why has my selection of examples emphasized the fallacies of equivocation and impact equivocation? My reasons are two. First, these two fallacies permeate discussions of educational matters, and thus need more attention from people interested in education. Second, combating the fallacy of impact equivocation was and still is the principle function of what has been called "ordinary-language philosophy of education." In this approach to philosophy great attention is devoted to getting clear about the ordinary (that is, standard) meaning of terms and to insisting that a term be used in its ordinary sense. The purpose was to avoid what Wittgenstein colorfully called "language gone on a holiday," that is, the creation of pseudo-problems and pseudo-proofs as a result of impact equivocation and regular equivocation. The suspicion that has sometimes been directed at this approach to philosophy of education is partly attributable to errors made in its practice, but more importantly to the fact that this function was often not recognized (or not remembered) by its practitioners and its audience. A primary reason for trying to determine what a word really means is to avoid employing it as though it expressed a different concept, thereby confusing ourselves and others.

A Detailed Conception of Rational Thinking

I have offered a broad picture of the conception of rational thinking, a conception consisting of proficiencies, tendencies, and good judgment. I also have provided a more detailed treatment of parts of that conception through the consideration of five examples suggesting its utility in various areas of educational practice for various sorts of education-oriented people. I hope that by now you are sufficiently intrigued to want to look at the conception in some detail. I shall present it in list form, interspersed with some commentary.

Generally, the way to approach the list is to sample it, reading a little at a time and thinking about how the items might apply in situations of concern to you and about how they applied in the situations I have described. Savor the items that interest you, but gradually try to get the whole picture. The list does not have all the answers, in some cases because the answers are not yet worked out satisfactorily, but more often because there can be no mechanical formula for rational thinking. Criteria can take us only so far. From there on, we need experienced, informed, intelligent judgment, tempered with a bit of humility and a heavy respect for evidence. It is for this reason that good judgment is presented as a major component of rational thinking.

PROFICIENCIES

One important starting point in doing rational thinking is *observing*. This is the first proficiency for which I suggest guides that may seem obvious but are still worth teaching. Note the use of qualifying words, like "by and large," "appropriate," and "sufficiently," and the use of words the application of which is not automatic, such as "area of experience," "full possession," and "good condition." The use of these words makes very clear the need for good judgment in the application of these criteria.

> A,1. *Rational thinkers are proficient at observing.* In order to observe well, one should by and large:
> a. be observing in an area of his or her experience;
> b. be careful;
> c. be in full possession of one's faculties;
> d. have no conflict of interest in making the observation;
> e. be skilled at observing the sort of thing observed, if skill is involved;
> f. have sensory equipment that is in sufficiently good condition;
> g. be as precise and use as sophisticated techniques as is appropriate for the situation; and
> h. avoid being influenced by preconceived notions about the outcome of the observation.

Note that this is not a list of necessary conditions for a successful or correct observation. It is a list of desirable characteristics of an observer. The violation of one of more of these conditions would on the face of it count against the trustworthiness of the observation. Note again the need for good judgment in determining when a characteristic of an observer should count against the trustworthiness of an observation "on the face of it."

A second mental activity that can be done rationally is *inferring explanatory hypotheses*, often based upon observations. Roughly speaking, a hypothesis is a proposition that is offered in explanation of some facts, data, observations, actions, and the like; is a candidate for testing; is tentatively put forward; and is at least conceivably capable of being tested. Inferring hypotheses is a basic skill and includes inferring a variety of key elements in thinking, as I indicated earlier in commenting on the five examples. Sometimes the product is so obvious that we do not elevate (or denigrate?) the result with the label "hypothesis" but rather speak of it as something that we can comprehend, as in "I see what you mean." If the result is controversial or not obvious, then it is usually best regarded as an explanatory hypothesis. Criteria for judging explanatory hypotheses are given later under A,6,c,(1) and A,6,d.

A,2. *Rational thinkers are proficient at inferring (or just seeing) explanatory hypotheses*, including the following:
  a. hypotheses to explain a set of physical events or states of affairs;
  b. interpretations of the presentations of others. Such interpretations include claims that some given proposition constitutes:
   (1) the point being made or at issue;
   (2) the structure of a line of reasoning;
   (3) the meaning of a statement;
   (4) the meaning of a term;
   (5) implicit reasons (unstated reasons consciously or unconsciously used by the reasoner); and
   (6) the implicit (but intended) conclusion(s).

In the examples, hypotheses that were inferred include the one about *the point* that the Supreme Court was *trying to prove* (b,1 in the above list); the one about *the structure* of the Court's line of reasoning (b,2 above); my allegation of the *meaning* of the editorial's claim that segregation exists in Chicago (b,3); the one about what Jim really *meant* by the word "propaganda" (b,4); the inference about Jim's *reason* for refusing to call his arguing with the referee propaganda (b,5); and the inference that Jim's *intended conclusion* was that the newspaper was somehow disreputable (b,6 above). I explicitly note these examples to emphasize the point that interpretations are to be regarded as hypotheses (except when obvious) just as much as are explanatory claims about the physical world.

Not all generalization can be regarded as inference to best explanation. Hence there is a third and separate kind of inferring, namely, inferring to a generalization:

A,3. *Rational thinkers are proficient at generalizing.*

Here is an example of a generalization that I believe: Teachers are generally successful at devising effective methods of teaching rational thinking when they understand what they are supposed to be teaching and when they are not overworked. Criteria for judging such generalizations appear later under A,6,c,(2).

A fourth sort of activity of rational thinkers is related to the second, although requiring even more creativity. It is conceiving and stating certain key devices in thinking. Here the result is not an explanatory hypothesis—with one exception. That one is "reported definition," currently embedded in A,4,f, which would be put under the category A,2,b,(4) if I were seeking a more elegant classification system.

A,4. *Rational thinkers are proficient at conceiving (or producing) and stating*:
  a. implicit assumptions, that is, items needed as a part of the structure of a line of reasoning, whether the reasoner used them or not (implicit assumptions fill the gaps in the strongest version of a line of reasoning, that is, the version that is most likely to justify the conclusion);
  b. other alternatives than the one(s) under consideration;
  c. reasonable plans for conducting investigations, including controlled experiments that are likely to rule out competing explanatory hypotheses;
  d. implications and conclusions, regardless of whether the grounds or bases are accepted;
  e. predictions; and
  f. definitions, in accord with criteria under A,6,f.

Please note the distinction between two kinds of assumption finding embodied in a separate listing of A,2,b,(5) and A,4,a. The first, locating implicit reasons, is concerned with finding out something that was in the assumer's mental operations. The claim that a person had a particular implicit reason is an explanatory hypothesis and is judged primarily by its ability best to explain the data (for example, the things the person said). The hypothesis that the editorial writer was defining "segregation" as statistical segregation in concluding that Chicago schools are segregated was such a hypothesis.

The second kind of assumption finding is the offering of something that a line of reasoning needs in order that it be as good as it can be, regardless of what the assumer was thinking. In dealing with the segregation editorial I might have approached the problem in a way that looks initially simpler by saying that the editorial assumes that the Supreme Court in 1954 prohibited segregation in the statistical sense. I did not do this because doing so in that case would not ultimately have avoided all the things I did anyway. But if I had only asserted that there is something on which the editorial depended, without necessarily challenging that thing, then I would have been identifying an assumption in this sense. The trouble is that moves to identify assumptions, although they are often appropriate, are more fragile than the equivocation strategy I used. To defend the move adequately in this context I would have had to show that the alleged assumption was *needed* by the argument. This is often difficult to show if the audience does not immediately assent. One way to go about it is to show that the argument is poor without the alleged assumption and is better with it. But we can often show this about more than one proposition, leaving us with more than one candidate for the assumption. (Remember that I am here concerned with identifying implicit assumptions, not implicit reasons. An implicit-reason claim is defended on the ground that it is the best explanation of a person's behavior, and this is generally more definitively determinable than a claim that a proposition is needed in an argument.) Thus, although moves to identify assumptions are initially more simple and sometimes more useful as a consequence, they do not stand up to scrutiny nearly as well as other approaches. It is often difficult to show, when sincerely challenged, that one has identified an assumption.

Please note here that I am risking the danger of impact equivocation in the sense I have stipulated a definition for the word "assumption." The word in its ordinary sense applies to many things from which I am for convenience withholding the application of my technical term, "assumption." For example, the things I am calling implicit reasons are regularly called assumptions in common parlance. I am stipulating the way I do in order to have one and only one word for each of the significantly different ideas to which I am referring. The price that we pay for this attempt to achieve clarity is the danger of impact equivocation. If you adopt my stipulation please be wary of confusing people with it.

A perhaps unnoticed feature of the fourth rational thinking proficiency is the inclusion of what is sometimes called "suppositional ability" as part of A,4,d: "regardless of whether the grounds or bases are accepted." I am here emphasizing the ability to reason, regardless of whether one believes the hypotheses or premises from which the reasoning proceeds. This is the sort of thing that Piaget apparently claimed (I think falsely) that children under ages eleven and twelve cannot do.[8] Such proficiency in a particular situation

---

8. Jean Piaget, *Judgment and Reasoning in the Child* (Patterson, N.J.: Littlefield, Adams and Co., 1959), p. 252.

is necessary for open-mindedness. One must think suppositionally in order to entertain a point of view with which one disagrees and see where it leads.

A fifth rational thinking activity involves putting it all together in a high quality presentation. Since to do so requires talking and writing, some might want to say that this goes beyond thinking. Perhaps, but given the ultimate practical purpose, I do not want to try to separate thinking from setting forth one's thoughts, a separation that, although generally conceptually possible, seems undesirable practically. Furthermore, the two are very close, perhaps identical, in those common cases where one thinks and talks at the same time, saying what one is thinking.

> A,5. *Rational thinkers are proficient at offering a well-organized, well-formulated line of reasoning, orally and in writing*:
> a. showing sensitivity to its weaknesses and existing challenges; and
> b. exhibiting awareness of its overall strength.

The previous five activities require monitoring in the form of evaluation of the product and of the bases upon which one operates. This evaluation activity is critical thinking. The following criteria for evaluation are organized in accord with the types of statements evaluated and the kinds of support available, beginning with the starting point for much of what we believe: authoritative-sounding statements made by others. These include statements by reputed authorities, as well as statements by a friend reporting some occurrence in the next room. Observation statements (by someone other than oneself) are included, since they are authoritative-sounding statements. The introductory language ("roughly to the extent that") should make it clear that this is not a list of necessary conditions; again good judgment is required. Thus qualified, the list of items is difficult to dispute, although eminently worthy of attention, judging by what I daily see and read.

> A,6,a. *Rational thinkers are proficient at evaluating authoritative-sounding statements.* A person's authoritative statement is believable roughly to the extent that:
> (1) the statement is in the person's area of experience or expertise, and the person has theoretical understanding of that area;
> (2) the person gave the statement careful consideration and

used appropriate procedures in deciding whether to accept it (established procedures, if any, are usually appropriate procedures);

(3) the person was in full possession of his or her faculties when making the statement;

(4) the person had no conflict of interest in making the statement;

(5) the person has a reputation for being honest and correct about the sort of thing considered;

(6) the person's reputation for being honest and correct could be affected by the statement, and the person was aware of this fact when making the statement;

(7) the person is not in disagreement with others who satisfy this set of criteria;

(8) the statement is not in conflict with what we otherwise have good reason to believe;

(9) the statement is close to being a statement of direct observation, as opposed to being an inference;

For observation statements the following additional criteria are applicable:

(10) the statement is made close to the time of observation;

(11) the statement is made by the person who made the observation;

(12) the statement, if based on a written record, is such that;

(a) the record was made at or close to the time of observation;

(b) the record was made by the person making the observation;

(c) the record was made by the person making the observation statement; and

(d) the statement is believed by the person making the statement to be correct, either because the statement maker so believed at the time the record was made, or believes that it was the record-maker's habit to make correct records;

(13) the statement is corroborated;

(14) the maker of the statement believes it can be corroborated;

(15) the observation conditions provided good access;

(16) high-quality, well-understood observation technology, if helpful, was used skillfully and with attention given to its limitations; and

(7) the observer

(a) has a reputation for honesty and correctness;

(b) believed that his or her reputation for honesty and correctness could be affected by the observation report;
(c) believed that the observation report was easily checkable by someone else, and
(d) satisfied the criteria in A,1.

From a set of starting points, including acceptable authoritative-sounding statements and observations, reasoning proceeds. This reasoning must also be evaluated. Reasoning can roughly be divided into three types—deductive, inductive, and value reasoning.

Deductive reasoning is that in which the conclusion is supposed to follow necessarily from the reasons given. The elaborate and elegant systems of symbolic deductive logic sometimes taught in logic courses have significant problems for our purposes. They are too elaborate; they avoid the most difficult part of applying deductive logic to practical cases—translating in and out of the system; and they seem to twist the meaning of basic words like "if," "or," and "some." But simple deductive logic plays a role in much of the rational thinking that we do. This role is not primarily in a direct necessary relationship from reasons to desired conclusions. Rather the role is, among other places, in a loosened relationship between reasons and conclusions, in inference to the best explanation, and in assumption finding, common candidates for assumptions and implicit reasons for being items that would fill the gap in a (loose) deductive argument.

A,6,b. *Rational thinkers are proficient at evaluating deductive (and loose deductive) reasoning.* One basic error to avoid in deductive reasoning is treating a necessary condition as though it were sufficient, and vice versa.

Whereas deduction can have as its conclusion any kind of statement, the next type of reasoning, inductive reasoning, is a way of supporting only empirical statements. It is, I believe, the fourth of four ways of supporting empirical statements, the other three being observation, taking someone else's word, and deduction. This fourth way, inductive reasoning, includes best-explanation reasoning and generalization. You will remember the large number of explanatory hypotheses that appeared in the five cases I considered earlier. They are to be evaluated by the criteria under A,6,c,(1).

A,6,c. *Rational thinkers are proficient at evaluating inductive reasoning leading to explanatory hypotheses (whether the conclusion be singular or general) and to simple generalizations (that are not necessarily explanatory).*
   (1) An explanatory hypothesis is justified to the extent that:
      (a) it would account for a bulk and variety of reliable data;
      (b) it itself fits into a satisfactory system of knowledge;
      (c) it is not inconsistent with any evidence;
      (d) its competitors are inconsistent with evidence (controlled experiments give such evidence an opportunity to appear); and
      (e) it is simpler than its competitors.
   (2) An empirical generalization is justified to the extent that:
      (a) there is a bulk of reliable instances of it;
      (b) it fits into a satisfactory system of knowledge; and
      (c) there is a variety of instances consonant with the degree of variety in the population covered by the generalization.
   (3) One standard way to seek variety within a limited population is through the use of procedures of unbiased sampling;
      (a) a pure random sample is unbiased;
      (b) a systematic sample is unbiased to the extent that a careful investigation fails to reveal a relevant cycle or trend followed by the sampling procedure;
      (c) stratification of a population on relevant variables (if known) and unbiased sampling within the strata are likely to be more efficient than a pure random sample or a pure systematic sample;
      (d) an unbiased sampling of clusters of the population followed by an unbiased sampling (or complete enumeration) within the clusters is likely to be a workable way of sampling when access to separate individual units is difficult.
   (4) Given an unlimited population or one which is not amenable to sampling:
      (a) a portion can be selected for sampling to determine the nature of that portion;
      (b) but in any case an extension is required beyond known portions of the population in which one has an interest, such extension ("the inductive leap") to be based upon background knowledge and context.
   (5) Often generalizations receive support, both as explanatory hypotheses and as empirical generalizations.

(6) Generally the degree of justification of inferring an inductive conclusion is weakened to the extent that the person doing the inferring is ignorant of the subject matter or area of concern.

Explanations are another product of rational thought that is to be evaluated, and attention to the "account-for" type of explanation is particularly needed because of the role played by such explanations in inference to the best explanation, a crucial type of inference, as I hope to have shown. Account-for explanations are those that attempt to account for some occurrence or state of affairs, and include interpretations. The proposed criteria are admittedly incomplete, as indicated by the words "only if" under A,6,d,(2), and must be regarded as provisionally offered. Much philosophical work yet needs to be done here.

In order to avoid confusion with account-for explanations, I distinguish between them and "justification" explanations, as indicated in A,6,d,(3). Justification explanation is explanation that attempts to prove or establish something that in the context is in doubt. Account-for explanation, on the other hand, assumes that the fact to be explained is true and attempts to account for it. Since evaluating justification explanation is the topic of most of this total section on evaluation, I only mention it here to distinguish it from account-for explanation.

A,6,d. *Rational thinkers are proficient at evaluating reason-giving explanations*:
  (1) One occurrence or state of affairs accounts for another if the following hold:
     (a) given the other conditions, the first was sufficient for the second; and
     (b) the first is appropriately deemed responsible for the other.
  (2) A generalization accounts for an event or state of affairs ('y') only if the relationship between y and another event or state of affairs ('x'), which accounts for y, can be subsumed under the generalization.
  (3) One set of reasons and evidence ('e') explains why someone would be justified in believing a proposition ('p'), if e establishes p.

A third kind of reasoning to be evaluated is that leading to value statements, commonly called "value judgments." I shall offer only a few relatively safe criteria in this complex area.

A,6,e. *Rational thinkers are proficient at evaluating value statements.*
   (1) The empirical bases of value statements should be correct.
   (2) A value statement should be consistent with acceptable higher-level value propositions, if there be any. In case of conflict it should be consistent with the most important one(s), if there be such.
   (3) The consequences of acting in accord with the value statement should be more acceptable than those of not acting in accord with it.

By way of illustration of the first criterion for value judgments, one of the empirical bases of the Supreme Court's implicit value judgment that (intentional) segregation is bad is the empirical statement that such segregation "may affect their hearts and minds in a way unlikely ever to be undone." If this empirical statement is false, then there would be less support for that value judgment.

In illustration of the second criterion, segregation is inconsistent with the broader value judgment that people should receive equal protection of the laws of a country. Thus the value judgment, "Segregation is wrong," is consistent with that broader value judgment.

The third criterion is more difficult to apply. (This is not to say that the first two are easy.) It is difficult to determine the consequences of acting in accord with the value judgment, "Segregation is wrong," for two reasons. First, it is not always obvious what someone acting in accord with a value judgment would do. In this case, for example, would we simply eliminate the legal restraints on racial mixing, or would we engage in an affirmative action program to compensate for the effects of past segregation? This is a difficult question calling for many other value judgments and debatable factual judgments.

Second, it is often very difficult to predict in advance what will happen if a course of action is selected, and to show afterwards which of the things that happened were actually a consequence of a course of action. Suppose, for example that the level of academic achievement of a particular racial group improves following the removal of legal barriers and the mixing of races in a particular school system. Was that a consequence of acting in accord with the value judgment, or of some unrelated outside occurrence, like a shift in curriculum emphasis? I am not saying that these are impossible problems. But they do show the need for good informed judgment and again the crucial role of best-explanation reasoning, which is the kind concerned with determining how to account for what happened.

Under the topic evaluation (A,6), I have so far considered some starting points in reasoning and three types of reasoning. The next concern under evaluation is something that is essential to clarity and understanding: definition.

Defining is best viewed as an act that has some form. Three rather different acts are commonly labeled "definition": *reporting* the meaning of a term; *stipulating* a meaning for a term; and *attaching criteria* to a term without giving its meaning. A reported definition, the result of the first of these kinds of acts, is judged by the criteria for an explanatory hypothesis. My reported definition of the term "segregation" as used by the Supreme Court is to be judged by these criteria. A stipulated definition (for example, Ms. Norko's stipulative definition) is judged for its convenience, although it may sometimes be controversial as to whose convenience is to be served and what constitutes convenience.

Criteria-attachment definition is judged on the basis of the justification for attaching the criteria to the concept expressed by the term in the context. An example of a criteria-attachment definition is the conception of rational thinking being presented in this chapter. A definition of segregation given by the Illinois Board of Education is another example of a criteria-attachment definition. According to it, segregation is judged to be present in a school if the racial composition of the school deviates more than 15 percent from the racial composition of the school district containing the school. This definition is to be judged satisfactory to the extent that one is justified in attaching that criterion to the concept "segregation" (presumably statistical). Whether this is justified depends upon the use to be made of the concept in the Illinois context. (Out of context there does not seem to be a basis for judgment.) In this context, segregation is a basis for legal action and a basis for withholding state aid to the schools. Thus the judgment whether the criterion attachment is justified in this context becomes roughly the judgment as to whether segregation so defined is a bad thing. More particularly the judgment is about whether segregation so defined is wrong to the degree that warrants the balance of legal, social, economic, and human consequences that are likely to arise from so defining it.

A common error is to behave as if a defense of one type of act constitutes a defense of another type of act, for example, treating justified convenience as a ground for criteria attachment. It might have been convenient to have accepted Jim's definition of "propaganda" but that is no reason for thinking that he offered justified criteria for the application of a pejorative term.

Another common error is to assume that people are more flexible than they are. Inflexibility often results in an accepted stipulated definition being treated as a justified criteria-attachment definition. (People often shift back to the original meaning in applying a statement that is justified when it is interpreted in accord with some stipulated meaning. This was the danger in the "propaganda" case, and is the essence of the impact equivocation problems.)

Each of these three definitional acts can be performed in any one of a variety of forms, depending on the context, the term being defined, and the audience. I start by listing several definition forms and then list the acts:

A,6,f. *Rational thinkers are proficient at evaluating definitions.*
   (1) Forms:
      (a) Equivalence forms. Equivalence between defined term and definition is desirable. Sometimes adjustments must be made in order to produce something to which a definition can be equivalent (for example, converting an adjective or adverb into its related noun).
        (i) Classification form. For precision and complete exhibition of the coverage of a noun, a classification definition is appropriate. It provides a general class and distinguishes features, each of which is a necessary condition for the application of the term. For most terms in everyday use, the precision of classification definition constitutes a frequently useful oversimplification. (Jim's definition of "propaganda" was in classification form.)
        (ii) Range form. In range form, which also is appropriate for nouns, a general class is provided, but the additional features characterize instead

of specifying all necessary conditions. That is, they constitute a set of conditions most of which hold for any given case properly labeled by the noun. For most nouns in everyday use the range form gives the most accurate portrayal of the meaning. (My definition of "hypothesis" on p. 167 is in range form.)

(iii) Equivalent-expression form. Here one embeds the defined term in a larger expression and presents another expression that is equivalent to the one containing the term. The danger is that, since someone must still infer the meaning of the defined term, a mistaken inference can be drawn. (My definitions of "equivocation" and "impact equivocation" on pages 151 and 152 are in the equivalent-expression form.)

(b) Nonequivalence forms. Provision of concrete interpretation is generally incompatible with equivalence in the same definition, although concrete interpretation and equivalence can be provided in different definitions.

(i) Example and nonexample form. Examples and nonexamples should be informative, examples by being central cases, and nonexamples by being fairly close to being cases, but instructively not so.

(ii) Operational definition. An operational definition specifies a condition institutable by an investigator, under which condition there holds a specified relation between an observation report and the application of the term. An operational definition provides an accurate but incomplete depiction of the meaning of a term, or criteria attachment for the term.

(2) Acts of defining. Although the following three acts are conceptually distinct, various combinations of these acts are possible.

(a) Reported definition. The most common act is reporting a meaning. Here one tries to give an accurate representation of the usage of a word for some individual, or more commonly, for some group, subculture, culture, or language community. Since usage changes over time, so do reported definitions. They can be correct or incorrect.

(b) Stipulated definition. Here one stipulates a meaning of a term for a given situation or set of situations.

The criterion is convenience.

(c) *Attaching criteria.* Here one attaches criteria to a term that often in the situation is a pro or con term. The criteria do not give the meaning of the term; but they tell how the term should be applied in the view of the person giving this kind of definition. Acceptance of these criteria is not simply a matter of convenience. The criteria, since their acceptance often implicitly embodies value judgments, can be justified or unjustified.

That completes the list of evaluation proficiencies, and in fact the logically-ordered part of the list of proficiencies. I should next like to offer a supplemental set of proficiencies, somewhat comparable to the informal fallacies of traditional logic. In my experience I have found a series of fairly standard mistakes in thinking continually recurring in a variety of contexts. And I have worked out and learned from other people some fairly standard moves to make in response to these standard problems. This last set of proficiencies is less rigorously organized than the first six, but for practical purposes this part of the presentation will be useful to many people.

A,7. *Rational thinkers are proficient at detecting standard problems and realizing appropriate action,* including such problems as the following and such standard action as is indicated:

a. Lack of offered reasons and/or clear connections between offered reasons and conclusions. Ask "Why?" or "How does that justify it?"

b. Lack of information. Figure out what you need to know. Ask for it. Seek it in an encyclopedia, newspaper file, library, and the like. Seek primary sources. Apply criteria for authoritative-sounding pronouncements. Conduct an investigation using controlled experimentation, appropriate survey and sampling techniques, and so forth. Make sure it all makes sense and is specific enough for the purpose.

c. Inconsistency. Point out the inconsistency and ask whether the person meant to say both things.

d. Equivocation fallacy (the exploitation in a line of reasoning of a shift in meaning of a key term). Lay out a rendition of the line of reasoning on each interpretation of the key term (or each combination of interpretations of the key terms) and evaluate each rendition. Alternatively, one might show that a key term is being used in one sense at one point, in a different sense at another point (these contentions should be judged as explanatory hypotheses), and that the reasoner treats the two senses as the same.

e. Impact equivocation fallacy (using a term in such a way that there is a good chance that one's audience will interpret the term in a different way in applying the conclusion). Offer a counterexample to a proposition that results from interpreting the terms in their ordinary sense; encourage flexibility by reminding the audience of the special meaning of a term, perhaps by using it in the special way in a context in which its use in the ordinary way would be strange; state or write both meanings and urge avoidance of the consequent invitation to equivocation.

f. A false starting point in a line of reasoning. Show it to be false, but see whether the conclusion might be justified in other ways.

g. The existence of a plausible competing explanation. Point out the alternative; design and implement controlled experiments that test the hypotheses.

h. Unclear concepts and statements. Ask for a definition; ask for an example and a nonexample, and then if necessary, ask why the reply constitutes an example or nonexample; ask, "What does that mean?" "Could you say some more about that?" Ask what might count as evidence in support of the statement, and what might count in opposition to the statement; ask what the statement implies in some real situation; ask what someone might do who believed the statement as opposed to what that person might do if he or she did not believe the statement.

i. Unnecessary request for a reported definition of a term. Say that you mean by the term whatever the requester means (if you think you do); if the requester protests that he or she does not have a particular meaning for the term, suggest a few everyday sentences containing the term, sentences that the requester would understand and employ.

j. Failure to join issue. Correct the misunderstanding, perhaps by noting that the parties are using a key term in different ways (an explanatory hypothesis) or by suggesting that they seem to be defending different statements (also an explanatory hypothesis).

k. Circularity. Ask what progress of the sort needed in the situation is made.

l. Irrelevance. Ask what bearing the item has on the issue or question.

m. Bandwagon appeals. Ask why others' doing something is a good reason.

n. Name calling and glittering language. Ask why such terms apply in the situation; reject as reasons their undefended use.
o. Slippery slope moves (alleging that since there is no sharp line between two sorts of thing, there is no difference). Point out clear cases of each side of the distinction and ask whether it is reasonable to deny the labeling; suggest that the approach assumes that lack of a sharp line implies no difference, and then offer a counterexample to that assumption (such as the difference between being bald and having a full head of hair).

That ends the perhaps overwhelming list of proficiency items. I do not expect anyone to grasp it all at one time, but I hope I have conveyed a general picture and that you have noted some particular features relevant to your work. But there is more. Proficiency is not enough. There must be a tendency to exercise the proficiency. Furthermore, there are a number of other tendencies that are in a way included in the list of proficiencies, but are so significant that they are worthy of separate attention. Lastly, and in a way redundantly, I offer the exercise of good judgment as the third major item in the conception. Although one cannot be proficient without exercising good judgment, the criteria listed under the proficiencies do require good judgment for their application. This fact is so important that I give it special attention.

B. *Rational thinkers are also characterized by a tendency to:*
1. exercise the proficiency that they possess;
2. take into account the total situation;
3. be well-informed;
4. demand as much precision as the subject matter permits;
5. deal with the parts of a complex situation in an orderly fashion, often one part at a time (but keeping the whole situation in mind when dealing with a part);
6. consider seriously other points of view than their own;
7. withhold judgment when the evidence and/or reasons are insufficient;
8. take a position and change the position when the evidence and reasons are sufficient to warrant so doing; and
9. accept the necessity of exercising informed judgment.

C. *Rational thinkers are characterized by the exercise of good judgment.*

Summary

I have presented a conception in terms of the characteristics of rational thinkers together with a set of loose criteria for deciding whether these characteristics are present. After exhibiting the need for some of these characteristics in a set of examples, I offered a set of proficiencies in certain thinking operations: observing, inferring explanation, generalizing, conceiving and stating, presenting one's thoughts, and evaluating (the basic constituent of critical thinking). These proficiencies are interdependent and interactive in operation, with the evaluation proficiency optimally providing continual feedback to the operations of the others. A last set of overlapping proficiencies consists of seeing some standard thinking problems and realizing appropriate counteraction.

But proficiencies are not enough. They must be exercised with discretion and good judgment. I hope to have covered these matters in the list of tendencies that comprise the second major component of the rational thinker, and in noting the third component, good judgment, which tends to increase with practice and experience.

This conception of rational thinking is relevant to all aspects of education: the specification of goals, the practice of teaching, the making of educational policy and the administration of it, and the practices of research and evaluation. Would it not be irrational to neglect the fourth R, rational thinking, in these important educational practices?

Ethics

The relationship between the Good, the Good Life, and education has been a persistent theme in the history of philosophy. Plato's ethical views were as basic and as important to his idea of education as were his epistemological and metaphysical views. The same is true of John Dewey, who ushered into twentieth century philosophical and educational thought the influential idea that ethics must be "experimental." Taking this view seriously, John Childs argued that the moral factor is pervasive throughout all of education and that educational choices are ultimately social choices. His 1950 work, *Education and Morals: An Experimentalist Philosophy of Education* (New York: Appleton-Century-Crofts, 1950) is a classic in this tradition. Since midcentury, other ethical views also have had their educational interpreters in the person of such philosophers of education as Philip H. Phenix, James D. Butler, Peter A. Bertocci, John Wilson, Richard S. Peters, among others. In recent years and with the popularization of Lawrence Kohlberg's psychological work on human moral development, the number of philosophers of education dealing with issues of moral education has steadily risen. Clive Beck, in this chapter, offers his views on this topic. (Editor)

CHAPTER VIII

The Reflective Approach to Values Education

CLIVE M. BECK

Overview

Ethics and education are related in many ways. For example, ethical questions must be explored in determining the aims of education; teachers and students should be ethical in their behavior toward each other; ethics is one subject that might be studied in a school program; education may be designed to promote ethical behavior in children; and so on.

In this chapter, I concentrate on one area of the field of ethics and education, namely, values education. In doing so, however, I outline a theory of ethics that could be used in tackling other educational problems. I hope, then, to give specific and immediate suggestions for the practice of values education and at the same time make a contribution to the general field of ethics and education.

The term "values education" is used to refer to education in a broad range of values—political, social, cultural—including moral values. My reasons for discussing values education rather than the narrower field of moral education are twofold. First, children need education in many other values areas, in addition to morals. Second, moral issues are difficult to resolve in isolation: one normally needs a perspective on human values in general in order to determine what is morally right or wrong.

The approach to values education I will advocate is the "reflective approach." According to this approach, there are certain basic human values that provide a common reference point for public education. Specific and intermediate-range values, many of them derived from culture and tradition, must be reflected upon in the light of basic values. The two main cognitive aspects of

185

values education, then, are (a) identification and refinement of basic values and (b) reflection upon specific and intermediate-range values in the light of basic values. In addition, values education has the affective goal of (c) relating feelings, attitudes, and behavior to specific, intermediate, and basic values arrived at or refined through reflection. The word "reflective" in the term "reflective values in education" has reference to both the cognitive and the affective component in values education.

The approach to ethics I will advocate is "reflective ethics." It has many features, but the main one for present purposes is the constant attempt to identify enduring, basic human values that can be used in reflecting on particular moral questions. Among moral philosophers, some have absolutized rather specific moral rules and principles and others have advocated a completely open approach that effectively leaves one with no guidance in everyday situations. I suggest that the correct approach lies between these two extreme positions: while theoretically anything *might* be valuable for human beings, in fact we rather consistently pursue an interconnected set of basic values over long periods of time. The task of ethics, prosaic though it may seem, is to identify these values, subject them to critical examination and refinement, and apply them to particular personal and social problems. Thus the tasks of reflective ethics overlap very considerably with the tasks of reflective values education.

Before describing in more detail the reflective approach to values education, I will review some recent discussions of issues in values education by educational philosophers and some specific approaches to values education that have been advocated for the schools. After discussing the reflective approach I will trace some of its roots in philosophy through the centuries.

Insights from Educational Philosophy

Perhaps the dominant view in modern Western society on how to be moral is that knowledge of right and wrong is not difficult to attain: the problem of morality is rather one of character or will, of having the moral fibre to do what is right and eschew what is wrong. Support for this view is sometimes derived from Christian teachings, going back to the New Testament itself: "I do not do the good I would, but the evil I would not is what I do." This view is deeply entrenched, however, in general secular outlooks, and many Christians in fact reject it as overly simplistic. It is no more (or less) the Christian view than it is the modern Western view.

Moral education based on this conception of how morality is attained involves reminding children of the key moral rules or principles that they "really know already" but "so easily forget." Further, it involves the use of activities, exercises, and procedures that habituate children in right modes of conduct, thus strengthening their character.

MORAL EDUCATION AS CRITICAL INQUIRY

John Dewey, who was brought up to see moral education as character development in the above sense, came to reject this view strongly and to place the emphasis squarely on the need to find out what is right rather than to do what one already knows to be right. His general assumption was that motivation is not the problem; children have all the motivation that is needed for moral conduct. The task of moral education is to help children discover what is right through constant critical inquiry and thus harness their inherent energies for the pursuit of sound values. Indeed, the dynamism of the child is taken as the starting point and basis for the process of value inquiry.[1]

For Dewey, the question of what is right is always complex and always open. Individual needs must be taken into account, along with the requirements of living in a society; new discoveries and changes in people's needs and circumstances inevitably condition what is right; and one's understanding of what is right or valuable constantly grows and hence changes. Moral education, then, may be defined as critical inquiry. Value inquiry is undertaken by the child (with the help of the teacher), and as the right and valuable is perceived by the child it is automatically embraced and followed, since it constitutes the solution to a problem that the energies of the child are bent on solving. There is no gap between discovery and action.

1. John Dewey, *Democracy and Education* (New York: Macmillan, 1916), chap. 26.

On the whole, the notion of moral education as critical inquiry is the one that has prevailed when philosophers of education since Dewey have ventured into this field. The emphasis has been strongly on finding out what is right rather than on habituation in an (already known) set of moral principles. Scheffler, for example, states that "the challenge of moral education is the challenge to develop critical thought in the sphere of practice and it is continuous with the challenge to develop critical thought in all aspects and phases of schooling."[2] Peters takes a similar position: "It might be said that my conception of moral education is indistinguishable from the ideal of a liberal education. I do not mind putting it this way provided that 'liberal' . . . is used with awareness of the distinct emphases that it intimates."[3]

While opinions may differ concerning the precise emphasis to be placed on finding out what is right and the extent of the problem of getting children to do what they know to be right, Dewey and the philosophers of education who have followed him must be credited with making a major contribution to moral education theory. They have rescued us from an obsessive preoccupation with strengthening the will and developing "character," and they have made us very aware that the question of what is right is by no means a simple one, and inquiry into what is right must be a major component in, if not the sum total of, any moral education program.

MORAL EDUCATION AS OPEN-ENDED INQUIRY

The open-ended nature of moral inquiry has been a favorite theme of philosophers of education from Dewey onward. They have applied to moral philosophy and moral education the familiar liberal academic notion that one should "follow the truth wherever it leads." And they have held that there is not an established body of moral knowledge that it is the business of moral education to impose on children.

In this vein, Peters criticizes the work of Lawrence Kohlberg

2. Israel Scheffler, *Reason and Teaching* (Indianapolis: Bobbs-Merrill, 1943), pp. 143-44.

3. Richard Peters, "Concrete Principles and the Rational Passions," in *Moral Education: Five Lectures*, ed. Nancy F. Sizer and Theodore R. Sizer (Cambridge: Harvard University Press, 1970), p. 55.

because it is based on a particular, narrow view of the nature of morality. Speaking of Kohlberg he says: "He suffers from the rather touching belief that a Kantian type of morality, represented in modern times most notably by Hare and Rawls, is the only one. . . . He fails to grasp that utilitarianism, in which the principle of justice is problematic, is an alternative type of morality and that people such as Winch have put forward a morality of integrity in which the principle of universalizability is problematic. . . . It is sheer legislation to say that Kohlberg's morality is the true one."[4]

Of course, openness in morality is a matter of degree. Dewey was open to letting the truth lead where it may to a greater extent than other philosophers of education have been. Even Peters, as we shall see later, imposes some limits. In general, however, modern philosophers of education have played a useful role in stressing that a satisfactory approach to moral education must be one in which one has not made up one's mind beforehand what is right or wrong or even what the nature of morality is.

THE PROBLEM OF INDOCTRINATION

Philosophers of education recognized early that the concept of indoctrination is a key one in education, and particularly in moral education. They have proceeded to show in some detail how indoctrination is antithetical to sound moral development, since it reduces the level of reason, critical awareness, and openness in ethical inquiry. Further, they have clarified to some extent the distinction between a legitimate initiation of children into morality and the inculcation of hard-and-fast moral beliefs that will be difficult for the child later to evaluate critically.

While Hare, for example, places considerable emphasis on the straightforward teaching of morality in early childhood, he objects to indoctrination in early childhood, which begins when we are "trying to stop the growth in our children of the capacity to think for themselves about moral questions."[5] Hare states that "if

---

4. Richard Peters, "Why Doesn't Lawrence Kohlberg Do His Homework?" in *Moral Education . . . It Comes with the Territory*, ed. David Purpel and Kevin Ryan (Berkeley, Calif.: McCutchan Publishing Corp., 1976), pp. 288-89.

5. Richard Hare, "Adolescents into Adults," in *Aims in Education*, ed. T. H. B. Hollins (Manchester: Manchester University Press, 1964), p. 52.

you are wanting your child in the end to become an adult and think for himself about moral questions, you will try, all the time that you are influencing him by nonrational methods (as you have to), to interest him in rational thinking about morality."[6] He adds that "this matter of the teacher himself really treating the questions as open ones is crucial."[7]

Wilson advocates a similar approach, saying that "it would be dangerous to use any method of teaching which did not allow the pupil the chance to reject the belief, either at the time or in the future."[8] In showing how we can place the child in a position to question a belief either now or in the future, he states that "to avoid indoctrination, we must be more concerned with putting forward the evidence for beliefs than with inculcating the beliefs themselves."[9]

The issue of indoctrination remains a difficult one, with disputes continuing about whether some degree of inculcation is appropriate in early childhood and whether some moral principles can be taught as established beyond reasonable doubt while others cannot. Nevertheless, considerable clarity has been arrived at with respect to the nature of indoctrination and the point has been made that a number of common forms of indoctrination are not compatible with sound moral education.

THE NEED FOR AN AFFECTIVE COMPONENT IN MORAL EDUCATION

While contemporary philosophers of education have performed a valuable service in emphasizing the place of critical, open inquiry in moral education, they have in recent years become more aware of the problem of a possible gap between moral knowledge and moral action, and have given us some useful pointers concerning how this gap might be closed.

Wilson's inventory of "moral components" has been particularly useful in displaying the range of conditions that must be ful-

6. Ibid.

7. Ibid., p. 53.

8. John Wilson, "Education and Indoctrination," in *Aims in Education*, ed. Hollins, p. 29.

9. Ibid.

filled if moral behavior is to take place. He has pointed out the necessity of an understanding of others and their needs, a concern for others, an awareness of one's own emotional life and that of others, knowledge of "hard facts" relevant to moral decisions, an ability to communicate with others both verbally and nonverbally, a capacity to give attention to moral problems and think them through, a capacity and tendency to carry one's feelings, understandings, and thoughts through to definite resolve, and freedom from "countermotivations" that may stand in the way of moral action.[10] Clearly, this list takes us beyond the purely cognitive goals of moral education into a solidly affective domain.

Peters also has recently placed increasing emphasis on affective elements in moral education. In criticizing Kohlberg he says:

> Kohlberg does not appreciate . . . that moral rules have to be learned in the face of counterinclinations. Otherwise there would, in general, be no point to them. Hence the necessity . . . for the type of reinforcement advocated by Skinner and others and for the modeling processes so stressed by Bronfenbrenner.
> . . . Kohlberg, like Piaget, is particularly weak on the development of the affective side of morality, of moral emotions such as "guilt," "concern for others," "remorse," and so on.
> . . . Kohlberg, in his references to ego strength, sees the importance of will in morality, but offers no account of the type of habit training which encourages or discourages its growth.[11]

In these statements by Wilson and Peters we note something of a return to the pre-Dewey emphasis on character building, strengthening of the will and dealing sternly with the willful self within us that may know the good and yet not do it. Indeed, Wilson with disarming dogmatism states that "the human situation is tragic, and original sin is an incontrovertible fact."[12] (Admittedly, he has a rather unconventional definition of original sin). There are dangers here, and we must maintain an appropriate balance between the cognitive and the affective and explore both domains further so that we know precisely how each is important

10. John Wilson, *A Teacher's Guide to Moral Education* (London: Geoffrey Chapman, 1973), pp. 136-37.

11. Peters, "Why Doesn't Lawrence Kohlberg Do His Homework?" pp. 289-90.

12. Wilson, "Education and Indoctrination," p. 36.

and how each should be approached. Nevertheless, we can see how educational philosophers in their earlier pronouncements on the importance of critical, open inquiry and their more recent attempts to explore the affective side of morality have made a significant contribution to the field of moral education.

Some Approaches to Values Education in the Schools

On the whole, philosophers of education have limited their remarks to broad philosophical and theoretical issues associated with moral education. They have not attempted to develop particular approaches to values education in the schools, which would require comprehensive knowledge of the curriculum needs and practical realities of the classroom. While it is probably appropriate for most philosophers of education to limit themselves in this way, some should take a more detailed interest in the important field of values education, critically evaluating particular approaches and perhaps developing approaches of their own. In this section, I examine briefly four approaches to values education that have recently been proposed.

THE REASONING SKILLS APPROACH

One of the earlier attempts to avoid the "problem" of indoctrination in values education involved teaching reasoning skills rather than "content" in values matters. This approach was popular at Harvard University in the 1960s in the area of social studies education and issued in Newmann and Oliver's book *Clarifying Public Controversy*.[13] As far as value content is concerned, the teacher is encouraged to maintain the stance of the neutral, objective, disinterested bystander or possibly the Socratic devil's advocate. The main positive teaching is of (a) an analytical scheme for clarifying the issues in controversial social problems and (b) reasoning skills for satisfactorily resolving the issues.

The main difficulty in this approach lies in the attempt to teach skills without content, in the notion that students should not, on the whole, be helped to arrive at viewpoints on substantive values in the classroom but rather be furnished with a set of reasoning

---

13. Fred Newmann and Donald Oliver, *Clarifying Public Controversy* (Boston: Little, Brown and Co., 1970).

skills, which they would then go off to use in the real world. Many people feel that it is necessary to resort to a skills approach in order to avoid indoctrination; but on the contrary, content must be dealt with in the classroom in order to overcome the tendency toward indoctrination. Despite this concern, however, it should be pointed out that it is essential to teach reasoning skills *among other things* in order to assist students in dealing with values issues and problems. Teaching problem-solving skills forms a major part of both the objective and the process of values education. Accordingly, the teaching of reasoning skills must be incorporated as one element in an adequate approach to values education.

THE DILEMMA DISCUSSION APPROACH

The discussion of dilemmas is a strategy of values education that in recent years has been associated most closely with Kohlberg, but it is also a key strategy for the values clarification movement and has been a traditional technique for the testing of moral ideas and principles through the ages. Some educators, following Kohlberg, have adopted it as *the* major approach in the classroom discussion of values, partly because it appears to avoid the inculcation of values and hence the problem of indoctrination.

It would seem that there are reasons for restricting rather severely the use of the dilemma method. Excessive preoccupation with dilemmas tends to reinforce the popular misconception that most values problems are of the dilemma type. In fact, values issues are seldom black-and-white, all-or-nothing in form and students must be strongly encouraged to see that there are almost always several better or worse solutions to a values problem rather than a single right solution. Further, since moral dilemmas are by their very nature so difficult to resolve, they tend to discourage students from engaging in value inquiry, or lead them to a highly relativistic view of value beliefs.

Dilemmas can be used to advantage, however, at certain points in values education: to open up a new line of thought, to test a principle, or to raise questions about a particular viewpoint that has been too easily taken for granted. Paradoxically, if one recognizes that there may not be a clear-cut answer to a moral dilemma (indeed, that is usually precisely why it is a dilemma), a dilemma can be used, when appropriate, to illustrate that a particular values issue is not of a black-and-white, all-or-nothing variety and that it is far more complex than had been assumed.

THE VALUES CLARIFICATION APPROACH

The values clarification approach has been associated with Louis Raths and more recently with Sidney Simon.[14] The main philosophical objection to values clarification is that it does not recognize that values can be objectively good or bad, sound or unsound, that one can *make a mistake* in values matters. The object of values education is seen to be that of helping students clarify the nature and consequences of their values and become thoroughly committed to their values, without judging whether the values are objectively sound for the people concerned. Clearly, this is contrary to the emphasis on inquiry and critical evaluation that has been stressed by educational philosophers. It is one thing to acknowledge that people will differ in their opinions regarding what is right and wrong, and quite another to maintain that right and wrong is "just a matter of opinion," that something is right if we sincerely believe it to be so.

It would be foolish, however, in rejecting the moral relativism and subjectivism of values clarification to reject also the many valuable strategies and techniques for clarifying values that have been developed within this approach. Clearly it is a crucial aspect of any sound approach to values education to become more aware of the values one has, precisely in order that one may evaluate them critically. While some of the techniques and activities advocated by values clarification move into very sensitive areas of a person's experience and so must be handled with great care, if at all, especially in a classroom setting, the body of values clarification strategies as a whole is a useful source of techniques for making the study of values more interesting and productive. Values clarification of this kind, however, should be seen as just one aspect of a much larger process in values education.

14. Louis E. Raths, Merrill Harmin, and Sidney B. Simon, *Values and Teaching* (Columbus, Ohio: Charles Merrill Publishing Co., 1966); Sidney Simon et al., *Values Clarification* (New York: Hart Publishing Co., 1972).

THE SCHOOL ORGANIZATION AND ATMOSPHERE APPROACH

There is a popular saying that "morality is caught, not taught," and with this notion in mind some educators have maintained that the only way to influence the values of children in school is through the organization and atmosphere of the school, including the personal example set by teachers. Others have not taken such an extreme position, but have suggested that the organization and atmosphere of the school is a major factor in moral development. (For example, see the work of Kohlberg on the "just school" and the work of Lickona on classroom relationships and atmosphere).[15]

In discussing the role of school organization and atmosphere in values education, two issues tend to be confused. One is the extent to which inquiry is an important aspect of values education; the other is the extent to which values inquiry can take place *through* the school organization and atmosphere. On the first issue, in the light of the stand taken by philosophers of education in recent times, one must emphasize the central role of inquiry in values education and reject categorically the notion that morality is caught, not taught. On the second issue, however, one must acknowledge that much of the teaching and learning of values that takes place in the school is mediated in part through organization and atmosphere. Hence, this must be seen as one important element in a total program of values education. A school that does not practice what it teaches in the area of values will teach very little.

The Reflective Approach in Values Education

The reflective approach, already introduced briefly, is among other things an attempt to arrive at a sound and comprehensive approach to values education.[16] It is felt that some projects or movements in values education have made the mistake of advocat-

---

15. See Elsa Wasserman, "Implementing Kohlberg's 'Just Community Concept' in an Alternative High School," *Social Education* 16 (April 1976); 203-7; Thomas Lickona, "Creating the Just Community with Children," *Theory Into Practice* 16 (April 1977): 97-104.

16. Material in this section is based in part on contract research funded by the Ministry of Education, Ontario, from 1972 to 1977. For reports on this research, see particularly Clive Beck et al., *The Moral Education Project, Year 3* (Toronto: Ontario Ministry of Education, 1976) and idem, *The Moral Education Project, Year 5* (Toronto: Ontario Ministry of Education, 1978).

ing a single strategy as *the* strategy, and that those of us who now have the benefit of hindsight should try to avoid making the same error. (Whether the reflective approach succeeds or not in this objective is for the reader to judge.) The term "reflective approach" has been chosen in order to give some impression of the emphases of the approach, and also in order to provide a name for the approach of my own choosing. But any name is somewhat unfortunate since it tends to suggest a narrow set of objectives and strategies. In describing the reflective approach, I will illustrate how it attempts to incorporate the strengths of other approaches while avoiding their weaknesses.

BASIC HUMAN VALUES AS A REFERENCE POINT FOR PUBLIC EDUCATION

Most people who have doubts about the feasibility of values education in a pluralistic society have not had the experience of engaging in it. If they had, they would have found that in fact students of different religious and cultural backgrounds have so many concerns in common that the scope for useful, joint values inquiry is enormous.

Values education in public schools is feasible because, despite the theoretical possibility of great diversity, we humans in fact share a common set of basic values: survival, happiness (enjoyment, pleasure, and so forth), health, fellowship (friendship, love, and so forth), helping others (to some extent), wisdom, fulfilment, freedom, self-respect, respect from others, a sense of meaning in life, and so on. Values education in the schools can (and must) proceed on the basis of these shared interests and pursuits. The nature of values inquiry in the schools can, then, be stated rather simply in terms of two elements: (a) identification and refinement of basic human values, and (b) assessment and development of specific and intermediate-range values in the light of basic values. Values education, which goes beyond values inquiry, involves also a third element, namely, (c) developing emotions, attitudes, and behavior patterns that accord with the values established through values inquiry.

A degree of complexity is introduced into this picture by the fact that people vary somewhat in the emphasis they place on different basic values. This does not, however, undermine significantly the possibility of joint value inquiry in the classroom since the variation is not extreme and the general form and substance of value inquiry remain much the same for different individuals. A perhaps more serious element of complexity lies in the fact that while different people have common values, they tend to favor themselves and their inner group in the pursuit of these goals. Once again, however, this factor is not fatal to joint classroom study of values. On the one hand, different students can help each other in working out how to pursue the same goal, even when they are pursuing it for different interest groups. On the other hand, since we must live together in the same world, considerable effort must be devoted to developing compromises or mutually beneficial arrangements between people who have similar goals but conflicting interests; and the classroom is one context in which this work can be done.

The acceptance of basic human values such as survival, happiness, and fellowship as a reference point for values education is seen by some as an easy, pragmatic solution that glosses over fundamental religious and metaphysical differences. I would claim, however, that these values are held in common even by people who are orthodox adherents of different religious or metaphysical positions. Differences exist in emphasis and in specific moral rules, and these differences must not be ignored. There are, however, extensive areas of overlap in the values concerns of different religions, and careful, systematic values education in these areas is possible in a pluralistic society and can only be of benefit to the respective religions and their adherents. To recognize the overlap is not "easy pragmatism" but simply good sense; to deny the overlap and discourage interreligious, intercultural values inquiry is to close off a major avenue of human (including religious) development.

It should be noted that the reflective approach to values education does not presuppose a humanism that stands as an alternative to or in opposition to religion. The basic human values, which on the reflective approach provide a basis for values education, are in turn influenced in part by the religious and cultural traditions (of which "humanism" may be one) from which the students come. The basic human values result from a constant interaction between, on the one hand, religious and cultural traditions and, on the other hand, elements that are in some sense "natural" in human beings. It is obvious that the development of religions has been influenced in major ways by human values that have some degree of independence from religions. But it is also apparent that religions have to some extent a life of their own and exercise a measure of independent influence on human values.

A "REFLECTIVE" APPROACH

The word "reflective" has been chosen to characterize the approach to values education being advocated in order to avoid the harsher connotations of terms such as "critical" or "questioning." While one engages in systematic appraisal of basic, intermediate, and specific values, one does so in a positive spirit. While one is reflective one is not skeptical or cynical. While all of our traditional values—religious, societal, parental—must be open to reflective assessment, each in its turn, one must not regard them as suspect simply because they are traditional.

The word "reflective" is also meant to suggest the inclusion of so-called "affective" approaches in values education. In a comprehensive program of values education the feelings and behavior of students must be engaged along with their thoughts. Sometimes a false dichotomy is made between "cognitive discussion" of values and "affective experiences" in values education. The dichotomy is false because, on the one hand, discussions can be highly affective in nature and, on the other hand, classroom experiences and activities must normally take place in a context of hard thinking if they are to be useful. But the fact remains that a major place must be given to affective elements in a values education program, and the term "reflective" has been chosen to allow for this concern. No label is perfect, however, and one must continually remind oneself of the wide range of components involved in an adequate values education program, whatever label is used to refer to it.

A PROBLEM-CENTERED APPROACH

The approach being advocated is one in which problems or topics are the main focus of inquiry, experience, and action. Units of study are centered on such topics as friendship, children in the family, myself and other people, punishment, sharing TV, bullying, trusting, getting even, differences in values, learning from parents, work and leisure, social conflict, prejudice, and so on.

Each topic is normally tackled through consideration of key questions, principles, and concepts, review of a wide variety of concrete examples, gathering of relevant information, having experiences appropriate to the problems in question, and, where feasible, engaging in related activities. There is a very strong input of ideas, theories, information, and experiences—it is a rather structured approach in many ways—but at the same time a high premium is placed on the freedom of students to disagree, modify the theories and principles presented, propose alternatives, respond differently, and so on.

Being problem-centered, the reflective approach is not just concerned with teaching principles. It is assumed that values principles can only be learned in the context of dealing with specific problem areas in life. Further, even if values principles could be taught in the abstract, students need help and practice in the classroom in applying them and in building up a set of substantive values beliefs and responses.

On the other hand, however, the reflective approach is not a case study or dilemma approach. In the course of dealing with a particular values issue there is a review of a wide range of examples rather than an extended consideration of a single case or dilemma. When too much attention is paid to a single situation, student interest is often low and the issues raised are often too numerous and varied to be manageable. A pure case study or dilemma approach leads at best to boredom and at worst to great frustration and complete loss of confidence in the possibility of arriving at solutions to values problems. In the reflective approach, there is a constant moving back and forth between key ideas or principles and specific cases.

A problem-centered approach also stands in contrast to a stage developmental approach such as that of Kohlberg. The focus is on helping particular students make progress in dealing with particular problem areas in their lives rather than on moving them up moral stages. A moral-stage orientation leads to a stereotyping of students and, very often, to an underestimation of what they are capable of achieving with respect to particular moral problems. A problem-centered approach, by contrast, leaves one free to help a student arrive at whatever degree of resolution is possible with respect to the problem in question.

THE REFLECTIVE APPROACH IN THE CURRICULUM

The reflective approach, then, is one that takes a set of shared, basic human values as a reference point, reflects on these values and on specific and intermediate-range values in the light of basic values, and centers on values topics or problems, dealing with general principles and specific cases in the context of topics or problems. How can such an approach to values education best be fitted into the school curriculum at the present time?

Within the school, there are four main ways in which a program in values education can be implemented: (a) through the organization and atmosphere of the school and classroom, (b) through the incidental treatment of values issues as they arise, (c) through an integration of values topics within other subject areas, and (d) through separate courses in values. The example set by teachers and students to each other also plays a significant role in values development, but this factor is one over which very little direct control can be exercised—there is nothing more pointless than contrived example—and so the use of examples can hardly be described as part of a values education program.

The organization and atmosphere of the school should be such as to encourage reflection on values. As far as possible, the values and rules of the school as an institution and of each classroom should be made explicit and subjected to open discussion. As far as possible, students should be involved in values decisions in the school, either personally or through representatives who in turn discuss the issues with the students whom they represent. Where a teacher or school administrator has to impose a rule or decision on students who hold a different point of view (and clearly this is often necessary), a serious attempt should be made to explain the reasons for the imposition. Often applying force and giving explanations are seen as mutually exclusive: teachers and parents feel that if they give an explanation it would be inconsistent to apply force and that if they are justified in applying force they have no responsibility to explain their actions. In fact, however, a combination of explanations and formal sanctions is possible and necessary in the school (and in society generally) since understanding alone and intrinsic motivation alone are usually not sufficient to lead to appropriate actions. Further, explanation of their actions by those in authority can be a major means of values education, provided of course the actions are indeed justifiable and the explanations are not merely rationalizations.

With respect to matters more closely associated with the traditional curriculum of the school, we have noted three possibilities: the incidental approach, the integrated approach, and the separate course approach. The main point to be made here is that *the three approaches are entirely compatible with one another and should as far as possible be used concurrently*. The work done under each approach complements and assists the work done under the others.

The incidental approach is one that has been employed since formal education began. Teachers take the opportunity to comment, usually rather briefly, on values issues as they arise incidentally (often accidentally) in the course of teaching other subjects (or running the school). The integrated approach is more explicit, systematic, and planned than the incidental approach but does not involve establishing separate courses in values. Individual units or series of units on values topics are built into existing school courses within the limitations imposed by the content and methodology of those courses. Separate courses in values may be taught on a full-year or single-term basis. They may be related to other school courses in the way that, say, geography is related to history and history to literature when these courses are taught well; but equally they may have as much autonomy as other courses.

The integrated approach, while it may be more ideal in some sense than the separate course approach, is rather impractical at the present time without the separate course approach. Without separate courses in values, values education is usually not taken seriously enough as a field of inquiry by either teachers or students, and an adequate reward structure is difficult to establish. Further, without separate courses both teachers and students have great difficulty acquiring the interest, theory, skills, and confidence required to deal with values adequately on an integrated basis.

The incidental approach is extremely important within the total structure of values education: much of the detailed working out of ideas and solutions takes place through it. It is also an inevitable element in any public school situation: teachers will always make known their views, whether implicitly or explicitly, on values issues as they arise in the school. However, values education is far too important, extensive, and difficult a field to be left to the incidental approach alone. If the integrated approach cannot take significant hold in a school without separate courses in values, the incidental approach is even more unlikely to do so. Incidental values "teaching" does not happen often enough, and when it does happen it too frequently takes the form of superficial moralizing, since teachers often lack the background and confidence to explore in depth the arguments and evidence for and against the views they are expressing.

Separate courses in values do not decrease the amount of integrated and incidental work in values that goes on in the school. In fact, they substantially increase it. Most school courses would be greatly improved if the values components inherent in them were adequately explored, without any loss to the disciplines involved. And the opportunities for incidental discussion of values in the school could be exploited much more than they are. The main obstacle in both cases appears to be the inability or disinclination of teachers and students to take advantage of the opportunities that exist. Separate courses in values, if supported by adequate learning materials, effective teacher education programs, and strong backing in the community and in the school system, could provide the momentum needed for increased and complementary work in values education using all three approaches.

Some Philosophical Roots of the Reflective Approach

The view of ethics that underlies the reflective approach to values education has similarities with a number of ethical theories which through the centuries have given a major place to human nature and human desires, without necessarily denying the importance of other considerations. Several of these theories will be reviewed here, both to explore the philosophical origins of the reflective approach to values education and to show the points at which its underlying ethical theory—which for convenience we will call "reflective ethics"—differs from other theories.

ARISTOTLE

The Greek philosophers of the fifth and fourth centuries B.C. whose theories have had such a significant impact on medieval and modern European thought, developed an account of ethics that was solidly based in human nature. In this tradition, the views of Aristotle (384-322 B.C.) are the most adequate in terms of scope. Like Plato (427-347 B.C.), Aristotle viewed the study of human nature as crucial in determining what is right and good for humans, and saw the pursuit of happiness and personal fulfillment as legitimate and central human activities. Going beyond Plato, he engaged in a detailed and practical analysis of the distinctive pursuits and experiences that make up "the good life" for humans.

A weakness in Aristotelean ethics, however, lay in its lack of clarity concerning the justification of specific ethical rules and judgments. While there was an emphasis on the importance of happiness, friendship, health, wisdom, self-respect, and so forth—the "basic values" identified in reflective ethics—it was not clear that ethical acts were right *because* they promoted these values. Rather, "human nature" tended to be given a metaphysical and normative status such that ethical acts were right and good because they constituted a fulfilling of one's nature. The fact that ethical acts also promoted one's well-being was seen as fortunate and a motivating factor in being ethical but as largely accidental: this was not *why* the acts were right and good.[17] From the point of view of reflective ethics this is unsatisfactory because it leaves one without a methodology for determining what is right. One cannot assess specific and intermediate-range values in the light of basic human values, as the reflective approach requires.

Reference to capacities and potentialities, after the manner of Aristotle (and Aquinas, in the natural domain), is unworkable as *the* guide for human conduct. We are all capable of all sorts of

---

17. *The Ethics of Aristotle, The Nicomachean Ethics*, trans. J. A. K. Thomson (New York: Penguin Books, 1955), pp. 37-66.

things. Some of these capacities are for human harm, but we cannot know what is harm by appealing to capacities alone. Many of these capacities are for human good (in terms of basic human values), but how will we determine what is the greater good, and hence which of several alternative capacities we should fulfill?

HOBBES

Thomas Hobbes (1588-1679) was the first major British moral and political philosopher of the modern period. In the *Leviathan* he outlined a theory of ethics that places a great deal of emphasis on human goals, which he claims consist simply in personal gain, safety, and reputation.[18] In his view these human strivings constitute the basis for ethics since they provide the motivation for humans to work out a social contract to deliver them from "the state of nature," in which no one can trust anyone and everyone's strivings are frustrated.

Hobbes's position is healthy in its realism and acceptance of human desires, but it is weak in terms of its pessimism and the very narrow range of basic human values it identifies. Another crucial weakness is that his system of ethics, once identified, is cut adrift from its foundations in human nature, and the stress is laid upon complete submission to a ruler accepted by the people as the one who will administer the social contract.[19] It remains quite unclear how this ruler will be constrained to take account of basic human values in ruling the people, and how individuals and small subgroups will make ethical decisions, given the authority that the ruler has to judge right and wrong. It is true that under any viable system of ethics, including reflective ethics, one has to take account of the hard reality of public authorities, both legitimate and illegitimate. However, in Hobbes's system we have the notion that "might makes right," and this is impossible to reconcile with a systematic and reflective derivation of right and wrong from basic human values.

BENTHAM

The relevance of human nature and human desires to ethical de-

18. Thomas Hobbes, *Leviathan* (New York: Everyman's Library, 1914), p. 64.

19. Ibid., pp. 64-65.

liberation remained an assumption of British moral philosophy for two centuries after Hobbes. It is to be found in the British utilitarian school, notably in the thought of Jeremy Bentham (1748-1832) who applied his utilitarianism in a systematic way in his recommendations concerning public education and moral education. According to Bentham, the maximization of human happiness in the long run and on the whole and across the entire human race is the sole end of morality. Further, he maintained, at least in his later years, that pursuit of one's own greatest happiness is entirely compatible with pursuit of "the greatest happiness of the greatest number."

Bentham's position was very close to reflective ethics in several respects. While it unfortunately restricted its range of attention to a single basic human value, namely happiness, it was uncompromising in its use of this value in reflecting upon particular ethical rules and judgments. Bentham was at pains to reject any traditional or "intuited" value that could not ultimately be justified in terms of the promotion of happiness. Further, within the category of enjoyments and satisfactions he refused to accept the notion of a hierarchy of pleasures, a concept that the later utilitarian J. S. Mill adopted, thereby greatly reducing the intelligibility and strength of the happiness criterion. Obviously, when one begins to talk of "higher pleasures" one has effectively abandoned the view that happiness is the sole criterion of right and wrong, for it is necessary to import additional criteria in order to determine which pleasures are higher and which are lower. This may be legitimate, but only if one spells out clearly the nature of these other criteria and how they are to be applied. Bentham's position was also close to reflective ethics in its emphasis on the importance of consequences. Moral acts were not right in themselves. In judging the rightness of an act it was necessary to pursue the consequences of the action, in the manner of reflective ethics, back further and further to its overall consequences for basic human values, in Bentham's case happiness.

The difficulties of Bentham's position lie not so much in its general form as in the specific content it gave to utilitarianism. A point that is often not understood today is that there are many different kinds of utilitarianism, and the nineteenth century British kind, which we might call "classical utilitarianism," had quite a distinctive content. The root idea of the term "utilitarianism" is that the rightness of an action derives from some further end. The action is right or good because it is *useful* in achieving something else: it has utility. The action is right and good because of its consequences. However, classical utilitarianism gives a general specification of the *type* of consequences that are relevant, namely, those that involve happiness in some way, and of the relevant *population*, namely, all people everywhere. Furthermore, it builds in a *time* and *space* dimension: the maximization of happiness is "in the long run and on the whole."

Thus classical utilitarianism is a relatively sophisticated position which escapes such common objections to "utilitarianism" as that it is self-centered, or that it is only concerned with the pleasures of the moment, or that it is success and achievement oriented without having regard for overall quality of life. The legitimate objections to Bentham's position, from the point of view of reflective ethics, lie elsewhere. They are threefold. First, happiness is not an adequate criterion of moral goodness and badness. Ethics has its basis in an interconnected set of basic human values, of which happiness is only one. Secondly, a theory that requires us to take account equally of the well-being of all people everywhere, without favoring ourselves or our inner group to any degree, is much too far removed from the facts of human nature and the human condition to be either workable or theoretically acceptable. Thirdly, Bentham is too naturalistic: he has taken the apparently genetic urge to pursue happiness as the sole ground of ethics, failing to take adequate account of the way in which human nature interacts with and is affected by human traditions of religion and culture.

DEWEY

John Dewey (1859-1952), with extensive roots in both British-style naturalism and continental idealism, was in a good position to resolve the tensions between the three main trends of thought we have identified so far: Aristotle's essentialism, Hobbes's social authoritarianism, and Bentham's naturalism. And in many respects Dewey did what needed to be done. He focussed attention on human experience in all its varied forms, refusing to opt for a particular type of experience as *the* authentic type, *the* basis of value. He was strongly naturalistic in his orientation, giving a major place to biological aspects of human nature. However, he also stressed the importance of social and cultural elements as constitutive of fundamental human experience. There was a healthy relativism in Dewey's position: *any* genuine experience is of value as long as it has had due cognitive input and is of such a type that it will extend experience in the future. He had the openness of Bentham, who said that anything can be a value if it maximizes happiness, but he was willing to go beyond happiness and indeed beyond human nature in the traditional sense in identifying sources of value.

There are many features of Dewey's position that are attractive to reflective ethics: the emphasis on openness, on reflection on consequences, on taking human nature seriously, on taking traditions seriously but evaluating them, and so on. The main shortcomings of the position lie in its unconditional openness and relativism, its excessive reaction against moral guidelines. At a theoretical level, Dewey was right to reject absolute values and maintain that everything is open, anything may be a value. But in practice it is possible and necessary to identify basic human values that persist despite (or because of) constant reappraisal and that indeed seem to be so much a part of human nature that it is difficult to conceive how they could cease to be fundamental to human life. In practice, also, it is important to bring these basic values to the attention of students in educational programs. These values need to be constantly reassessed in case they are not in fact of enduring value or in case they require major reinterpretation. But it is neither realistic nor responsible to proceed as if they did not exist.

There is a sense in which Dewey knew all this. At the end of *Theory of the Moral Life* he says:

> The facts of desiring, purpose, social demand and law, sympathetic approval and hostile disapproval are constant. We cannot imagine them disappearing as long as human nature remains human nature, and lives in association with others. . . . Particular aspects of morals are transient;

they are often, in their actual manifestation, defective and perverted. But the framework of moral conceptions is as permanent as human life itself.[20]

Dewey did not seem to realize, however, that it is not sufficient for a moral or educational philosopher to *say* that there is an enduring framework of moral conceptions. One must go on to spell out with some degree of specificity what this framework is. Otherwise people will not know what one means, even at the theoretical level, and in practice the moral theory propounded will have very little pull on people's lives. Reference to "growth" and "experience" does not solve the problem: there are so many different directions of growth and kinds of experience. In many respects Dewey fell into the same trap as those who in recent years have propounded a skills approach to values education, according to which if you teach children a set of moral reasoning skills they can then go off into the world and solve their moral problems. In practice, of course, one cannot teach moral reasoning skills without content, and even if one could, without a set of substantive moral ideas and principles (as well as skills) people cannot solve moral problems.

GINSBERG

Morris Ginsberg (1889-1970) was a philosopher and sociologist who explored the realm of enduring and basic human values in the way that is necessary to supplement Dewey's more abstract metaethics. He stated that "the moralist needs to have as accurate a knowledge as he can get of human needs and the possibilities of satisfying them."[21] Ginsberg not only identified such basic values; he also went to considerable lengths to establish the point, assumed in reflective ethics, that these basic values are held in common by people of different religious and cultural persuasions. He states:

---

20. John Dewey, *Theory of the Moral Life* (New York: Holt, Rinehart and Winston, 1960), pp. 175-76. *Theory of the Moral Life* appeared originally as Part II of John Dewey and James Tufts, *Ethics*, rev. ed. (New York: Henry Holt and Co., 1932).

21. Morris Ginsburg, *On the Diversity of Morals* (London: Heinemann, 1956), p. vii.

Relativists generally stress the great diversity of morals. Yet the similarity is far greater. Westermarck—himself, be it noted, a relativist—concluded on the basis of his elaborate survey that "the moral rules laid down by the customs of savage peoples ... in a very large measure resemble the rules of civilized nations,"[22] and, so far as I can judge, later anthropological work strongly confirms his conclusion. The higher religions converge in their teaching of the inward nature of morality and the universality of love and its obligations. The philosophers, after the manner of their trade, emphasize their differences from each other. But in their accounts of the good for man they move within a restricted circle of ideas—happiness, wisdom, virtue, fulfilment. These are, except on superficial analysis, interrelated, and, taking large stretches of social life, none can be attained or maintained without the others.[23]

Ginsberg lists a number of basic needs—needs of the body, needs of the mind, and social needs[24]—that correspond very closely to the basic human values given at the beginning of this chapter. He then goes on to state that "moral problems, always related to basic needs, emerge into consciousness with the formation of ideals. These are ends which are built up out of the basic needs by a process of constructive imagination, spurred on by disappointments and failures, directly experienced or vividly realized through sympathy with others."[25]

While I have not chosen to make a distinction between basic needs and the basic values that are "built up out of" them, since in my view "need" is already a value word and so-called "basic needs" are already in part an imaginative and theoretical product, it seems clear that Ginsberg's position is very close to that of reflective ethics. He holds that there is an interconnected set of basic human values that are common to people of different cultures and which can and must form the basis for judgments concerning more specific ethical issues.

22. Edward Westermarck, *Ethical Relativity* (New York: Harcourt Brace and Co., 1932), p. 197.

23. Ginsberg, *On the Diversity of Morals*, p. 124.

24. Ibid., p. 134.

25. Ibid., p. 135.

Conclusion

It should now be apparent why ethics is so fundamental to values education, from the point of view of reflective ethics and reflective values education. From this viewpoint, one's approach to ethics and one's substantive ethical position affect significantly the form and substance of values education. Indeed, in large measure values education and ethical inquiry are one and the same thing, no matter how elementary the level, and accordingly have methodologies and contents in common.

It is important to keep in mind, however, that values education is both cognitive and affective. It involves *both* inquiry into basic human values and corresponding intermediate-range and specific values *and* development of emotions, attitudes, and behavior patterns that accord with the values established or refined through inquiry. The word "reflective" in the term "reflective values education" is intended to signal a strong emphasis on both components and a close interaction between the two.

Because of the emphasis on values inquiry, then, reflective values education is heavily dependent upon the study of ethics both for its formulation and its ongoing inspiration. However, it is based on a particular view of ethics, namely, that ethics includes the study and refinement of a complex of basic human values in the light of which intermediate-range and specific values are assessed. Thus it rejects narrow approaches to ethics that absolutize specific moral rules, but it also rejects totally open approaches to ethics that do not generate substantive value principles to serve as guidelines in making particular judgments and decisions. (It accepts, however, that value issues are always *in principle* entirely open). Most ethical theories are seen as erring either in the direction of undue prescriptiveness in specific matters or in the direction of unconditioned openness such that they are of no practical use.

Because of its emphasis on the affective component, reflective values education is clearly dependent upon other disciplines and subdisciplines in addition to ethics for insight into the context and manner in which values are formed and acted upon. Further work on values education would require that attention be given to the sociology of values, moral psychology, political theory, curriculum theory, and so forth. The emphasis in this chapter on the roots of reflective values education in moral philosophy or philosophy of values is simply because of our choice of a particular field of concentration in this chapter, namely, ethics and education.

Social Philosophy

Philosophy of education has been a part of social philosophy since antiquity. Plato's *Republic* dwells on the function of the kind of education required to develop citizens for a just and stable state. Aristotle's political discussions likewise address the issue of how people are to be properly educated under different constitutions. Both saw a state's constitution as an educational device. For the Greeks the laws teach. Americans have devoted much attention to similar matters. The progressive movement in American education spawned a generation of educational philosophers concerned with the relationship of education to democratic social life. John Dewey's *Democracy and Education* (New York: Macmillan, 1916) is the classic instance. During the Great Depression, George Counts asked *Dare the School Build a New Social Order?* (New York: John Day, 1932). William H. Kilpatrick edited the "reconstructionist" volume describing the challenges of *The Educational Frontier* (New York: Century Co., 1931) and Boyd Bode examined schooling and *Democracy as a Way of Life* (New York: Macmillan, 1937). The 1950s and 1960s witnessed a decrease in the interest in social philosophy. In recent years, however, this interest has been reborn in philosophy with the publication of John Rawls's *A Theory of Justice* (Cambridge, Mass.: Harvard University Press, 1971) and in education with the recognition of the need to deal with the undeniable relationships between school and society. In this chapter Kenneth Strike deals with one such relationship between school desegregation and social justice. (Editor)

CHAPTER IX

Toward a Moral Theory of Desegregation

KENNETH A. STRIKE

Introduction

The U.S. Supreme Court is not only the nation's highest legal authority. It is often our conscience. The Court's role as moral spokesman for America is nowhere more important than in *Brown v. Board of Education*.[1] This decision not only signaled the beginning of the end of state-enforced racial segregation in American public schools; it announced a moral point of view. It held that the exclusion of blacks from full participation in American institutions was wrong.

No doubt it would be unwise to overstate the effects of this moral judgment. A quarter century after *Brown* outright bigotry has hardly been erased from the soul of America. Certainly the effects of a history of discrimination have only begun to be remedied. Yet we should give credit where credit is due. It is no longer easy to profit from the public advocacy of racism. Public racism must be hidden in euphemism and layered over with false issues. And most white Americans, while they may not support busing and are uneasy about affirmative action, also seem sincerely committed to some notion of equal rights. Few wish to return to pre-*Brown* days. These changes are not to be credited entirely to the moral courage of the Supreme Court. Yet the Court took a strong and unpopular stand and did much to affect a change in moral climate.

The stand may have been strong, but it was less than clear. Neither the legal nor the moral grounds on which *Brown* was decided are very obvious. *Brown* can be read as saying that segre-

---

1. *Brown v. Board of Education*, 347 U.S. 483 (1954).

gation is wrong because it does psychological and educational damage to black children. No doubt it does. But suppose it did not. Suppose that the consequences of a segregated education were benign or even beneficial for the self-respect and achievement of black children. Would this make segregation morally permissible or even morally obligatory? Such a view seems counterintuitive. And its counterintuitiveness suggests that the educational consequences of segregation cannot be the only morally relevant factor. But what else is relevant? And must not the consequences of segregation be *a* relevant factor in its moral appraisal?

These questions are at heart philosophical questions. They fall within the domain of social philosophy and are specifically issues of what philosophers call distributive justice. To answer them we need to get clear about some fundamental issues concerning what counts as fairness in the institutions by means of which our society distributes good and services. We need to know what is meant by equality, what is to count as equal opportunity, and particularly whether (and how) the pattern of effects of a given institution counts for or against a determination of its basic fairness.

Brown failed to answer such questions clearly. Moreover, this failure is in part responsible for the uncertainty of much of recent desegregation policy. We are not, for example, very sure what counts as desegregation. One view maintains that desegregated schools are those that result from a racially neutral policy for assignment of pupils. Such a view is compatible with the existence of largely black or largely white schools so long as that is an artifact of residential choice rather than a consequence of public action. The opposed view holds that a desegregated school is one in which black and white children actually go to school with one another. Given present residential patterns such desegregation will often require race-conscious pupil assignment, and in many urban areas it will require interdistrict busing. To choose between such views it is important first and foremost to have a moral point of view about segregation and desegregation. What precisely is the evil of segregation and what is the nature of the good or the right that is served by desegregation?

In this chapter I shall describe alternative moral points of view concerning desegregation. I will focus on the question of the relevance of information concerning the consequences of segregation and desegregation on achievement and income for the moral appraisal of desegregation policy. This question is important because the legal community and the social science community have generated different and conflicting attitudes toward the importance of empirical knowledge of the consequences of desegregation policy. This difference, I shall argue, reflects differing needs for information that are rooted ultimately in differing moral attitudes toward desegregation. Thus the question will enable me to pose some moral options concerning desegregation and will have the added merit of allowing us to examine the moral assumptions of legal and social science thought on the topic. It will perhaps be helpful to remember that lawyers and social scientists, while not always our best social philosophers, are often our most influential ones.

A Moral Theory for Brown

I shall begin by constructing a moral theory for *Brown*. Let me note at the outset that this is not the most viable reading (given recent Court decisions), but its conceptual properties are quite interesting.

Brown reversed the "separate but equal" doctrine established by the Court in *Plessy v. Ferguson*.[2] Consider some of the following remarks of Chief Justice Warren in expressing the Court's opinion:

In these days, it is doubtful that any child may reasonably be expected to succeed in life if he is denied the opportunity of an education. Such an opportunity, where the state has undertaken to provide it, is a right which must be made available to all on equal terms.[3]

Justice Warren then quotes with favor the following remarks from a lower court:

Segregation of white and colored children in public schools has a detrimental effect upon the colored children. The impact is greater when it has the sanction of law; for the policy of separating the races is usually interpreted as denoting the inferiority of the Negro group. A

2. *Plessy v. Ferguson*, 163 U.S. 537 (1896).
3. *Brown v. Board of Education*, p. 493.

sense of inferiority affects the motivation of a child to learn. Segregation with the sanction of law, therefore, has a tendency to retard the educational and mental development of Negro children and to deprive them of some of the benefits they would receive in a racially integrated school system.[4]

On the basis of these arguments, Warren states the Court's conclusion as follows: "In the field of public education the doctrine of separate but equal has no place. Separate facilities are inherently unequal." [5]

These remarks suggest a considerable concern for the consequences of segregation. Segregation was held to be psychologically damaging, and this psychological damage is said to contribute to the low achievement of black children and ultimately to the inability of black children to compete successfully in American society. Consider now how these kinds of observations might be incorporated into a systematic argument relating views about the role and functioning of schools to a more general social theory.

Initially, we shall need an abstract moral principle of some sort. Since part of the Court's concern in *Brown* seems to be for fairness in matters affecting success in life, we shall need a principle which formulates that notion. Consider, then, the following candidate: *Fairness as pertains to success in life consists in the existence of a set of social institutions for the distribution or allocation of social goods such that social goods are allocated on relevant rather than irrelevant criteria.*

This principle is similar to the equal protection clause of the Fourteenth Amendment, which is the piece of the Constitution pertinent to *Brown*. The equal protection clause is often read as a requirement that governments employ rational classifications in their dealings. Since any criterion used as the basis for a decision implicitly generates a class of persons to whom that criterion applies, the demand that decisions be based on relevant criteria and the demand that decisions employ rational classifications are equivalent. This is not to say that my principle and the equal protection clause are equivalent. That would be to ignore the peculiar history of the Fourteenth Amendment and the differences between phil-

4. Ibid., p. 494.
5. Ibid., p. 495.

osophical and legal reasoning. Let us rather say that they express a common concern that decisions be made on rational and appropriate grounds.

My principle expresses the demand that social goods be distributed on relevant grounds. To apply such a principle one must specify at the outset what is being distributed and what counts as relevant grounds for its distribution. Here I do not want to be overly concerned with what counts as social goods. Perhaps an illustrative list will suffice. It seems intuitively plausible to count as social goods things such as wealth or income, status, jobs, and job opportunities. These are the sorts of things that are normally assumed to be part of that amorphous notion, success in life. Given also our concern with schools and their consequences, we might include achievement and a notion suitably related to the sort of psychological damage referred to in *Brown*, let us say the notion of self-concept or self-respect.

The more difficult part of applying our principle is to develop a theory of relevant and irrelevant factors for decision making. Here too we might sketch an intuitive view. It should be readily granted that ability is and race is not per se relevant to the allocation of jobs. (The per se here is meant to exclude considerations such as compensation for past injury, which can make race relevant to job allocation, but which also makes the present analysis needlessly complex.[6]) But ultimately a more systematic account of our sense of what is and is not relevant will be required. Thus the following sketch of a theory of relevant reasons.

A society whose goods and services are largely distributed by free markets may hold that economic benefits should primarily be a function of social contribution as measured by the free choices of consumers. That is to say that what a person will get is determined by his ability to provide something valued by others. The scarcity of the service provided in relation to the demand for it is supposed to determine its actual price. People will then be rewarded according to their realized and applied talent for meeting

---

6. For my views on this matter, see Kenneth A. Strike, "Justice and Reverse Discrimination," *School Review* 84 (August 1976): 516-37, and idem, "The Justice of Affirmative Action," in Cynthia J. Smith, *Advancing Equality of Opportunity: A Matter of Justice* (Washington, D.C.: Institute for the Study of Educational Policy, 1978), pp. 56-63.

the needs of others or (more accurately) according to the scarcity of their talent.

The above account provides some systematic basis for the intuitive assumption that talent or ability is a relevant basis for social rewards, but race is not. Talent has a plausible connection with the satisfaction of the wants and needs of others which race does not.[7] The view does, of course, have its difficulties. For one, it makes no provision for the care and feeding of those who have no marketable skill. The view thus is not a sufficient account of fairness in the treatment of individuals.

For my purposes its major shortcoming is that it makes no provision for fairness in the acquisition of marketable talent. Imagine a society that was scrupulous in making sure that rewards were attached only to an individual's productivity, not to his race, but at the same time allowed only members of a given race to acquire those talents that pertain to the better rewarded economic niches. Such an arrangement seems clearly unjust. Fairness thus requires not only that economic rewards be allocated on relevant rather than irrelevant criteria, but that the opportunity to acquire those talents and skills that are relevantly rewarded also be allocated on relevant criteria.

Thus, we need a second theory of relevant reasons. This time we need to know not what counts as relevant grounds for allocating jobs and income, but what counts as relevant grounds for assigning opportunity. This question can be answered much along the lines of its predecessor. That is, a society whose goods and services are distributed by free markets may also wish to allocate its opportunities in ways that yield optimal social benefit, again as measured by the free choices of consumers. This leads to the conclusion that the relevant basis for allocating opportunities for a given talent is the ability to acquire that talent. Race again can be assumed to be irrelevant.

7. But consider the following problem: Suppose a large number of persons in a society have a preference not just for television sets, but for television sets made only by white persons. A society that formulates its notion of fairness solely in terms of what is effective in satisfying consumer preferences will in this case find race relevant. The objection to using race as a criterion for allocating social goods must, therefore, be more fundamental than that race is not connected to the satisfaction of consumer preferences.

The view that emerges from such considerations can be summarized in the following four points:

1. Fairness in the distribution of economic goods and services is viewed as fair competition rather than as a function of some property of the actual distribution of goods and services. This kind of equality is quite consistent with significant variance in actual economic benefits so long as the competition for these benefits is fair.

2. Fair competition has two components: (a) economic benefits need to be assigned on relevant grounds; and (b) the opportunity to acquire whatever talents and skills are relevant under (a) must be assigned on relevant grounds.[8]

3. What counts as relevant in each case is determined by what best serves society as determined by free markets, which in turn are thought to represent the expressed desires of consumers.[9]

4. The consequence is to justify attaching economic rewards to scarce talents and skills and attaching opportunity to acquire these talents and skills to ability to profit.

This view, then, provides a meritocratic view of society in which the chief value is the satisfaction of consumer preferences and equality is valued essentially because it is an efficient way of achieving this goal.

To see the impact of this view on public education, we need merely to note that public schools are thought to be the central institution in our society for distributing opportunities. Justice Warren seems to express just this sentiment in the passages quoted from *Brown*.

It should be added that the notion that schools are a basic dispenser of opportunities for success in later life assumes that whatever is learned in school is a central ingredient in life success. It is easy to assume, since schools are primarily concerned with cog-

---

8. This notion of fair competition is roughly equivalent to part (b) of Rawls's second principle. See page 230 of this chapter.

9. The use of cost benefit analysis to evaluate educational programs assumes something like this. Cost benefit analysis is commonly described as a device to simulate consumer sovereignty in public institutions. See Burton Weisbrod, "Education and Investment in Human Capital," *Journal of Political Economy* 70, Part 2 (October 1962): 106-123.

nitive attainment, that cognitive achievement is the **relevant variable**. Such a view, of course, is not implausible, although there is much evidence to suggest both that the economic effects of cognitive achievement are overrated and the economic effects of other consequences of schooling are underrated.[10] For this discussion I shall assume that cognitive attainment is the primary school-related variable in life success not because I am persuaded that this is true, but because this has been the operating assumption in much of the literature I shall discuss.

These various ideas generate a view of how schools should function in our society. It can be diagrammed as shown in figure 1.

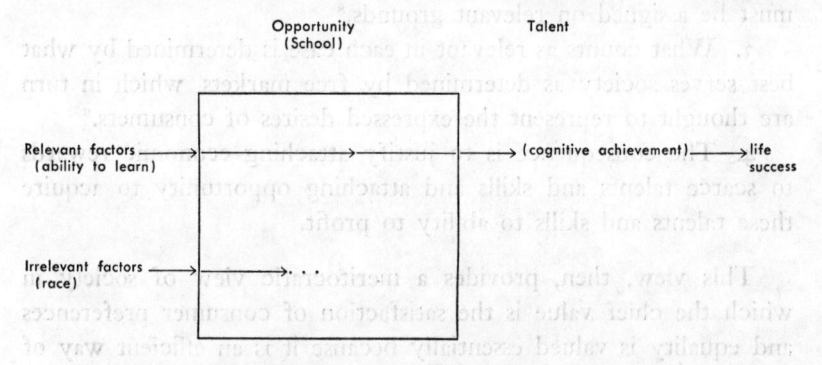

Fig. 1. How schools should function in our society.

The idea is that schools are to distribute the opportunity for achievement on relevant grounds rather than on irrelevant grounds. The discussion and the diagram assume that race is the basic irrelevant factor of concern and that schools distribute cognitive achievement, which is the basis of life success.

An Empirical Interpretation of the Moral Theory

This theory can now be used as a device for constructing an interpretation of *Brown*. What needs to be added to the above is the Court's view of how segregation functions. According to

---

10. See, for example, Christopher Jencks et al., *Inequality: A Reassessment of the Effect of Family and Schooling in America* (New York: Basic Books, 1972) and Samuel Bowles and Herbert Gintis, *Schooling in Capitalist America: Educational Reform and the Contradictions of Economic Life* (New York: Basic Books, 1976).

Justice Warren, segregated schools are predicated on the notion that blacks are inferior. This sense of inferiority affects the motivation of the black child to learn. Consequently, black children do less well than white children in school and pursuantly are less able to compete for the various components of life success. Because segregation itself is responsible for the educational failures of black children, these failures cannot be alleviated by separate but equivalent facilities. Thus, segregated schools are inherently unequal, and since they are inherently unequal the separate but equal doctrine has no place in American education.

The argument of *Brown* (in this interpretation) thus has two basic aspects. First, it assumes that any social institution is noxious if it can be shown to result in the distribution of some important class of social goods on the irrelevant criterion of race. Second, the Court propounds an empirical theory that purports to show that segregated schools inevitably have this consequence. The empirical theory connects segregation with life success, via the variables of self-concept and achievement. The path of connections Justice Warren seems to have had in mind, as it applies to black children, can be sketched as shown in figure 2.

Race⟶Segregated⟶Feelings of ⟶Low achiev-⟶Low life
         school   inferiority   ment   success

Fig. 2. How segregation connects with life success.

The Court cited a fair amount of evidence, much of it based on research by Kenneth Clark, to support the connection between segregation and the self-image of black children.[11] The rest of the connections in the theory are largely assumed.

One further comment on this theory is in order. It is not clear what importance the Court attaches to psychological harm and low achievement. These can be viewed as important solely because they mediate between school segregation and whatever variables comprise life success. However, they can also plausibly be viewed as a central part of life success. Indeed, there are grounds for believing that the self-concept of black children is far more important

---

11. This material is cited in the famous footnote 11 in *Brown v. Board of Education*, pp. 494-95.

to the issues than this reading of *Brown* suggests.[12]

That this reading of *Brown* depends on a sociological theory has gotten the Court in a good deal of difficulty, for it makes it appear that the primary differences between the *Brown* Court and the *Plessy* Court are empirical rather than legal. This view prompted the charge that the Court had abandoned the task of interpreting the Constitution in favor of social engineering based on sociological speculations. Moreover, many critics noted the weakness of the empirical evidence cited by the Court. The noted legal scholar Edmond Cahn suggests the need for a firmer base for *Brown*, noting that "I would not have the Constitutional rights of Negroes—or of other Americans—rest on any such flimsy foundation as some of the scientific demonstrations in these records."[13] The weakness of the apparent empirical basis of *Brown* is best suggested by the fact that at least one federal district judge attempted to "overrule" *Brown* on the facts.[14] Having collected substantial evidence from "expert" witnesses that segregation was in fact good for black children, Judge Scarlett upheld its legality in Savannah, Georgia. Griffin Bell, then an appellate court judge, overruled, holding this testimony to be irrelevant.[15]

A Second Empirical Interpretation of the Moral Theory

Perhaps the most interesting consequence of this way of thinking about the evils of desegregation can be seen if one continues to accept the moral theory outlined for *Brown*, but alters the empirical claims. Now it so happens that a significantly different view of the connections between race, school, and achievement was generated by a 1966 document commissioned by Congress in the 1964 Civil Rights Act. The document is officially entitled *Equality of*

12. See Kenneth A. Strike, "Education, Justice and Self-Respect: A School for Rodney Dangerfield," in *Philosophy of Education 1979*, Proceedings of the Thirty-fifth Annual Meeting of the Philosophy of Education Society (Normal, Ill.: The Society, 1980), pp. 41-49.

13. Edmond Cahn, "Jurisprudence," *New York University Law Review* 30 (January 1955): 150-69.

14. *Stell v. Savannah-Chatham County Board of Education*, 333 F. Supp. 667 (1963).

15. *Stell v. Savannah-Chatham County Board of Education*, 333 F.2d 55 (1964).

Educational Opportunity and is popularly known as the Coleman Report.[16] It was Coleman's intent in the research reported in this study both to document the substantial inequalities between schooling available to black and white students and to show that these inequalities were responsible for the achievement gap between black and white students.

The study, however, produced surprising results. Coleman summarizes these results as they pertain to black students as follows:

> The magnitude of differences between schools attended by Negroes and those attended by whites were as follows: least, facilities and curriculum; next, teacher quality; and greatest, educational background of fellow students. The order of importance of these inputs on the achievement of Negro students is precisely the same: facilities and curriculum least, teacher quality next, and background of fellow students, most.[17]

In short, black and white schools do not differ greatly in the quality of material and personnel resources they make available to students. They do differ in the background characteristics of the student body. Second, it is not the school but with whom you go to school that is important.

What difference does it make if we view schools and segregation through the sociology of James Coleman rather than that of Kenneth Clark? If we continue to ascribe to the moral theory sketched above, then our basic concern will continue to be with how schools mediate the connection between background variables such as race with those variables that comprise life success. Our conception of justice requires us to manage social institutions in such a way that life success does not turn out to depend on irrelevant factors such as race. Coleman's views, however, suggest some rather different ideas concerning what would count as sensible school policy to achieve these goals. These differences are numerous and complex, but the basic idea can be communicated by focusing on the concept of segregation and on the remedies for it generated by each view. Consider then the following three points of contrast. For convenience I shall label the two views the

---

16. James Coleman et al., *Equality of Educational Opportunity*, 2 vols. (Washington, D.C.: U.S. Government Printing Office, 1966).

17. James Coleman, "The Concept of Equality of Educational Opportunity," *Harvard Educational Review* 38 (Winter 1968): 7-22.

"stigma" theory and the "background" theory, since Clark's views focus on the stigma of segregation while Coleman's focus on students' background.[18]

1. *The agency of the state is the crucial feature of segregation on the Stigma theory, whereas on the Background theory it is racial imbalance.* On Clark's theory it is the diminished motivation consequent on the imputation of inferiority involved in state-sponsored segregation that has a negative effect on achievement. That blacks go to school only with blacks is accidental to the harm of segregation. The harm results from the fact that blacks *must* go to school only with blacks. It is the act of the state, not the actual racial composition of schools, that carries the suggestion of inferiority. On Coleman's theory, however, it is the racial and socio-economic imbalance that is the relevant causal factor in black achievement. Whether this results from state policy or not is not seen as pertinent to the effects the imbalances produce.

2. *The purpose of desegregation on the Stigma theory is to eliminate the imputation of inferiority involved in state imposed segregation. The purpose of desegregation on the Background theory, however, is to effect a racial balance.*

3. *The means necessary to effect desegregation on the Background theory are far more radical than those necessary to effect desegregation on the Stigma theory.* On the Stigma theory it is sufficient in order to have eliminated segregation to have effected a racially neutral policy for assignment of pupils or, when identifiably white and black schools exist as a consequence of a history of segregation, to eliminate racially identifiable schools. On the Background theory, however, the elimination of segregation requires a proper racial balance. The crucial point at which these remedies diverge is in those school districts that are predominantly black. In these cases to effect a Stigma-type remedy requires only the elimination of identifiably white schools, but a Background-type remedy will require interdistrict pupil transfer.

Perhaps, then, the case of *Milliken v. Bradley* (1974) can be viewed as the crucial test of the willingness of the Court to "Cole-

---

18. I do not assume, however, that either Clark or Coleman would agree with my construction of what follows from their views.

manize" the Constitution.[19] The school district of Detroit has a substantial and growing black majority. Achieving a plausible racial balance within the limits of the district therefore was implausible. Moreover, many feared that a "Detroit only" remedy would merely hasten "white flight" from Detroit, producing a virtually all black and unintegratable city.

The plaintiffs in the case therefore requested an interdistrict remedy for Detroit, and the federal district court granted such a remedy, in effect constituting a super school district of Detroit and its near suburbs. The district court's view on the matter seems moreover to have been much influenced by various social science evidence concerning the beneficial effects of a suitable racial balance on the achievement of black children.

The Supreme Court, however, rejected this remedy, ordering instead a "Detroit only" desegregation plan. The basic argument of the Court was the notion that the scope of the remedy should not exceed that of the violation. Since Detroit's suburbs had not been shown to have been involved in producing segregation in Detroit, they could not be involved in its remedy. The desegregation plan that resulted thus focused on eliminating identifiably white schools in the city.

The results of *Milliken* exhibit the basic features of the Stigma theory. *Milliken* makes the agency of the state the defining feature of segregation and limits the remedy accordingly. It is thus not necessary to achieve any particular racial balance. What is necessary is to remove the stigma involved in segregation by eliminating the vestiges of a dual school system. Thus desegregation in Detroit in effect means the creation of a system in which *every* school is a predominately black school.

How might this result be justified? The account thus far suggests two options. On one hand, the Court may simply prefer Clark's sociology to Coleman's. But almost nothing in the record suggests this. A more interesting possibility is that the court has a somewhat different moral theory in mind—one which seems to give Stigma-type results, but does not require a preference for Clark's ideology. It is this second option that we need to explore.

19. *Milliken v. Bradley*, 418 U.S. 717 (1974).

A Second Moral Theory for Brown

Perhaps we might get some clues concerning this second possibility by looking at quotations from two noted jurists about the impact of social science evidence on judicial deliberations on desegregation. The first is taken from the opinion of Judge Soboloff in *Brunson v. Board of Trustees* concerning the testimony of Thomas Pettigrew, a Harvard sociologist, in *Brewer v. Norfolk*:

> [Pettigrew's] central proposition is that the value of a school depends on the characteristics of a majority of its students and superiority is related to whiteness, inferiority to blackness. . . . It rests on the generalization that, educationally speaking, white pupils are somehow better or more desirable than black pupils.
>
> The . . . proponents of this theory misapprehend the philosophical basis for desegregation. It is not founded on the concept that white children are a precious resource which should be fairly apportioned. . . . Segregation is forbidden simply because its perpetuation is a living insult to the black children and immeasurably taints the education they receive. This is the precise lesson of *Brown*.[20]

Here Judge Soboloff seems not to be disputing the truth of Pettigrew's claims, but their relevance. The focus is not on the conditions which affect achievement and life chances, but on the insult to black children. The insult itself and not its consequences seems to be the wrong done. Even the substitution of the phrase "taints the education they receive" for *Brown's* comments on achievement can be construed as an attempt to focus on the stigma of segregation as distinct from its consequences.

These notions can be augmented with some similar observations by Judge William Doyle.

> No person would argue that any race or group is inferior to another, that it is to be considered unworthy to associate with the excluding group. I submit thus that this is the actual key to the *Brown* decision. . . . *Brown* [and others] were not predicated on the studies of sociologists and psychologists. They are all based on the fundamental invalidity of isolating people from other people.[21]

20. *Brunson v. Board of Trustees*, 429 F.2d 820 (1970), p. 826.

21. William E. Doyle, "Social Science Evidence in Court Cases," in *Education, Social Science, and the Judicial Process*, ed. Ray Rist and Ronald Anson (New York: Teachers College Press, 1977), p. 13.

Judge Doyle's remarks suggest, I think, that *Brown* relies on the existence of a kind of equality more fundamental than the sort at issue in the fair distribution of goods and services. Doyle seems to say that there is a sense of equality in which all men are equal regardless of whatever properties according to which they differ— a kind of equality that stems merely from the fact of being human. It is this kind of equality which is denied when one group of men deems another group unworthy of their association. Thus Doyle views segregation as based on the state's assumption that the black man is somehow less of a person than the white man and is thus entitled to a lesser respect and lesser consideration. This being the case, desegregation is not primarily intended to equalize the achievement or income of black children or to establish conditions of fair competition. It is intended instead to affirm the state's commitment to a principle—let us call it the *equal humanity of all persons*—which segregation seemed to deny. *Brown*, thus, is based on an affirmation of this principle.

Does this make any sense of *Brown*? It does for at least four reasons. First, it makes sense of the rather constant insistence of the judicial community that *Brown* was not based on social science, and it thereby explains why the Supreme Court is reluctant to revise its concept of segregation to accommodate recent sociological trends. It is the treatment of segregation as a problem of distributive justice which generates a need to understand how schools affect the allocation of social goods and which creates a need for social science data.

Second, this reading makes sense of *Brown's* discussion of the psychological damage done to black children by segregation. The loss of self-respect resulting from state-imposed segregation is the subjective side of the judgment of inherent inferiority implied in segregation. Indeed, the black child whose self-respect is injured is simply drawing the logical conclusion on the state's judgment. For the rational basis of self-respect is fundamentally that one is a person.[22] (At least many Western philosophies and religions have so taught.) Loss of self-respect is thus the reasonable result of an institution such as segregation, which is based on the assumption that blacks are not fully persons. Empirical studies on black chil-

22. See Strike, "Education, Justice, and Self-Respect."

dren may help confirm that segregation is harmful, but they are hardly necessary to show that it is an attack on the personhood of blacks.

Third, this reading of *Brown* suggests the importance of the agency of the state in defining segregation. After all, it is not the fact of who goes to school with whom that carries the imputation that blacks are not fully human. What carries this noxious insinuation is that the facts about who goes to school with whom are a result of state policy and state action. A racial imbalance does not require an agent, but an insult does. The policy requirements of this view of *Brown* thus appear to be rather similar to the Stigma theory.

Finally, this reading of *Brown* is consistent with much of the legal background of *Brown*. *Plessy* deals with the argument that segregation is tantamount to a state affirmation of the inferiority of blacks with the following comment:

We consider the underlying fallacy of the plaintiff's arguments to consist in the assumption that the enforced separation of the two races stamps the colored race with a badge of inferiority. If this be so, it is not by reason of anything found in the act, but solely because the colored race chooses to put that construction upon it.[23]

The second reading of *Brown* makes this the heart of the matter. The basis of the rejection of *Plessy* which *Brown* expresses is the recognition that the above passage is nonsense and that segregation is a state-sponsored attack on the full humanity of blacks.

Synthesizing the Moral Theories

Where does this leave us? At this point I do not wish to argue that any one of the constructions of *Brown* is the correct interpretation or is to be preferred on moral or philosophical grounds. It will be more profitable to explore the relations between them. For as things now stand we seem to have two distinctly yet plausible views of the moral issues in desegregation. And these two views generate different ways of thinking about desegregation and perhaps different policies. On one hand we have a point of view that regards desegregation as essentially an issue

23. *Plessy v. Ferguson*, p. 551.

about the fair distribution of social goods. This view, if it is to be applied to schools, requires not only a clear theory of distributive justice but also a detailed picture of how schools function in the overall distributive system. This in turn requires knowledge concerning the interaction of such variables as race, schooling, achievement, and income. It is not surprising, then, that economists and sociologists intuitively treat problems of race and schooling as issues of distributive justice. They must if their work is to be relevant.

On the other hand, the judicial community has tended to see issues of race and school in terms of a principle that I have characterized as the equal humanity of persons. This notion does not seem overly concerned with the just distribution of much of anything. Rather, the concern is the eradication of any suggestion of racial disparagement from public policy or public behavior. For schools this means basically that school officials cannot act nor school districts be operated in any way which suggests that blacks are less human and thus less worthy of respect and consideration than whites.

Now since these moral points of view and their pursuant ways of thinking about desegregation have been and are vastly influential concerning public educational policy, it is a matter of some interest as to whether they are consistent and as to whether they can be integrated into a conceptually unified point of view. I shall now turn to this topic. My approach will be to sketch briefly two views of distributive justice and to ask how these views relate to the equal humanity of all persons. These two accounts are both taken from John Rawls's *A Theory of Justice*.[24] The first, utilitarianism, is Rawls's foil. The second is his own view.

Utilitarianism can be simply expressed. It is the view that questions of justice are to be decided on the criterion of the greatest good for the greatest number. Good here means pleasure or satisfaction. In more recent versions the notion is made less subjective by tying it to expressed preferences. The greatest good for the greatest number is understood as the sum of satisfaction divided by the number of persons in society. This is usually called the

---

24. John Rawls, *A Theory of Justice* (Cambridge, Mass.: Harvard University Press, 1971).

average utility. For utilitarians, then, just institutions are those that maximize the average utility. When notions of equality appear in utilitarian theory they are justified in these terms. Thus, equal opportunity will be justified in that it leads to efficient employment of manpower.[25]

Rawls's rejection of utilitarianism is based primarily on the contention that utilitarianism is sensitive only to the quantity of satisfaction, but not its distribution. Thus it can tolerate and may even require situations that are intuitively unfair. Substantial inequalities and exploitation can be justified if they increase the average utility.

In contrast, Rawls puts forth the following view, which he terms justice as fairness. A just society, he claims, is one that is regulated by principles which would be selected by self-interested rational agents choosing under conditions where they are unaware of how their choice would affect their particular social position or life chances. Rawls claims that persons choosing under these conditions, which he calls the original position, would select the following two principles:

First principle: Each person is to have an equal right to the most extensive total system of equal basic liberties compatible with a similar system of liberty for all.

Second principle: Social and economic inequalities are to be arranged so that they are both (a) to the greatest benefit of the least advantaged . . . and (b) attached to offices and positions open to all under conditions of fair equality of opportunity.[26]

The point (roughly) of the first principle is to grant to everyone freedom of conscience and an equal right to influence decisions that affect their interests. The second principle provides for fairness in allocating opportunity and positions and income.

These principles do not govern the distribution of satisfaction, but a set of universal instrumentalities which Rawls calls primary goods. These he lists as rights and liberties, opportunities and powers, income and wealth. He later adds self-respect.

Now how does the notion of the equal humanity of all persons relate to these conceptions of distributive justice? The first part of

---

25. Note that the first moral theory for interpreting *Brown* was argued in utilitarian terms.

26. Rawls, *A Theory of Justice*, p. 302.

the answer to this question is that they presuppose it. To see why, it may be helpful to consider Jeremy Bentham's claim that in calculating total satisfaction each person is to count as one and no more than one. Thus one may not claim that because he is a person of a certain sort his satisfaction is to be multiplied by a factor in excess of one when the average utility is being computed. Nor may he claim that someone else's satisfaction is to be multiplied by a factor of less than one. What this says, in effect, is that while the desire to maximize the average utility may lead to inequalities in the distribution of satisfaction one may not claim prior to the application of the principle that some people are inherently entitled to more satisfaction than others. There may be inequality of results, but there may not be unequal consideration of interests. Everyone's interests have the same *prima facie* claim to be considered.

The average utility principle thus presupposes a notion that I shall call the equal consideration of interests. This in turn seems to require for its justification some concept like the equal humanity of all persons. Consider why. To apply a principle of justice as Bentham suggests, one must first formulate some notion of the class of beings to whom that principle applies. Let us assume that principles of justice apply to the class of persons.[27] Next one must show that principles of justice apply equally or impartially to persons—that no one counts more or less than one. There are two ways to do this. One may either hold that persons do not vary in whatever property the possession of which makes them a person, or one may hold that whatever variations there may be in that property are not relevant grounds for distinguishing gradations among persons or for differential application of principles of justice.[28] Either of these formulations will adequately express the idea of the equal humanity of persons. Such principles require equal respect for all persons and equal consideration of their in-

27. This is problematic for utilitarians. It is arguable that if one's central commitment is the maximization of happiness, then principles of justice should extend to all beings capable of experiencing pleasure and pain.

28. Note, incidentally, that there is nothing odd in this second formulation. If intelligence is part of our concept of a person it does not follow that superior intelligence qualifies one to be treated as more of a person any more than it follows that high SAT scores make one more of a freshman.

terests regardless of how persons may differ from one another.

Rawls's theory of justice also assumes some such principle. It is the basis of the sort of equality that obtains in the original position. Indeed, the affirmation of this sort of fundamental equality can be regarded as the point of the original position.[29]

Now the fact that theories of distributive justice of the sort described above assume the equal humanity of persons has a most interesting corollary. What follows is that a society's willful failure to provide for fairness in the distribution of its goods and services or to redress extant forms of economic inequality can be reasonably construed as implying a judgment concerning the personhood of the aggrieved individuals. Indeed, if the failure is genuinely willful, it is hard to see what other conclusion is available. A society which can but fails to provide just treatment for some of its members implies that the interests of those oppressed members are somehow less worthy of consideration than the interests of others, and this in turn implies a failure to treat them fully as humans.

This argument has some obvious implications for the two theories of the moral point of *Brown*. Particularly, it suggests that one cannot exclude considerations of distributive justice from the moral appraisal of segregation because one's concern is for a different and more fundamental kind of equality. This view cannot be successfully defended because failures to provide for the fair distribution of social goods *are* failures to provide equal respect for all persons. There are not then two kinds of segregation, one which maligns the basic humanity of blacks and a second which "merely" maldistributes social goods. There are just different ways to fail to extend to blacks a recognition of their full humanity.

There is a second way in which these two kinds of moral theory for desegregation interact. I have already indicated that self-respect is the subjective side of the principle of the equal humanity of persons. This as well as its connection to achievement is the reason for its importance in *Brown*. Now, insofar as self-respect is contingent on social arrangements, it can be viewed as something that a society distributes. We might, then, attempt to

29. See Ronald Dworkin, *Taking Rights Seriously* (Cambridge, Mass.: Harvard University Press, 1977), chap. 6.

further the pursuits of a more integrated moral theory for desegregation by looking at the role self-respect can play in a view of distributive justice.

Recall that Rawls includes self-respect among the primary goods. It is something that any rational person wants whatever else he wants. Indeed, Rawls claims that self-respect is the most important primary good.[30] Why should this be the case? According to Rawls, the reason is that self-respect is a condition of feeling that our plans and our own good are worth pursuing. A person who lacks a sense of his own worth fails to find the fact that he wants something a reason why he should have it. Without self-respect "nothing may seem worth doing. . . . All desire and activity become empty and vain, and we sink into apathy and cynicism."[31]

Rawls's point here is correct, but he understates his case. It is not just that lack of self-respect leads to the inability to affirm one's own good. More importantly, a lack of self-respect can lead a person to be unable to affirm his own rights. It will seem only natural and right to someone who questions his own worth that others' interests are given preferential consideration. Unequal or unfair treatment may seem justifiable, or a lack of security in one's worth may lead to hesitation or refusal to take action in one's own behalf or defense.

This suggests why self-respect is a crucial commodity in any sensible theory of distributive justice. People who lack self-respect will not only be apathetic in pursuing their own good; they will acquiesce in their own oppression. To enslave a man thoroughly one must make him feel worthless.

How then, do people acquire self-respect? Certainly having a sense of one's own value depends in part on the extent to which other persons and institutions affirm that value. Few people will feel secure in their own worth when the messages expressed in their personal and social life constantly deny it. And if this is the case then what follows for views concerning desegregation is that even if the primary concern is for the fair distribution of economic goods, one cannot be indifferent to whether or not public policy

---

30. Rawls, *A Theory of Justice*, p. 440.
31. Ibid.

seems to be based on the rejection or the affirmation of the humanity of blacks. There may then be a more fundamental reason why separate schools are inherently unequal than that they do psychological damage that lowers the achievement of black children. The psychological damage resulting from segregation can lessen the ability of blacks to see themselves as fully human and thereby create a willingness to acquiesce in their oppression. Self-respect, thus, has a central place in distributive justice.

Conclusion

These arguments indicate, then, that the two moral theories under discussion imply one another and that when separated each gives an incomplete view of what is at stake in issues of segregation and desegregation. If we start with a theory that views segregation as noxious primarily because it maligns the humanity of blacks, we are soon led to a concern for how schools effect the fair distribution of various social goods. For the failure to distribute economic goods equitably on a criterion of race is a way of maligning the full humanity of blacks. If, on the other hand, we start with a concern for the fair distribution of even purely economic goods, we are led to a concern for self-respect and thereby to a recognition that the affirmation of the dignity and worth of all persons in our public educational policy is a fundamental consideration. One simply cannot divorce a concern that public policy affirms the worth of all persons and a concern for fair institutions for allocating goods and services from the evaluation of the moral issues raised by school segregation.

The arguments lead to the further conclusion that the moral theory that seems implicit in the views of many jurists and the moral theory implicit in much of the literature on the effects of schooling are overly narrow. The judicial insistence that *Brown* and subsequent cases were based on legal and moral considerations, not economics and sociology, has begun to border on a refusal by the courts to take into consideration relevant information on how schooling effects achievement and income. A concern for distributive justice is thereby thrown out of court. On the other hand much recent sociological and legal literature shows a fixation on the connections between race, schooling, achievement and income, and a comparative lack of interest in self-respect,[32] and a lack of recognition of the importance of institutions that publicly affirm the equal worth of all people. My arguments show these concerns to be part of a larger view.

This larger view requires us to be fundamentally concerned that schools be operated in ways which express the equal worth of all persons and provide all children the chance to acquire a sense of their own worth. It requires this both because it recognizes that the equal humanity of all persons is a fundamental moral commitment of our society, and because it recognizes the crucial role of self-respect for the fair allocation of social goods. It thus requires us to understand better how public policy conveys messages (institutional body language, if you will) and how schools affect self-respect. We are not, I think, adequately knowledgeable on these topics.

The view also requires us to understand how schooling affects achievement, income, and indeed the entire range of relevant social outcomes, because fairness here is a significant moral issue in its own right and because failure to achieve justice here impugns the basic humanity of the oppressed.

Finally, this view requires us to get our policy making act together. That is, we need to be able to take into consideration all of the morally relevant considerations in the judicial and legislative forums where desegregation decisions are made. The questions this larger view raises are not easy ones. We shall need wisdom and research to answer them. The somewhat myopic intellectual division of labor that seems to be developing between the legal and social science communities is not helpful in this regard.

---

32. There is a literature on how desegregation affects the self-concept of black students. See Edgar G. Epps, "The Impact of School Desegregation on Aspirations, Self-Concepts, and Other Aspects of Personality," *Law and Contemporary Problems* 39 (Spring 1975): 300-313. The question at issue is whether or not competing with often better-prepared white students lessens the black child's sense of personal efficacy or personal competence. I would suggest, however, that measures of self-image that turn out to be linked to comparative competence are not measures of self-respect as I have employed the notion. To lack self-respect is to feel unworthy as a person, which is not the same as feeling less academically competent than someone else. On the other hand, it is possible that many children have an irrational view of the basis of self-respect. They might then lose their self-respect on finding themselves to be less than academically able. It is important in any case to distinguish self-respect from the broader notion of self-image.

Philosophy of Science

"Science" leads three lives in education. It is the name for a subject in the curriculum, it often serves as the example—*par excellence*—of knowledge, and it is a model for carrying out educational research. In all cases, what we believe science to be determines to a large extent how we will teach science, how we will think about knowledge in general, and how we will investigate educational phenomena. Joseph J. Schwab's program of "enquiry" teaching illustrates the first of these; writings as diverse as those of John Dewey and the numerous people influenced by twentieth-century positivism reflect the second; and the Seventy-first Yearbook of the Society, *Philosophical Redirection of Educational Research* (Chicago: University of Chicago Press, 1972) speaks to the third. There is a long tradition of concern over the question, How scientific can the study of the art of education be? Dewey's 1929 discussion of *The Sources of a Science of Education* (New York: Horace Liveright and Co., 1929) is an early classic which argued that if there is to be a science of education, the ultimate test of its theory must be made in actual practice. More recently, such philosophers as May Brodbeck and Michael Scriven have brought ideas from Philosophy of Science to bear on what it means to be a "scientific" educational researcher. But the greatest recent impact on the idea of educational research has come from T. S. Kuhn's influential work *The Structure of Scientific Revolutions* (Chicago: University of Chicago Press, 1962) and the number of philosophical discussions it has spawned not only in education, but also in other academic fields. Denis Phillips turns in this chapter to examine some of the impact Kuhn and his critics have had on educational matters. (Editor)

CHAPTER X

Post-Kuhnian Reflections on Educational Research

D. C. PHILLIPS

Introduction

Over the years, there have been many admirers of the famous passage written by William James:

> I say moreover that you make a great, a very great mistake, if you think that psychology, being the science of the mind's laws, is something from which you can deduce definite programs and schemes and methods of instruction for immediate schoolroom use. Psychology is a science, and teaching an art; and sciences never generate arts directly out of themselves. ... A science only lays down lines within which the rules of the art must fall, laws which the follower of the art must not transgress; but what particular thing he shall positively do within those lines is left exclusively to his own genius.[1]

The work of the educational researcher N. L. Gage exemplifies the Jamesian orientation. In his recent book, *The Scientific Basis of the Art of Teaching*, Gage argues that modern scientific endeavor has, indeed, established guidelines that teachers should follow in the practice of their art.[2]

But if James were still on the scene he would be forced to acknowledge that all is not well, although his fundamental thesis would remain unshaken. At the very least, a few caveats would have to be added to his famous paragraph. It is a matter of dispute

---

I am indebted to Gary Fenstermacher, Jennie Nicolayev, Nel Noddings, and my fellow contributors to this volume for helpful comments on earlier drafts of this chapter.

1. William James, *Talks to Teachers on Psychology, and to Students on Some of Life's Ideals* (London: Longmans, 1925), pp. 7-8.

2. N. L. Gage, *The Scientific Basis of the Art of Teaching* (New York: Teachers College Press, 1978).

whether certain branches of psychology are scientific (Freudianism is a prime example); and even those branches widely acknowledged as being scientific are increasingly subject to attack for embodying an unduly narrow and positivistically oriented view of the nature of science.[3] Furthermore, some eminent researchers in the behavioral sciences, among them Lee J. Cronbach,[4] have come to believe that scientific inquiry has a limited capacity to pin down the basic regularities in nature, and as a result are advocating something of a shift in the researcher's role, making it more of an adjunct to the political and decision-making processes that determine educational policy. Finally, philosophers of science are piecing together a new account of science in the wake of Kuhn's *The Structure of Scientific Revolutions*, and to many it seems that the specter of relativism looms large and presents a serious challenge to the view that science is an objective and rational enterprise. In other words, from some points of view science is becoming less demarcated from art.

The purpose of the following discussion is to highlight some of the ramifications for the field of education of these developments concerning our understanding of science. No doubt the work of educational researchers and evaluators is directly affected; but there are wider implications if only for the reason that science has often been considered the paradigm case of a body of knowledge (Dewey, for instance, viewed it in this light), and if our view of the nature of knowledge undergoes revolutionary change, who can say what fields of activity will remain unaffected? As one philosopher put it recently:

Scientific change cannot be analyzed in terms of logic or empirical methodology. . . . If this view, or one even close to it, is correct, it raises serious problems about the validity of scientific knowledge and the rationality of the scientific enterprise. Indeed if we extend the extreme historicist thesis to encompass all knowledge, as we must if we

---

3. See, for example, Romano Harré and Paul F. Secord, *The Explanation of Social Behavior* (Totowa, N.J.: Littlefield, Adams and Co., 1973), and Brian D. Mackenzie, *Behaviorism and the Limits of Scientific Method* (London: Routledge and Kegan Paul, 1977), where the impact of positivistic philosophy on the behaviorists is discussed.

4. Lee J. Cronbach, "Beyond the Two Disciplines of Scientific Psychology," *American Psychologist* 30 (February 1975): 116-27; idem, "Remarks to the New Society," *Evaluation Research Society Newsletter*, April 1977.

are to take it seriously, it is difficult to understand how any knowledge or any theory of knowledge is possible.[5]

These recent developments in philosophy of science are complex and not easy to summarize, as witnessed by the fact that in 1973 it took Frederick Suppe well over two hundred pages to sketch the "recent background" by way of introduction to a conference on the structure of scientific theories.[6] And a great deal of water has flowed under the bridge since then. But hopefully it will be no distortion to highlight some key contributions from one particular area of philosophy of science before moving on to delineate their significance for the field of education.

The Kuhnian and Wittgensteinian Perspectives and the Emergence of Relativism

In 1962 Kuhn challenged the view that the history of science is a story of unremitting progress marked by the steady "accumulation of individual discoveries and inventions."[7] Instead, his perception was that scientists throughout history were working within a series of discontinuous or incommensurable paradigms. At any one time, Kuhn was saying, a particular paradigm acted as a framework that determined the key concepts and methods, the problems that were of significance, and so on. Scientists working within this paradigm were filling out the details and perhaps slightly extending it, a process Kuhn labelled as "puzzle-solving."

Few people who are not actually practitioners of a mature science realize how much mop-up work of this sort a paradigm leaves to be done or quite how fascinating such work can prove in the execution. . . . Mopping-up operations are what engage most scientists throughout their careers. They constitute what I am here calling normal science. Closely examined, whether historically or in the contemporary laboratory, that enterprise seems an attempt to force nature into the preformed and relatively inflexible box that the paradigm supplies.[8]

5. Harold I. Brown, "For a Modest Historicism," *The Monist* 60 (October 1977): 540-41.

6. Frederick Suppe, *The Structure of Scientific Theories* (Urbana: University of Illinois Press, 1974).

7. Thomas S. Kuhn, *The Structure of Scientific Revolutions* (Chicago: University of Chicago Press, 1962), p. 2.

8. Ibid., p. 24.

This portion of Kuhn's work has proven to be controversial; one critic has noted that he used his key term "paradigm" in at least twenty-one different senses.[9] But the reaction here has been mild in comparison to the invective heaped upon the remainder of Kuhn's theses.

For those scientists working within a given paradigm, Kuhn asserted, difficulties or anomalies arise from time to time but these would usually be set aside as being of minor importance. Eventually a revolutionary scientist would treat them as signs of decay, and would be inspired to devise a new paradigm, a new framework of concepts and methods, and so forth. The development of this new paradigm, and its competition for dominance with the older one, constituted a scientific revolution.

Now, if a paradigm delineates the key concepts of a science and the methodological rules to be followed, then it is apparent that the adherents of one paradigm will think harshly of a rival paradigm—by the rules and criteria appropriate to the first, the second is likely to appear deficient, and of course, vice versa. As a consequence of this, the movement of a scientist from one paradigm to another is, in a sense, not a rational affair. The making of the judgments that presumably accompany a rational shift in position is dependent upon the existence of rules or criteria, and these are always embedded *within* a paradigm. So it is not clear how adherents of one paradigm could *rationally decide* to switch positions, for the criteria they would be using would necessarily be inappropriate for the new paradigm. Kuhn put the issue vividly:

> Like the choice between competing political institutions, that between competing paradigms proves to be a choice between incompatible modes of community life. Because it has that character, the choice is not and cannot be determined merely by the evaluative procedures characteristic of normal science, for these depend in part upon a particular paradigm, and that paradigm is at issue. When paradigms enter, as they must, into a debate about paradigm choice, their role is necessarily circular. Each group uses its own paradigm to argue in that paradigm's defense.[10]

9. Margaret Masterman, "The Nature of a Paradigm," in *Criticism and the Growth of Knowledge*, ed. Imre Lakatos and Alan Musgrave (Cambridge: Cambridge University Press, 1970), p. 61.

10. Kuhn, *The Structure of Scientific Revolutions*, p. 93.

Kuhn's reference, in the passage above, to a paradigm as a form of community life highlights the similarity between his position and that of members of the Wittgensteinian tradition in philosophy. For in his *Philosophical Investigations* Wittgenstein discussed the multitude of games that are played with language, such as giving orders, reporting events, speculating, testing hypotheses, making jokes, "asking, thanking, cursing, greeting, praying,"[11] and presumably each of these activities had its own set of rules or criteria (no matter how fuzzy a set). So, it would be inappropriate to judge the game of making hypotheses about nature in terms of the criteria appropriate to the game of making jokes. Furthermore, Wittgenstein claimed that a language game is part of a "form of life." In essence, then, games are a species of paradigm—or perhaps vice versa.

Peter Winch has approached various issues in philosophy of social science from this general Wittgensteinian orientation, and his work brings out clearly the similarity between the Wittgensteinian and Kuhnian theses. In his influential book, *The Idea of a Social Science*, which appeared about four years before Kuhn's volume, and also in several papers written later, Winch made use of some fascinating examples—a sociologist studying religions, and a Western anthropologist studying the "primitive culture" of the Azande. The sociologist or anthropologist, on one hand, is working within a particular scientific framework (or game or form of life or paradigm, to use the Kuhnian and Wittgensteinian terminology somewhat liberally), whereas, on the other hand, the religious zealot or the Azande tribesman is working and living within another.

The point Winch was making here was a sophisticated one not fully appreciated by his opponents.[12] It is *not* that Western scientists cannot validly criticize cross-culturally; but before they can do so, the scientists must be able to identify relevant aspects of the form of life under study, and to do this they must make use of

11. Ludwig Wittgenstein, *Philosophical Investigations* (New York: Macmillan, 1968), p. 23.

12. See the exchange between I. C. Jarvie and Peter Winch, under the heading "Understanding and Explanation in Sociology and Social Anthropology," in *Explanation in the Behavioral Sciences*, ed. Robert Borger and Frank Cioffi (Cambridge: Cambridge University Press, 1970), pp. 231-48.

the criteria used within that particular form. For instance, if a Pharisee is chanting or performing some ritual action, is that an example of a religious practice? To identify it as such, the sociologists of religion have to make use of the criteria for demarcating religious practices not that they use, but which are used in the Pharisee's culture. Hence, as Winch puts it:

> But if the judgments of identity—and hence the generalizations—of the sociologist of religion rest on criteria taken from religion, then his relation to the performers of religious activity cannot be just that of observer to the observed. . . . A historian or sociologist of religion must himself have some religious feeling if he is to make sense of the religious movement he is studying and understand the considerations which govern the lives of its participants.[13]

A follower of Kuhn might make the same point; to take a dramatic case, if psychologists in the Skinnerian behavioristic paradigm (assuming it is a paradigm[14]) wished to criticize the types of evidence considered by Freudians, they would have to use (and hence understand) the Freudian criteria for judging the admissibility of evidence.

In general terms, then, the essentials of Winch's position are as follows: (a) before we can criticize some activity or belief, in either our own society or a foreign culture, we have first to identify what game (or form of life or paradigm) it belongs to; (b) in order to do this we must use the appropriate rules or criteria, and these will be the ones that are *internal* to that form of life; (c) when we come to criticize the identified activity or belief, we may well see that it is inappropriate to judge it in terms of the rules apposite to Western science—there are many forms of life or paradigms or ways of knowing, and, to repeat Wittgenstein's point, religion or telling jokes or doing philosophy and so forth are activities that have a different point from the point of science (or, for that matter, from the point of each other); (d) the point

---

13. Peter Winch, *The Idea of a Social Science* (London: Routledge and Kegan Paul, 1967), pp. 87-88. The distinction between a framework or paradigm as seen from within, and as seen by an outsider, is often drawn by ethnographers, who use the terms "emic" and "etic."

14. Although it resembles a paradigm in many ways, there are reasons for denying it has this status (whatever precisely this status is!). See Mackenzie, *Behaviorism and the Limits of Scientific Method*, especially chap. 1.

of a paradigm or form of life is really only apparent to those *within* that particular form.

The general Wittgensteinian-Winchian-Kuhnian orientation delineated in the foregoing discussion has been strongly criticized by those who occupy what might be identified as the Popperian end of the philosophical spectrum.

It is clear that one of the latter group, I. C. Jarvie, did not fully appreciate the sophistication of Winch's position, but nevertheless his critical points have force. For while he admits that much of Winch's argument is "a plausible, even a beguiling one,"[15] Jarvie correctly notes that essentially it makes external criticism of forms of life an impossibility. Thus the practice of some primitive tribe, whose members engage in a rite such as ritual sacrifice before the planting of crops, cannot be criticized by an outsider on, for example, moral or religious or even agricultural grounds; for it may well be that the form (or paradigm or game) being engaged in has a point that cannot be translated as being the same as the point of our Western science or agriculture or morality or religion. The ritual may well be part of a form of life or game that we do not have, and which we therefore cannot identify in our own terms, and hence cannot properly criticize. As Jarvie puts it, Winch's view is that "our universe of discourse cannot appraise other universes of discourse, or appraise itself as the only true universe of discourse. Reality is built into a universe of discourse."[16] And a little later he adds that Winch "maintains in his book that understanding a society is a kind of conceptual empathy which imprisons you in a universe of discourse that cannot evaluate itself."[17]

From the point of view of Karl Popper this is an entirely unsatisfactory position. The essence of rationality, for Popperians, is the delivery (and acceptance) of strong criticism, particularly that aimed at the bases or foundations of a position. But this is precisely what seems excluded by the Winchian-Wittgensteinian argument. A form of relativism seems to have been established.

15. Jarvie, in "Understanding and Explanation in Sociology and Social Anthropology," p. 235.

16. Ibid., p. 236.

17. Ibid., p. 246.

Jarvie, and Stephen Toulmin in a different context, both identify what appears to be a flaw in this line of argument. If paradigms or games or forms of life are incommensurable, that is, if there are no common or overlapping elements, then indeed Winch's argument is beguiling. But is it the case that forms of life and so on, even forms from quite disparate societies, are *completely* incommensurable? Both Jarvie and Toulmin answer this in the negative; in essence both hold that there is a type of "methodological" overlap or commonality between forms of life or paradigms. Jarvie puts the point in terms of rationality. There is, he argues,

... something like a community of rationality shared by all men, but recognized or fostered by different societies in varying degrees (none being perfect). This rationality consists at the very least in learning from experience, and especially from mistakes.[18]

It is this that allows rational argument to take place across frameworks, not only between "primitives and primitives, primitives and westerners, but even between Einsteins and Bohrs."[19]

In discussing both Kuhn and Wittgenstein, Toulmin shows that "the central paradox in the classical theory of scientific revolutions is the implication that, between supporters of different paradigms, mutual incomprehension is unavoidable."[20] Toulmin resolves the paradox by distinguishing between two elements of a paradigm: the set of basic "theoretical" principles that embodies the key concepts and relationships of the paradigm (such as Newton's principle of gravitation, or Mendel's law of genetics), and the set of "disciplinary" principles that defines the general goals and underlying "philosophy" of the paradigm. In a scientific revolution, Toulmin points out, both of these two basic elements never change completely, and even within one of them (say, within the set of theoretical principles) there is rarely if ever a complete discontinuity between an old and a new paradigm. Hence, "paradigm-switches certainly need not lead to inescapable incomprehension."[21] Toulmin believes there is enough overlap be-

---

18. Ibid., p. 238.
19. Ibid., p. 239.
20. Stephen Toulmin, *Human Understanding* (Princeton, N.J.: Princeton University Press, 1972), p. 123.
21. Ibid., p. 124. For a different approach to many of these issues, see Israel Scheffler, *Science and Subjectivity* (Indianapolis: Bobbs-Merrill Co., 1967).

tween either the theoretical principles or the disciplinary principles (or both of them) of the old and the new paradigm to ensure the possibility of communication.

Lest it appear from this brief summary that unanimity has been reached between Jarvie, who is a neo-Popperian, and Toulmin, who no less than Winch is a Wittgensteinian, it should be noted that there is still a great chasm between them. In reviewing Toulmin's book, Jarvie wrote that "despite its display of learning and its fluency, *Human Understanding*, volume one, is open to shoals of criticisms and objections to everything from its broadest claims, down to the minutiae of its formulations and index."[22] Which only goes to show that men who recognize a common enemy are not necessarily allies—and so the debate continues.

Fruitful Applications to Education, I

Before continuing the account of some post-Kuhnian developments in philosophy of science, it may be fruitful to sketch a few of the interesting perspectives on education that are opened up by the ideas already discussed.

1. In the first place, it is evident even from the few pieces of work already mentioned, which are only the tip of a large iceberg,[23] that cross-cultural study raises thorny issues. Some types of research avoid the problems, for they are essentially studies within some Western framework or paradigm that merely requires straightforward cross-cultural observational data. A simple example would be the study of various national dietary habits and their correlation with the incidence of various types of intestinal

22. I. C. Jarvie, "Toulmin and the Rationality of Science," in *Essays in Memory of Imre Lakatos*, ed. Robert S. Cohen, Paul K. Feyerabend, and Marx W. Wartofsky, Boston Studies in the Philosophy of Science, vol. 39 (Boston: D. Reidel, 1976), p. 323.

23. Other important papers are collected in Ernest Gellner, *Cause and Meaning in the Social Sciences* (London: Routledge and Kegan Paul, 1973), of which the second chapter is especially important; Bryan R. Wilson, ed. *Rationality* (Oxford: Blackwell, 1970); Stanley I. Benn and G. W. Mortimore, eds., *Rationality and the Social Sciences: Contributions to the Philosophy and Methodology of the Social Sciences* (London: Routledge and Kegan Paul, 1976). Many of W. V. O. Quine's papers also are pertinent, as is Morris Zelditch, Jr., "Intelligible Comparisons," in *Comparative Methods in Sociology*, ed. Ivan Vallier (Berkeley: University of California Press, 1971), pp. 267-307.

cancer. (Is the incidence of stomach cancer in Japan due to the high rate of consumption of ingredients that we do not imbibe so frequently, such as teriyaki sauce?)

The situation is entirely different if the behavior being studied in the other culture is inseparably bound up with the rules, mores, or understandings within that culture. The study of discipline in schools, of interaction between teachers and pupils or teachers and parents, or moral behavior and moral cognition, or the use (or nonuse) by pupils in their out-of-school life of science and other subjects studied in school—these and a host of other research problems are plagued by the difficulties discussed earlier. For even to describe the observed behavior involves the researcher in categorizing it (" 'A' is an example of pupil disobedience to authority," "it is an example of parent disinterest in the school curriculum"), and this involves understanding the distinctions made and the rules followed within the culture or group under investigation. What looks like disobedience to us may count as high spirits or healthy independence to others, and what looks like parent disinterest may in fact be highly ritualized respect for the great importance of the teacher's role when seen through the eyes of the other culture.

An important contemporary example to illustrate the importance and complexity of these general issues is provided by the work of Kohlberg and his associates on the stages of development of moral cognition. It is worth emphasizing that the example is illustrative of the issues; the aim is not to give either a thorough exposition or a far-reaching critique of Kohlberg's research.

Kohlberg has developed a theory with universal pretensions in two respects—he claims that it applies to children of all times and places, and that it applies without exception. What is important for the present is Kohlberg's oft-repeated assertion that his hierarchy of six stages is culturally invariant. Repeating his research, originally conceived and tested in Chicago, he claims to have obtained consistent results in Taiwan, Mexico, Turkey, and Yucatan.[24]

---

24. The same brief discussion and several graphs reappear in many of Kohlberg's papers. A source easy to locate is Lawrence Kohlberg, "Stages of Moral Development as a Basis for Moral Education," in *Moral Education: Interdisciplinary Approaches,* ed. Clive M. Beck, Brian S. Crittenden, and Edmund V. Sullivan (New York: Newman Press, 1971), p. 37.

Now, the relevant thing about this research is that it is based on a standard test instrument that involves presenting subjects with a series of stories embodying "moral dilemmas." What interests Kohlberg is not the specific answers his experimental subjects give, but rather the form of reasoning they use to resolve the various dilemmas. The best known of Kohlberg's stories involves Heinz, whose wife is dying of cancer, and who has not enough cash to buy the expensive medication for her from the pharmacist who developed a new drug. Should Heinz steal the chemical, or should he allow his wife to succumb? It is safe to assume that residents of Chicago are acquainted with both pharmacists and cancer, and there are particular mores in our society with respect to property and to life. But it is not clear that the same degree of familiarity, or the same mores, can be assumed in Yucatan, Turkey, or even Taiwan and Mexico. So the stories not only require translation into the foreign language; it is evident that the characters and the situations depicted in the stories have to be modified to accommodate the foreign culture. But then the stories might not embody moral dilemmas that are exact equivalents, with respect to impact or seriousness, to the dilemmas embodied in the English stories. They might not raise dilemmas at all in the foreign culture, in which case the researcher is being misled if he uses data about the reasoning used in such examples to infer the presence or absence of cognitive structures or of stages in people from other cultures.

The cross-cultural research of Michael Cole and his coworkers makes an interesting comparison here.[25] Working in Liberia, Cole quickly realized that "standard" tasks given to Western children in experiments on cognitive development had completely different significance in the African setting, and he abandoned them and instead attempted to adopt an "ethnographical" approach to his psychological research—an approach that was far more sophisticated, and more philosophically defensible.

It is not clear to what extent Kohlberg is aware of these issues.

25. See, for example, Michael Cole et al., *The Cultural Context of Learning and Thinking* (New York: Basic Books, 1971), and Michael Cole, "An Ethnographic Psychology of Cognition," in *Thinking: Readings in Cognitive Science*, ed. Philip N. Johnson-Laird and Peter C. Wason (Cambridge: Cambridge University Press, 1977), pp. 468-82.

The precise details of his cross-cultural work have been an enigma for many years. It is not clear how Kohlberg did, or could, check that a particular story or dilemma used in research on another culture was, in fact, equivalent in its force to a dilemma presented to the subjects of his original experiment in Chicago. Following the perceptive remarks of Ernest Gellner in his paper "Concepts and Society," it appears that there is a simple (but dubious) procedure: one could "translate" the story embodying the dilemma, but if the subjects of the experiment give responses that are "wrong," that is, if they do not respond in the way predicted by the theory, then it could be judged that the original translation was wrong; one could try other versions until the responses came out in the way predicted by the theory. As Gellner put it, this "is unwittingly quite a priori" and it may "delude" researchers into thinking they have "found" something whereas in fact the principle that they have been using has "ensured in advance" that the particular result would be obtained.[26] Thus, Kohlberg's cross-cultural "findings" may not be findings at all; his procedures may have ensured that his theory came out looking as if it were valid cross-culturally.

2. Apart from its bearing on the conduct of cross-cultural or comparative research in education, the issue of whether or not different paradigms or frameworks or ways of life are incommensurable has relevance nearer home. The field of educational research is replete with rival theories and contrasting approaches, and in many cases it is not apparent whether these are, in fact, conflicting or complementary. The field of history of education has been shaken by the work of the so-called revisionists; educational psychology is the home of Skinnerians, Bandurians, information-processing theorists, Eriksonians, Rogerians, and Freudians; and in sociology of education the descendants of the functionalists face up to neo-Marxists, symbolic interactionists, and sociobiologists. The amount of dialogue and mutual comprehension between these various "rivals" covers the entire spectrum.

Followers of Freud and Skinner provide the neatest example.

---

26. Ernest Gellner, "Concepts and Society," in Gellner, *Cause and Meaning in the Social Sciences*, p. 34.

Researchers who accept the radical behaviorist framework deny that it is scientific to speculate about "inner" causes, especially "ghostly" entities that are in principle unobservable, such as ego, id, and thanatos; and of course they focus upon behavior and its observable antecedents and consequences. Many Freudians take the diametrically opposite view; and some would argue that the Skinnerians have adopted an untenable positivistic account of the nature of science, and that they fail to take seriously phenomena about human beings that all of us are directly acquainted with through personal experience. There are some Freudians, however, who would acknowledge that they are not playing the scientific game; the point of their game is different, and can only be fully appreciated from inside the framework.

A follower of Winch and Wittgenstein would gleefully point to the incommensurability of frameworks or ways of life that is illustrated here. On the other hand, a follower of Popper and Jarvie (and perhaps of Toulmin) would point to the work of Paul Meehl. A former president of the American Psychological Association, Meehl coauthored (with Lee J. Cronbach) a "hard-nosed" paper on construct validity and in numerous works has displayed his expertise in the classic statistical and experimental methods of psychological research. Yet Meehl is a psychoanalyst; and he has attempted to show that on strict Popperian criteria the Freudian framework is scientific, and that it is commensurable with other branches of behavioral science.[27]

A different example can be presented to illustrate another point, namely, that differences in paradigms or frameworks can sometimes present insuperable problems for decision makers or those who set educational policy. If some way could be found to catalyze dialogue across the boundaries of different theoretical frames in the spirit of the Popperians, then these problems might be attenuated. Working for the U.S. Commission on Civil Rights, the Rand Corporation published in 1974 a report entitled *Design for a National Longitudinal Study of School Desegregation*. The re-

27. Paul Meehl, "Some Methodological Reflections on the Difficulties of Psychoanalytic Research," in *Analyses of Theories and Methods of Physics and Psychology*, ed. Michael Radner and Stephen Winokur, Minnesota Studies in Philosophy of Science, vol. 4 (Minneapolis: University of Minnesota Press, 1970), pp. 403-16.

search design envisioned a study of 1600 schools carried out over five years, plus the establishment of a mammoth national data bank. Before funding the research, the Commission submitted the detailed proposal for evaluation to a nation-wide panel of twenty-five distinguished social scientists and makers of desegregation policy. No steps were taken to ensure that the members of the panel had compatible or commensurable frameworks; as a result, the twenty-five evaluations from these experts contained a startling variety of opinions ranging from very favorable to very unfavorable. There was no clear consensus on any of the major issues raised by the design, and it was apparent from the specific comments that the experts were differing among themselves over paradigmatic issues (what counts as an adequate research design, what statistical analyses are permissible, and so on).[28] Something of the flavor can be indicated by quoting one referee who commented that "the proposed research, even in its nonexperimental form, is well worth undertaking"; he went on to state that the "knowledgeability and technical competence of the authors of the proposal are impressively high." On the other hand, another referee wrote that he was firmly opposed to the study, and that on many technical issues "I judge Rand to be wrong. . . . I certainly am not prepared to endorse those studies as presently designed." When so many experts disagree about so much, it is not clear what the policy makers are to do. As nonexperts on the matters in dispute, they cannot be expected to resolve the problems and paradigm clashes, and yet to fund the research—and also to withdraw the funding—is to take sides. Members of the Commission, perhaps wisely, evidently decided that discretion was the better part of valor, and the data bank remained empty.

3. The literature on paradigms, games, and forms of life also is directly relevant to the field of education by way of the light it throws on certain curriculum issues. In particular, the "structure of knowledge" theorists—Joseph Schwab and Philip H. Phenix in the United States and Paul Hirst, R. S. Peters, and J. P. White in

28. For fuller discussion of this case and documentation, see D. C. Phillips, "When Evaluators Disagree: Perplexities and Perspectives," *Policy Sciences* 8 (June 1977): 147-59.

Britain[29]—treat the various forms of knowledge that traditionally constitute the main body of school and university curricula in a way that closely relates them to Kuhnian paradigms and Wittgensteinian forms of life.

Schwab and Hirst have given similar analyses of the structure possessed by a form of knowledge. In general terms, they stress that each form has a set of distinctive concepts which are related in, again, distinctive ways; and that each form has its own characteristic "methodological" features, such as tests against experience and manipulative techniques. The difficulties associated with this position have been thoroughly aired in the literature of philosophy of education over the last decade or so.[30] Jane Martin discusses some of them in chapter 3 of the present volume.

For the present purposes, the relevant issue is that the various forms of knowledge (Hirst identified some seven separate forms—mathematics, the physical sciences, history, and so on), each with its own distinctive structure, give incommensurable views of reality, and to understand the viewpoint of each form it is necessary to become immersed in it (to absorb, one might say, its distinctive "form of life"). In the words of Peters and Hirst:

> What we are suggesting is that within the domain of objective experience and knowledge, there are such radical differences of kind that experience and knowledge of one form is neither equatable with, nor reducible to, that of any other form. In each case it is only by a grasp of the appropriate concepts and tests that experience and knowledge of that kind become available to the individual. Achievements in one do-

---

29. Joseph J. Schwab, "Structure of the Disciplines: Meanings and Significances," in *The Structure of Knowledge and the Curriculum,* ed. G. W. Ford and Lawrence Pugno (Chicago: Rand McNally, 1965), pp. 1-30; Philip H. Phenix, *Realms of Meaning* (New York: McGraw-Hill, 1964); Paul H. Hirst, "Liberal Education and the Nature of Knowledge," in *Philosophical Analysis and Education,* ed. Reginald D. Archambault (London: Routledge and Kegan Paul, 1965), pp. 113-38; R. S. Peters and Paul H. Hirst, *The Logic of Education* (London: Routledge and Kegan Paul, 1970); J. P. White, *Towards a Compulsory Curriculum* (London: Routledge and Kegan Paul, 1973).

30. For a discussion of some of the problems see D. C. Phillips, "Perspectives on Structure of Knowledge and the Curriculum," in *Contemporary Studies in the Curriculum,* ed. Peter W. Musgrave (Sydney: Angus and Robertson, 1974), pp. 15-29.

main must be recognized as radically different from those in any other.[31]

This position has some important implications. In the first place, Hirst and Peters recognize that some subjects (geography is a good case to consider) are really "fields" to which several disciplines or forms of knowledge can make a contribution. In other terminology, subjects such as geography are "multidisciplinary" fields. But it would appear to follow from the analysis of Hirst and Peters that a genuine interdisciplinary subject (that is, an integrated blend of several forms) is a *logical* impossibility, for the forms of knowledge are incommensurable.[32]

Another implication of the structure of knowledge approach has been traced by J. P. White. Although disagreeing with Hirst and Peters on some matters, White has recognized that some school subjects or activities are such that pupils cannot have any understanding of them until they have pursued some serious study of them—pure mathematics and physical science, for example. Therefore, it does not seem to make sense to give students a choice as to whether to study these subjects, for there are no reasoned grounds on which an uninformed pupil could decide. Thus a pupil "must be compelled to engage in those activities which are unintelligible without such engagement. One comes back to the principle of liberty and justified overridings of it."[33]

It is little wonder that White's book is titled *Towards a Compulsory Curriculum*; but it should also be noted that he carefully delineates areas where compulsion is not warranted.

The "New Methodology" of Science

Within the field of philosophy of science, attention in the post-Kuhnian period has not focused merely upon questions about the nature, and incommensurability, of paradigms. The whole topic of the way in which the corpus of science undergoes change (and possibly development) has been thrown open to vigorous debate;

31. Peters and Hirst, *The Logic of Education*, p. 65.

32. All this requires further discussion. Syed Shahab is writing a doctoral dissertation at Stanford University on the matter.

33. White, *Towards a Compulsory Curriculum*, p. 35.

and accompanying this debate has been a renewed effort to use case studies from the history of science to inform the discussion. Once again, a brief sampling will be presented from the available material, before the discussion turns to the application of the relevant ideas to the field of education.

In his now classic paper "Falsification and the Methodology of Scientific Research Programs," written for a conference discussing Kuhn's views, Lakatos reached a number of important and controversial conclusions about the nature of scientific inquiry.[34] He argued that there is no magic method of "instant rationality" and that there is no watertight way to take a piece of scientific work and decide upon its merits. Work that appears of crucial importance at one time may shrink into insignificance; work that now is apparently sound may later be judged as faulty; and the grounds offered by a scientist for ignoring difficulties or even clear counterevidence may seem entirely cavalier at one time, but remarkably insightful at some other date.

So Lakatos turned to *ongoing* science, to *programs* of scientific research. Here it is possible to make judgments; the direction in which the program has been moving over time can be assessed as either progressive or degenerative. Changes or "improvements" to a research program, the stratagems adopted to accommodate difficult experimental findings, and so forth, should always be progressive; they should be content-increasing by anticipating new facts. In Lakatos's view, a scientific research program is rather like a game with evolving rules. Central to the activity are certain ingredients that the players do not want to change under any circumstances (in baseball, for example, there are certain rules and procedures that cannot be changed without the game losing its identity and changing into something entirely different). This is what Lakatos calls the "hard core." To preserve this core, there must be other elements that are expendable or subject to change in the light of experience. (Baseball has its "designated hitter" rule, rules governing the replacement of pitchers, and so on). These

34. Imre Lakatos, "Falsification and the Methodology of Scientific Research Programs," in *Criticism and the Growth of Knowledge*, ed. Lakatos and Musgrave, pp. 91-196. (It should be noted that page references here are to the 1976 edition; Lakatos made revisions of his 1970 version in several subsequent editions of the volume).

form the "protective belt." And finally, changes in the program are directed by the "positive heuristic." (In baseball, presumably, changes in the game are directed by the heuristic principle of making it more of a thrilling competition and spectacle.) This is how one of Lakatos's colleagues summarizes his theory, in a memorial volume of essays:

> According to this methodology the basic unit of scientific discovery is not an isolated theory but rather a research program. Such a program, developing under the guidance of its heuristic, issues in a series of theories. Each such theory though it may contain an irrefutable ("metaphysical") part, will be refutable, but the typical response of the proponent of the program to an experimental refutation will be to amend his theory—leaving certain assumptions (the "hard core" of the program) unchanged, whilst replacing other ("auxiliary") assumptions.[35]

In this same memorial volume, the controversial nature of Lakatos's position is underscored by a number of critical essays, including several by former colleagues and students. A variety of historical examples are dissected to see if, in fact, they bear out Lakatos's account.

One more or less sympathetic critic who deserves special mention is Paul K. Feyerabend, who developed many of his own views through vigorous dialogue with Lakatos. Feyerabend calls himself an anarchist, and he asserts that while it is not, perhaps, the most attractive political view, it "is certainly excellent medicine for *epistemology,* and for the philosophy of science."[36] (In a footnote added at a later date he noted that he now preferred to think of himself as a Dadaist, to avoid certain unpleasant connotations of the term "anarchist").

Feyerabend goes further than Lakatos, and asserts that there is no way at all in which we can pass definitive judgment on the work of scientists. "Anything goes," he constantly argues, for there is no way in advance that we can determine what methods will force nature to yield her secrets. And the greater the diversity of methods and theories that are being used the better the quest

---

35. John Worrall, "Imre Lakatos (1922-1974)," in *Essays in Memory of Imre Lakatos,* ed. Cohen, Feyerabend, and Wartofsky, pp. 5-6.
36. Paul Feyerabend, *Against Method* (London: Verso, 1978), p. 17.

will be because there will be constant challenge, criticism, stimulation, and interchange.[37]

The idea of a method that contains firm, unchanging, and absolutely binding principles for conducting the business of science meets considerable difficulty when confronted with the results of historical research. We find then, that there is not a single rule, however plausible, and however firmly grounded in epistemology, that is not violated at some time or other. It becomes evident that such violations are not accidental events. . . . On the contrary, we see that they are necessary for progress.[38]

To sum up this brief discussion, then: although there is little overall unanimity, it would not be entirely reckless to assert that contemporary philosophy of science does emphasize the importance of research programs progressively opening up new phenomena, the exposing of assumptions (including ones that are difficult to give up as well as the ones that are expendable), and the giving and receiving of strong criticism (and especially valuable here is "external" criticism, criticism from outside one's own theoretical frame). Together with all this goes a rather more charitable attitude than existed in the past; scientists can no longer be condemned automatically if they are caught making ad hoc hypotheses. The main focus of attention in all this obviously is the process of scientific change.

Fruitful Applications to Education, II

The most direct application of the material emerging from these recent debates is to the field of educational research. Over recent decades there has been a constant stream of criticism of the whole educational research enterprise. The misconceived, misdirected, trivial, and fruitless nature of much research has been touted in many journals including the *Harvard Educational Review*, *Educational Researcher*, *Educational Theory*, and *Educational Philosophy and Theory*. There have been conferences and

---

37. This, perhaps, is the main theme of Feyerabend's paper "How To Be a Good Empiricist—A Plea for Tolerance in Matters Epistemological," in *The Philosophy of Science*, ed. Peter H. Nidditch (Oxford: Oxford University Press, 1974), pp. 12-39.

38. Feyerabend, *Against Method*, p. 23.

symposia to discuss the lack of impact of research on practice.[39] And a number of books either offer guidance in fruitful ways to critique research,[40] or suggest how to redirect the research efforts,[41] or else they attack the very cornerstones of educational and social science research methods.[42] To this list must now be added work inspired both by Lakatos's "methodology of scientific research programs," and Feyerabend's "anarchistic Dadaism."

The benefits that can be expected to accrue from application of these new viewpoints can be highlighted through contrast with work done from a more conventional position. In their book, *Appraising Educational Research*,[43] Millman and Gowin set out to train students in the field of education to think critically about cases of educational research. The book reprints eight research papers—none of which is a "straw-man," but all of which are in some way useful pieces of work—and then a critique is given of each paper in a "question-answer" format. The critiques focus upon such issues as whether the research achieves its stated aims, the type of evidence or data adduced and whether it is compelling or ambiguous, whether the overall design of the research seemed sound, and use of key concepts throughout the research paper.

Clearly, all these matters are important, especially for researchers in training who must learn to profit from both the positive and negative features of preceding work; but there are many vital issues left unaddressed.

One striking feature of the eight individual case studies presented by Millman and Gowin is that they are, indeed, *individual*.

39. See also Fred N. Kerlinger, "The Influence of Research on Education Practice," *Educational Researcher* 6 (September 1977): 5-12, and Philip W. Jackson and Sara B. Kieslar, "Fundamental Research and Education," ibid., 13-18.

40. For example, Jason Millman and D. Bob Gowin, *Appraising Educational Research* (Englewood Cliffs, N.J.: Prentice-Hall, 1974).

41. Lawrence G. Thomas, ed., *Philosophical Redirection of Educational Research*, Seventy-first Yearbook of the National Society for the Study of Education, Part 1 (Chicago: University of Chicago Press, 1972).

42. See Harré and Secord, *The Explanation of Social Behavior* and the papers attacking the statistical test of significance that have been collected by Denton E. Morrison and Ramon E. Henkel, eds., *The Significance Test Controversy* (Chicago: Aldine-Atherton, 1970).

43. Millman and Gowin, *Appraising Educational Research*.

Their book does not grapple with the *dynamics* of research—the fact that research usually is inspired by a theoretical position, and is part of an ongoing program or loosely defined movement. Furthermore, an individual researcher usually will criticize earlier work, and try to improve upon it (the full ruminations here might not be included in the final published paper or report); and in turn the researcher's own efforts will be subject to scrutiny by the peer group, and will be rejected, or revised, or perhaps even emulated. If full justice is to be done to educational research, then some way must be found to incorporate evaluation of the ongoing stream of work plus the basic theoretical orientation that has inspired it (and which may be modified a little as a result of it). Even a casual reader of Lakatos or Feyerabend, not to mention Popper and Kuhn, or the person who occasionally browses through the *British Journal for the Philosophy of Science*, cannot help but become sensitized to these issues.

Two examples may help to clarify the newly emerging mode of criticism or appraisal, especially in its application to educational research.

In 1969, the age-old "environment versus heredity" dispute was revitalized by the appearance, in the *Harvard Educational Review*, of Jensen's paper "How Much Can We Boost IQ and Scholastic Achievement?"[44] This, together with the related work of H. J. Eysenck in Britain, suggested that intelligence (as measured by IQ tests) was largely genetically determined; the issue was taken up vigorously by supporters of the environmentalist school of thought. Rebuttal followed upon rebuttal; the *Harvard Educational Review* alone was able to fill two volumes with reprints of the articles it had published on the matters in dispute. It is apparent that the two rival viewpoints here can be treated as competing research programs; the dynamic interaction between them (one position rebutting the other, and in turn trying to fortify itself against new arguments and new data from the opposition) can be evaluated in terms of some of Lakatos's ideas. Are the rival programs progressing or degenerating? Are the changes in the respective "protective belts" such that new phenomena are un-

---

44. Arthur R. Jensen, "How Much Can We Boost IQ and Scholastic Achievement?" *Harvard Educational Review* 39 (Winter 1969): 1-123.

covered? Peter Urbach, Lakatos's colleague at the London School of Economics, made a study along these lines and concluded that the hereditarian or Jensenist position was stronger, considered as a research program.[45] However, a supporter of Feyerabend would emphasize that this does not mean the environmentalist position is the *wrong* one; there are no sure criteria for judging the long-term outcome of rivalry between several research programs. One that is weaker now may be stronger later.

It is worth returning to a familiar example, and treating it in more detail in order to highlight and clarify the novel features of the Lakatosian approach. Kohlberg's theory dominates the whole field of research on moral development; there is no forceful and coherent rival position.[46] Along with Lakatos and Feyerabend, one can mourn over this situation; there are obvious signs that the field is considerably weaker as a result of the lack of criticism and clash of opinion. This is not to say that no problems have been pointed out in the Kohlbergians' work; but scattered criticism is less effective, and probably less penetrating, than criticism that comes from a coherent alternative framework. As Feyerabend once put it:

> You can be a good empiricist only if you are prepared to work with many alternative theories rather than with a single point of view and "experience." This plurality of theories must not be regarded as a preliminary stage of knowledge which will at some time in the future be replaced by the One True Theory.[47]

The Lakatosian approach focuses attention upon the hard core of Kohlberg's program, and how this has been protected as anomalies and criticisms arise. Now, the hard core consists of at least three elements which, as Kohlberg has made abundantly clear, he

---

45. Peter Urbach, "Progress and Degeneration in the 'IQ Debate'," Parts I and II, *British Journal for the Philosophy of Science* 25 (June 1974): 99-135; (September 1974): 235-59.

46. The discussion here is indebted to D. C. Phillips and Jennie Nicolayev, "Kohlbergian Moral Development: A Progressing or Degenerating Research Program?" *Educational Theory* 28 (Fall 1978): 286-301. A slightly different version of this paper is in *The Domain of Moral Education*, ed. Don B. Cochrane, C. Hamm, and A. C. Kazepides (New York: Paulist Press, 1979), pp. 231-50.

47. Feyerabend, "How To Be a Good Empiricist," p. 14.

is not prepared to surrender and which he could not surrender without his program completely disintegrating: there are distinct developmental stages (six have been identified, but one is now in doubt), the order of occurrence of which is logically necessary and invariant.

Even before proceeding to look at the auxiliary hypotheses or protective belt, some serious problems emerge. In the first place, in what *sense* are the stages logically necessary? Next, why is Kohlberg so intent on having a theory that is logically necessary when it is a hallmark of science that it does not have this feature? (The theories of Newton, Einstein, Darwin, and so on, certainly are not logically necessary.) Finally, why do Kohlberg and his associates offer empirical evidence here? Logical truths neither require such evidential support, nor in fact can they be supported by such means (although, of course, a claim for logical necessity might under some conditions be discredited by empirical evidence).

However, there is empirical evidence to challenge the two remaining hard-core assumptions, namely, that there are distinct stages, and that the developmental order is invariant (movement through the stages occurs in a set order, and there is no omission of stages or any regression). Kohlbergians themselves constantly find that the majority of their experimental subjects use reasoning that is a blend of several stages, and they even come across not insignificant numbers of people who use a mixture of reasoning from all the stages. So it is not clear why a skeptic should believe that there are stages at all; Kohlberg's stages are not analogous, for example, to the clear-cut stages of insect development. Furthermore, Kohlberg and his coworkers explicitly identify several groups of people who do show regression in their moral cognition.[48]

How does the protective belt handle these problems? Do the modifications that are made enable the prediction of new and previously unexpected phenomena? To summarize briefly, the Kohlbergians use a variety of devices: they constantly revise the scoring procedures by which subjects are assigned to stages, the

---

48. Fuller discussion and documentation is given in the references detailed in footnote 46. See also, William Kurtines and Esther B. Greif, "The Development of Moral Thought: Review and Evaluation of Kohlberg's Approach," *Psychological Bulletin* 81 (August 1974): 453-70.

effect being that certain responses preventing clear allocation to a stage are ignored; they incorporate in an ad hoc way new categories into their scoring manual ("ambiguous," "transitional," "unscorable"); they simply ignore the fact that one case of regression, let alone the much more substantial number actually found, refutes the invariance claim (invariance means that there is *never* an invariant case); and they systematically claim that probabilistic results which at best only support the existence of developmental *trends*, actually support strong universal generalizations. And throughout all this tinkering, no new predictions have been made possible. The words of Lakatos bear quoting:

> This requirement of *continuous growth* is my rational reconstruction of the widely acknowledged requirement of "unity" or "beauty" of science. . . . It hits patched-up unimaginative series of pedestrian "empirical" adjustments which are so frequent, for instance, in modern social psychology.[49]

One positive point should be added here, something that Lakatos himself stressed and with which Kohlberg would concur. A "fledgeling version" of a program must be treated with some lenience; it takes even the most gifted scientific workers considerable time to perfect their framework, and to be too harsh too early would be counterproductive. Nevertheless, it would seem that the Lakatosian approach highlights some startling deficiencies in the work of the Kohlbergians and it is apparent that a rival program is sorely needed in this important area of study.

Concluding Remarks on Epistemology

The recent debates over the nature of science that have been surveyed in the preceding discussion are closely connected with debates over an even more general issue: the nature of knowledge. Educational theorists from Plato to Dewey have been greatly influenced by their reflections upon this general problem, and so it seems relevant to close the discussion by indicating the epistemological relevance of post-Kuhnian philosophy of science.

The history of Western philosophy is packed with rival perspectives on knowledge: Platonic idealism, Lockean empiricism,

---

49. Lakatos, "Falsification and the Methodology of Scientific Research Programs," pp. 175-76.

Cartesian rationalism, Kantianism, Deweyan interactionism, and so forth. Most (but perhaps not all) of these have been justificationist positions. As Walter Weimer has put it,

> Justificationism's two cardinal traits are the identification of knowledge with *proof* and the identification of knowledge with *authority*. Historically this is the central unity in Western philosophy. . . . A putative knowledge claim cannot be accepted as genuine knowledge unless it can be proven, and it cannot be proven except by submission to the appropriate epistemological authority. For the empiricist such as Locke, *the epistemological* authority is sense experience. For the intellectualist such as Descartes, *the* supreme epistemological authority needed to certify a knowledge claim is rational intuition.[50]

The work of Popper, Lakatos, and others offers a challenge: no knowledge claim can be proven; nothing, not even science, is infallible; everything is open to revision in the light of new experience or strong criticism. A nonjustificationist position must be built. Again in Weimer's words,

> Knowledge claims must be defended, to be sure; however the defense of such a claim is not an attempt to prove it, but rather the marshalling of "good reasons" in its behalf. . . . The only way to defend fallible knowledge claims is by marshalling other fallible knowledge claims—such as the best contingent theories that we possess. There are no "ultimate" sources of knowledge or epistemological authorities.[51]

The issues here, as with the ones discussed earlier, are still matters of controversy.

One thing is clear: there can be little doubt about the vigor, interest, and educational relevance of the debates that have been spawned in philosophy of science and epistemology by the work of Kuhn, Popper, Lakatos, and Feyerabend. Perhaps it is worth closing the discussion where it began, with William James. After his death, a paper was found on his desk with the following prophetic words written on it: "There is no conclusion. What has concluded that we might conclude in regard to it? There are no fortunes to be told and there is no advice to be given." [52]

50. Walter B. Weimer, *Notes on the Methodology of Scientific Research* (Hillsdale, N.J.: Lawrence Erlbaum Associates, 1979), pp. 8-9.

51. Ibid., p. 41.

52. Quoted by Will Durant in *The Story of Philosophy* (New York: Pocket Library, 1954), p. 519.

Metaphysics

The fundamental philosophical questions (What is real? and What is life all about?) are linked naturally in the minds of educators to such questions as What shall we teach? and What are the aims of education? From one perspective, philosophy is the answer to these questions formulated as a coherent and systematic world view based on a belief about ultimate reality. This century has produced a number of defenders of such different metaphysical-educational views as idealism (Herman H. Horne), pragmatism (John Dewey, Boyd Bode), realism (Frederick S. Breed, Harry S. Broudy), Thomism (William F. Cunningham, Robert J. Henle, Jacques Maritain), and existentialism (George Kneller, Van Cleve Morris). Generally, the chapters in this yearbook reflect the way in which more recent philosophy of education has tended less to define, defend, and extend such basic metaphysical views than to deal with other kinds of philosophical topics. This does not mean, however, that metaphysical issues are unimportant for educators to puzzle over, as James McClellan reminds us in this last chapter with his contemporary treatment of "first philosophy"—the search for ultimate reality. (Editor)

CHAPTER XI

First Philosophy and Education

JAMES E. MC CLELLAN

More than any other field of learning, philosophy goes to the roots of things. It explores the basic sources and aims of life. It asks and tries to answer the deepest questions that man can ask or answer. . . .

You and I live at a grim and fearful junction of history. Events of grave significance have occurred within our lifetime. You know of these events, but . . . we have scarcely begun to estimate their monstrous impact upon all of us. Especially, we have not begun to appreciate their revolutionary meaning for education.

THEODORE BRAMELD
Philosophy of Education in Cultural Perspective (1956)

How to Get to Basics

First philosophy is a union of two more familiar branches of philosophy—epistemology and ontology (metaphysics), theory of Knowledge and theory of Being. The reader of this yearbook most likely has learned to regard both metaphysics and epistemology (except for some of Piaget's work) at best as interesting intellectual pastimes devoid of practical utility, at worst as covers for selling buncombe. Hook once put the case against them with great verve:

To encourage philosophers . . . "to derive [a philosophy of education] from some philosophic position such as Idealism, Realism, Thomism, Pragmatism, or Existentialism" is to encourage them to perpetrate garrulous absurdities. . . . Similarly [to] write that "the epistemology of education consists in an attempt to derive from an epistemological study of the method of knowledge a description of the procedures by which learning may be furthered, and consequent recommendation that such courses be pursued in the schools" [is to] put the cart before the horse. Epistemology is bad enough in its confusions of logic and psychology: epistemology of education is worse. No one ever derived a single item of new knowledge about learning from either epistemology or epistemology of education. What we know about reliable procedures by which learning may be furthered, we know through scientific or empirical psychology without benefit of epistemology. . . . What is true of "the epistemology of education" is true also of "the metaphysics of education," only more so.

But Hook continues, and what he says continues to be true:

A philosophy of education, worthy of consideration, will develop [only] when philosophers and educators, as well as other intelligent citizens, concern themselves with questions of education, explore their bearing on conflicting value commitments and seek some comprehensive theory of human values to guide us in the resolution of conflicts.[1]

Exactly. But when we essay philosophy of education "worthy of consideration" we cannot escape issues of metaphysics-cum-epistemology. We can try. Suppose we start with the traditional questions that define philosophy of education: What is teaching? What is learning? What is indoctrination? and so forth. We build the best answers we can to those questions, using the rich resources of contemporary work in philosophical analysis of the Anglo-American tradition. A recent effort of that sort came up with a set of interrelated answers, holding, among many other unsurprising things, that if it is true that person A is teaching something to B, then is it true that A intends that B should learn that something.[2] What is it to learn something? It is to come to know, or, under certain conditions, to come to believe, something. Indoctrination is defined, in part, as A's teaching B something as if it were knowledge when, in fact, what is being taught is not the sort of thing that *can* be known, in a scientific sense of "know."

Following out those and similar answers, we build a network of logically consistent concepts defining the standard terms of educational theory and practice, as the work cited demonstrates. And questions of first philosophy "do not arise," as we say.

But one *can* ask all sorts of questions. To follow the examples above: What is it to know something, to believe something? What

---

1. Sidney Hook, "The Scope of Philosophy of Education," in *What Is Philosophy of Education?* ed. Christopher J. Lucas (London: Collier-Macmillan, 1969), p. 139.

2. James E. McClellan, *Philosophy of Education* (Englewood Cliffs, N.J.: Prentice-Hall, 1976), pp. 140 and passim.

is it to *be* true or false? More provocatively, What is it to *be* something intended (an intention or an intension), something known or believed? What is it to be an entity that *can* be true or false? We have not gone to the roots until we have a systematic way of either answering those questions or, in a non-ad hoc manner, proving that they do not arise. So I say "Amen" to Hook's condemnation of the misuses of epistemology and metaphysics, but I think we are irresponsible if we let it deter us from following our questions as far as they lead.

In sum, then, we are practicing first philosophy when we set after questions like those mentioned, with careful attention both to the historical canon of philosophical thought in which they have been the subject of sustained inquiry, and also to the systematic interconnectedness of the epistemological and ontological considerations that go into answering them. That is to say, we must keep metaphysics and epistemology tied together so that (a) our explanation of Knowledge does not leave us committed to there being things we cannot account for in our theory of Being, and (b) our theory of Knowledge (thus restricted) can accommodate our claim to know what Being is. Thus our theories of teaching and learning very directly lead to questions that can be answered only from the perspective of first philosophy.

Or so it seems to me. I might add, for Hook's benefit, that our "comprehensive theory of human values" will likewise be built on first philosophy, for value commitments presuppose ontological commitments. We are irresponsible if we do not examine those presuppositions carefully and critically, using the most advanced philosophical resources we can master. Is any philosophy of education that fails to do so "worthy of consideration?"

Before attempting to fulfill the promises implicit above, I invite the reader to consider with me, in the painfully brief section that follows, certain antecedents to the snippet of contemporary first philosophy that will be set out in a later section.

Excerpts from the Historical Canon of First Philosophy
ARISTOTLE FINDS GOD

The expression "first philosophy" enters Western thought in the *Metaphysics*, that is, in the book that came "After Physics."

Aristotle's route to the roots of things had started with: Why do things change? Particularly, Why do things move, that is, change location? Aristotle's explanation for the motion of any particular body, say A, is communicated motion from some other body, say B, which received that motion in turn from C, *sic ad infinitum*, it would appear.

But that conclusion is unacceptable to Aristotle; for in Aristotle's scientific schema there is simply no place for the materially infinite. If we are to have a *rational* explanation for A's motion, we must find some principle in addition to communicated motion —cue stick to billiard ball—for explaining motion in general. Wherefore:

It is clear then from what has been said that there is a substance which is external and unmovable and separate from sensible things. It has been shown also that this substance cannot have any magnitude, but is without parts and indivisible (... because there is no infinite magnitude at all).... The first mover, then, exists of necessity; and insofar as it exists by necessity, its mode of being is good, and it is in this sense a first principle.... And life also belongs to God; for the actuality of thought is life, and God's self-dependent actuality is life most good and eternal. We say, therefore, that God is a living being, eternal, most good, so that life and duration continuous and eternal belong to God; for this is God.[3]

But how, one may ask, does that which is eternal and necessary cause motion in that which is finite and contingent? By being pure contemplation, hence pure pleasure, the prime mover is to all other beings the object of desire. "The final cause, then, produces motion as being loved, but all other things move by being moved." And the first motion is "motion in a circle ...; and this the first mover *produces*."[4] As Max Fisch puts it: According to Aristotle, love makes the world go 'round. (Sir Isaac Newton's explanation of celestial motion was more direct and democratic: everybody is attractive to and attracted by everybody else, each pair along the shortest path between them.)

From the explanation of the (apparently) circular motion of

3. Aristotle, *Metaphysics*, tr. W. D. Ross (Oxford: Clarendon Press, 1924), 1072b-1073a.

4. Ibid., 1072b.

the fixed stars to the explanation of all the other movements of all other bodies, including human beings and their thoughts, is a long journey indeed. Aristotelian science scarcely traverses that distance, although the history of Western thought reveals no individual attempt equal to Aristotle's in scope, detail, and logical consistency. First philosophy stands squarely within that corpus of science. Eschewing myths of the sort without which Plato could not *do* philosophy, Aristotle followed the question of motion back to a principle of pure actuality, which he called god (*theos*), but pronominalized as "it." Questioned about the ontological status of his Prime Mover, Aristotle can answer simply: Its being, which means being perfect, complete, and unchanging, is *necessary*. Other objects exist contingently, but there is not an iota of contingency in the First Cause.

Its epistemological status, however, can be accounted for only by a complex indirect argument. We know that there is a first mover having those properties only because its denial leaves our questioning with no stopping point:

If there is no substance other than those which are formed by nature, natural science will be the first science; but if there is an immovable substance, the science of this must be prior and must be first philosophy, and universal in this way, because it is first. And it will belong to this [science] to consider being *qua* being—both what it is and the attributes which belong to it *qua* being.[5]

But how do we *know* that there is an immovable substance? How do we *know* that our question must have a stopping point? Well, "if there is no such term [question stopper] there will be no final cause, those who maintain the infinite series eliminate the Good without knowing it . . . nor would there be reason in the world."[6]

And who could doubt that there is reason in the world? Consider the utterly magnificent corpus of Aristotelian science: as Alexander is said to have grieved for the lack of new worlds to conquer, so might his teacher Aristotle have grieved for the lack of new realms of knowledge to incorporate into his conceptual empire. This structure could not hold if there were no Prime

5. Ibid., 1926a.
6. Ibid., 994b.

Mover as keystone. Our knowledge of its existence is based not on direct experience of any kind, but on the clear demonstration that otherwise absurdity has usurped the throne of reason in the practical as well as the theoretical sciences.

That *reductio ad absurdum* was sufficient epistemological grounding for first philosophy in Aristotle's view, but the winds of skepticism must have their season to test any philosophy. Equally so, the passion for faith. To trace the course of first philosophy from Aristotle to Descartes is to see the Unmoved Mover take on the guise of a personal God, to observe the change—one dare not call it progress—in the roles played by Reason, Doubt, Faith, and Knowledge in the search for the ultimate Cause, to feel the impulse toward surrender to mystical experience and the unconquerable resistance to that impulse, a resistance that gradually came to dominance as Aristotle's philosophy returned to the West.

DESCARTES LOSES THE SACRED FACULTY

The remains from the once majestic Aristotelian-Thomistic science were long past repairing when Descartes could say to himself: "I had attained an age so mature that I could not hope that at any later date I should be better fitted to execute my design" of providing a new keystone for the sciences. In his dedication "To the Most Wise and Illustrious the Dean and Doctors of the Sacred Faculty of Theology in Paris," Descartes pled that his *Meditations on First Philosophy* be extended the protection of that holy body "in consideration of the cause of God and religion."[7] It was to no avail; the sacred faculty was wise enough to see that, despite Descartes' sincerity, the structure to which a Cartesian keystone can be fitted will not support the philosophical and theological claims of the Holy Catholic Church. They sensed the revolutionary implications of Descartes' philosophy even if they dared not attempt to refute it.

7. Rene Descartes, *Meditations on First Philosophy*, in *Philosophical Works of Descartes*, vol. 1, ed. Elizabeth S. Haldane and G. T. R. Ross (Cambridge: Cambridge University Press, 1931). Quoted passages appear on pages 133, 145, 149, 160, 165, 198. The account here follows May Brodbeck, "Descartes and the Notion of a Criterion of External Reality," in *Reason and Reality*, Royal Institute of Philosophy Lectures, vol. 5 (London: Macmillan, 1972), pp. 1-14.

When Descartes treated "God and the Soul" he used the technique of skeptical doubt that he had employed earlier in his *Rules for the Direction of the Mind* and in his most widely read work, *Discourse on Method*. He would develop that same method into a pedagogical technique in his unfinished dialogue, *The Search after Truth*. And that technique turns Aristotle upside down. By making the epistemological question primary, by following the question "How do I know?" back to *its* starting/stopping point, by accepting whatever ontology comes with that epistemological grounding, Descartes reversed Aristotle, who had made the mechanical question primary and accepted the epistemological complexity required to sustain the ontological stopping point he reached.

If we take "How do I *know* that p?" as Descartes took it, that is, to mean "How can I be certain beyond any possible doubt that p?" we require an argument of this form:

> I *know* that p if and only if I *know* that q, *and* I *know* that q entails p.
> Let $p =$ I have a book in my hand.
> Let $q =$ I see a book with my eyes.
>   I feel a book with my fingers.
>   I taste a book with my tongue.
>   I smell a book with my nose.
>   I hear a book when I riffle the pages.

Now, says Descartes, I cannot treat every case of p and q, "which would be an endless undertaking." Since the "destruction of the foundation of necessity brings with it the destruction of the rest of the edifice, I shall only . . . attack those principles upon which all my former opinions rested," for example, the opinion that I hold a book in my hand. How is the "foundation" of the required argument unsound? Can we *know* that q beyond any possible doubt? No, "for it is sometimes proved to me that these senses are deceptive, and it is wiser not to trust entirely to anything by which we have once been deceived," where "entirely" means beyond possible doubt.

Exactly how and where do our senses deceive us? Descartes gives many examples, enough to establish that it is *possible* that they are deceptive in this case. The only way we could *know* that *q*, then, is to *know* that *r* (*r*: my senses *are* sending me those book-in-my-hand messages) *and* to *know* that *r*, receiving those messages, entails *q*, seeing, touching, and so forth a *book*. But I cannot claim to know either of those propositions beyond a possible doubt. Therefore, there is no way to establish *q*. Therefore, no *q* to establish *p*. Therefore, by induction, we cannot *know* anything that requires sensory evidence.

That argument may sound a trifle weak to pull the foundation from the edifice of science, but notice that Descartes wrote his *Meditations on First Philosophy* in the first person singular, a very different form from the magisterial impersonality of Aristotle's *Metaphysics*. In the seventeenth century people were sincerely claiming to have seen, heard, smelled all *sorts* of queer things—witches, goblins, angels, spirits, ghosts, "sirens, hippogryphs," and so forth. If I allow the slightest possibility of doubt in any belief I accept, Descartes says, I may well end up believing anything! Just look at the nonsense people around me believe. (Remember Salem, Massachusetts?) It is a grave danger, requiring heroic measures. I have to give up trusting my senses. But if I cannot trust my senses, then what, in God's name, can I trust? I have to live "the course of my ordinary life" as if my senses were sources of knowledge. But that is like living in a dream world where "agreeable illusions" protect me from "the excessive darkness of the difficulties that have just been discussed."

The oft-told story of how Descartes rescued himself from that epistemological abyss can be summarized as three steps:

1. He advanced the logical truism—*Cogito, ergo sum* (I think, therefore I am)—as an example of a sentence that *can* be known beyond possible doubt.

2. He accepted the ontology that that solution to the epistemological problem required. Being is divided into two kinds—*res cogitans* (thinking stuff) and *res extensa* (extended stuff, that which occupies space). If there were no bridge between the two, my only certain knowledge would be of my own existence as a locus of *res cogitans*. But by the necessary laws of thinking, says Descartes, although no one now believes him, we can prove that there exists "a substance that is infinite, eternal, immutable, inde-

pendent, all-knowing, all-powerful, and by which I myself and everything else, if there is anything else, have been created"—an argument from which "we must conclude that God necessarily exists."

3. He proved (or so he believed) the existence of other material objects and their properties, so thoroughly to his satisfaction that at the end he could look back somewhat contemptuously to his earlier "hyperbolical doubts."

We cannot pause to finish the story of Descartes' futile efforts to secure the blessing of the Sacred Faculty of Theology. They knew, if he did not, that the method of radical doubt would blow away the tattered remnants of scholasticism. They apparently recognized that *no* orthodoxy could grow on the ground that Descartes had cleared. If at the very root of things lies this individual mental act, this personal acceptance of a conclusion grounded in nothing but the mind's own inherent activity, then all Authority has been superceded. In philosophy, the Age of Individualism must succeed the Age of Faith, just as capitalism must, over time, succeed feudalism in the production of the material goods of life.

We Seek a First Philosophy

The history of Western philosophy contains many figures beyond Aristotle and Descartes who deserve our attention, but space is short and names are dull. And there are philosophies other than Western, but Western philosophy, let us never forget, is the seed-bed of modern science, that mode of thought in which there is no East nor West. We can see in the transition from Aristotle's first philosophy to that of Descartes certain elements essential to a scientific world view. Cartesian doubt eliminates *all* claims to special knowledge, that is, knowledge that cannot be communicated *in toto* by logical argument, each step of which is as obvious and necessary as proof of a theorem in analytic geometry, that branch of science in which Descartes gained early repute. It is a radical democratization in epistemology, one that Descartes pursued quite consciously, holding that "all men" (generic term) have the necessary "good sense" to follow "clear and distinct ideas."[8]

[8]. Rene Descartes, "Discourse on the Method of Rightly Conducting the Reason and Seeking for Truth in the Sciences," in *Philosophical Works*, vol. 1, ed. Haldane and Ross, p. 81.

His insistence that sensory evidence must itself be justified by appeal to a more general theory of the world before it can gain admittance to the body of science was as progressive in Descartes' day as it is in ours, when people have numerous "encounters" with all sorts of nonexistent entities. The listing of positive elements in Descartes could go on for some time.

A major task of first philosophy today, however, is to remove the traces of Cartesianism still found in every branch of philosophy, especially, I believe, in philosophy of education. I mention only two:

1. *Cartesian method.* When talking about his philosophical work, Descartes speaks of "razing" existing structures, "clearing" the debris, finding "bedrock" on which to "build unshakable foundations," and so forth. As if the philosopher were manning a bulldozer in an urban renewal project!

There are two interrelated errors in that figure. First, it is an error to think of philosophy as somehow occupying a spot outside science from which to remake the structure of science as a whole. That mistake was understandable in Descartes' era when modern science, mathematics first, was painfully emerging from the womb of scholasticism. There is no excuse for that mistake today.

Second, it is an error to think that science must have absolutely certain premises on which to build theories. Most philosophers today have learned that "the quest for certainty" (to borrow Dewey's phrase) is futile even in pure mathematics; they remain Cartesian in holding that such a foundation is nonetheless necessary for scientific knowledge. They then become vicious relativists—one opinion is as good as the next. They become vulgar Kuhnians—science is just one damned paradigm after another.

2. *Cartesian ontology.* Descartes found problems with the dualism required by his epistemology. How are thinking and extended stuff connected, for example, when the thought of last evening's faux pas brings the physical reaction of blushing to my cheeks? No philosopher *likes* dualism; the twentieth century (like every century since the seventeenth) has seen innumerable efforts to restore the monism that is our conceptual birthright, according to the first chapter of Genesis. But dualism survives; this yearbook, just for example, is full of it. If the arguments in the following

section are sound, however, the excuses for its continuance are undermined; Cartesianism *can* be expunged.

I apologize for the space devoted to philosophy so old and out of date. The reader will understand that attention to historical roots is required in the responsible practice of the philosophical craft. I put those data in the text because I imagine that educators see themselves as operating within the body of science or social science. (It is of interest to note that until 1910, the National Society for the Study of Education was known as the National Society for the *Scientific* Study of Education). I imagine that educators regard philosophers, especially those concerned with ethics and politics, as outside science. One should recognize, however, that the division between philosophy and science is a recent historical aberration, contemporaneous with the growth of industrial capitalism, like the latter doomed either to become extinct or else to extinguish *us*—in either case, fairly soon.

Toward a Scientific First Philosophy
THE ROUTE TO THE ROOTS OF THINGS

In practicing first philosophy, Aristotle adopted a standpoint outside Nature and asked what else there must *be* to set it in motion. Descartes sought an Archimedean point outside science on which to hang his scale and weigh human knowledge as a whole. To adopt either stance toward philosophy today would be to perpetuate the garrulous absurdities that Hook condemns. Today first philosophy must be practiced from a self-conscious standpoint within science.

Why *must* we stay within science? Why not direct our attention to the realm of "consciousness" or "values" or *anywhere* that we can escape the application of scientific criteria to our knowledge claims? Why not say that the scientific way (Tao) of knowing is one alongside many other ways of knowing? There are two ways of treating the question. One is to see it as requiring a proof that there *is* no way of being other than natural or no way of knowing other than scientific. A negative universal can be *proved* only indirectly by showing that its contradictory itself leads to contradiction. But it is not clear to me that we could frame the hypothesis that there *is* a mode of being that is nonnatural (or a "Tao" of knowing that is nonscientific) according to accepted criteria for framing hypotheses, such that proof procedures could be applied to it; in short, if we seek proof that first philosophy must start and stay within science, we shall be disappointed.

But if we take the question in a practical sense, we can see many obvious, commonsensical arguments for adopting the standpoint of the natural scientist in the practice of first philosophy, arguments that would not have been available to Aristotle or even to Descartes. To me the most convincing is the historical, political case. Before an activity like first philosophy can go on, those who practice it must be supplied with the specific molecules without which the human organism is not "viable," as they say. *Erst zum fressen, dann kommt die Prima Philosophia*, to paraphrase Brecht. Now for any species of animal, the set of conditionals that determine an individual organism's responses to the environment (and thus determine its success in getting what it needs to survive and avoiding what would destroy it) is called that species' theory of the world. For a frog sitting on the bank of the pond, the theory is fairly simple: if it is small and moves fast in the visual field, eat it; if it is large and moves slowly, jump in the pond and wait till it leaves; if it is neither, it ain't—to a frog.

Those who practice first philosophy usually lack that direct connection with either food or danger. We require a whole social system in which the simple conditionals of the frog have proliferated into vast, often competing, conflicting, contradictory theories, all of which somehow get put together as a set of routines such that Aristotle or Descartes or you or I receive the material bases of life. There is, however, a crucial difference between you and me on one hand and Aristotle and Descartes on the other. The conditionals that actually guide *our* collective human effort to produce the material requirements for life have coalesced, at an ever increasing rate, into engineering (including medical, agricultural, educational [?], and so forth) sciences that are ontologically and epistemologically continuous with physics. Thus natural science has become *our* theory of the world; it is the theory *we* depend on for our daily bread. The animistic theories that the peasants of Attica or Brittany followed in sowing, cultivating, harvesting, and then surrendering their crops to landlords, so that Aristotle or Descartes could eat, were definitely *not* continuous with the theories Aristotle or Descartes propounded. Before science could liberate common sense it had to be liberated from common sense. When Willard V. O. Quine insists that philosophical research must be conducted from within science, he is but acknowledging that his work is, at whatever apparent remove, continuous with the theories that guide the productive acts without which no food would appear in the dining rooms of the Harvard Faculty Club. Thus, there is no snobbery in Quine's use of "*our* theory of the world"; it is the theory we depend on as a species to maintain our dangerously preeminent ecological niche on this increasingly fragile planet.

Assuming that you will *try* the scientific route, let me explain how it works. Hook was quite correct to condemn the alleged derivation of practical educational directives from ontological or epistemological premises. Considerations of first philosophy enter, rather, as criteria to be applied to the engineering theories we actually use in practical decision making, at the level of both policy and individual case. We hold our engineering theory up to the light; we ask: Does this theory refer to "things that ain't," given our scientific theory of Being? Does it constitute a claim to know something that cannot be justified according to our theory of Knowledge? If the answer to either question is "yes," shall we "commit it then to the flames"?[9] Hume's treatment of "sophistry and illusion" may have been drastic. Even flawed practical theories contain much that is true and real; applying first philosophy is radical surgery, not capital punishment.

EXISTENTIALISM

In our theory of the world there are many mansions—astronomy to zoology. Where does one knock and ask for a theory of Being? If one is serious about doing first philosophy one goes to that rather remote room in philosophy called foundations of mathematics where such geniuses as Quine, Kurt Gödel, Bertrand Russell, Gottlob Frege (names *are* dull) have done their major work.

---

9. David Hume, *Enquiries Concerning Human Understanding and Concerning the Principles of Morals* (Oxford: Clarendon Press, 1975), p. 165.

In the anteroom one finds arguments written for the general public (well, at least for other denizens in the mansion of philosophy) to explain what goes on inside. Thanks to those efforts, it is possible to believe that one understands "On What There Is" even if one (for example, the present author) is not privy to the mysteries of the inner sanctum.[10] I touch only such points as seem noncontroversial among those so privileged.

The basic unit in any theory is a sentence, the smallest grammatical entity that has a truth value—T or F. When displayed in what Quine calls "full canonical notation," any scientific sentence will begin (left-most inscription) either as Sentence 1 or as Sentence 2 following:

Sentence 1: $(\exists y)(Fy \text{ and } Gy)$
Sentence 2: $(y)(\text{If } Fy, \text{ then } Gy)$

The symbols '$(\exists y)$' and '(y)' are called quantifiers, existential and universal respectively. The first may be read: "*Something*, let's just say 'y,' *is*, such that . . ." The second says: "For *all y*, everything that *is*, . . ." Thus a scientific sentence begins, as should we all, by making clear whether it is talking about all or only some.

Sentences Number 1 and Number 2 are thus consistent. The first says that something both F's and G's; the second says that if anything F's, then that same thing also G's. Sentence 1 might be an experimental finding: an electron has a certain mass, a plant grows at a certain rate, a child learns a certain skill, and so forth. Sentence 2 might be a generalization tested and, to a specific degree, confirmed by Sentence 1. In its logically simplest form, any scientific theory consists of sentences ordered as Sentences 1 and 2. A theory containing Sentences 1 and 2 is, we say, *ontologically committed* to there being entities that F and entities that G.

We are entering first philosophy through the door opened by Quine's magic key: "To *be* is to be the value of a variable."[11] Inside, we see Being entire: the class of *all* values of y in all true

10. Willard V. O. Quine, *From a Logical Point of View* (Cambridge, Mass.: Harvard University Press, 1953), pp. 1-19.

11. Willard V. O. Quine, "A Logistical Approach to the Ontological Problem," in *The Ways of Paradox and Other Essays* (Cambridge, Mass.: Harvard University Press, 1976), p. 199. This essay was first published in 1939.

existentially quantified sentences of the form of Sentence 1 above. Thus we might think to construct an ontology continuous with physics by treating as real only such entities as can be measured (or resolved or aggregated *into* entities that can be measured) in centimeters, grams, and seconds, that is, on *cgs* scales. Common sense and science agree that such entities are indeed real. But science, as we understand it, simply could not operate with such a limited ontology; the criterion of *cgs* measurement specifies a sufficient but not a necessary condition for Being (real) in our theory of the world. For we *have* to be able to say, for example, that the square root of 2 is a real entity; that $(\exists z)(z = \sqrt{2})$ where whatever it is that '$\sqrt{2}$' refers to does not seem to be (nor to aggregate or resolve into anything that is) measurable in the fundamental quantities of physics.

What sort of thing *does* '$\sqrt{2}$' refer to? Various answers are advanced from inside foundations of mathematics; they come as formal systems, none of which, we are told, can entirely escape all the problems of paradox, incompleteness, truth gaps, and so forth that led Bertrand Russell to create his pioneering formal system in the first decade of this century. We may leave such matters to the current crop of geniuses who practice that most demanding philosophy, for the conclusion comes out simple and straightforward enough: Everything that *is* in our theory of the world—the theory that contains set theory, quantum mechanics, applied astrophysical kinesthetics, *all* theories in all branches of science—is either the sort of thing, like an electron, which is measurable in physically fundamental terms, or else the sort of thing that '$\sqrt{2}$' refers to or both sorts of things together. For (and here is the extraordinary point in logic) as far as the use of the existential quantifier is concerned, it makes no difference that the *number* $\sqrt{2}$ as defined in mathematics, what '$\sqrt{2}$' refers to, does not have mass and spin. The latter is simply a fact in our theory of the world. We say that some z is equal to $\sqrt{2}$, and we say that some y is an electron and has a certain mass: the "some . . . is" has *exactly* the same logical force and form and function in the two sentences. And in some rooms of science (for example, in the computer center where the set theory which defined the number $\sqrt{2}$

has been set in circuits), the question whether or not, in a specific system, there is some z such that $z = \sqrt{2}$ is equally a question about numbers and a question about the flow of electrons.

Let me emphasize the point beyond any possible misunderstanding. That humble little quantifier which announces the Holy Presence of Being-in-the-World, '$(\exists y)$', is *univocal*. *We* feel intuitively that there is an unbridgeable gap between being a tangible object composed of atoms, molecules, and so forth and being an abstract entity like the number $\sqrt{2}$. But in our theory of the world there is no more ground for that feeling than for the intuition that the earth is the center of the universe: ontological dualism, like geocentrism, is anthropomorphic prejudice!

EPISTEMOLOGICAL REALISM

But can one account for Knowledge if one is restricted to an ontology continuous with physics? Let us consider the class of all true sentences constructed on the schema

Sentence 3: B know(s) _____ X.

We let 'B' range over all organisms that can be said to know anything. Let 'know' range throughout its lovely Anglo-Saxon conjugation. Let the blank '_____' be filled with any of the vast range of relation-indicators: 'that', 'how to', 'to', 'the', 'where', 'a', or let '_____' remain blank. For 'X': put in a grammatically correct verb, a phrase, or a sentence, and so forth. We have a *very* large class of sentences:

> Mary knows how to factor binomials.
> George knows that Brutus killed Caesar.
> This experimental animal knows which lever to operate for food.
> Fido always knew his master's voice.
> That horse knows to avoid the electric fence.

All those sentences appear all right on the surface. We should protest were the ontology section of our first philosophy committee to prohibit sentences of that general form in responsible educational discourse. So we begin with the presumption that talk about knowledge is talk about real things. But first philosophy requires us, nonetheless, to study that class of sentences constructed on Sentence 3 above, a class we may henceforth speak of as the *concept* of knowledge. (Please note the ontological grounding of "concept." [12] If what I say henceforth makes ontological commitments not continuous with those of physics, consign it appropriately.) Is there *any* value of *any* variable in any sentence in that entire *concept* that constitutes or entails an ontological commitment discontinuous with physics? An awfully big question to be answered with a simple "no," but there it is.

How to sustain such a claim? First, distinguish out a subset of sentences from the concept of knowledge—those following the form "B knows *that s*," "George knows that Brutus killed Caesar," and so forth. Such sentences constitute the concept of propositional knowledge. Special problems in ontology arise in the analysis of that subconcept, as will be noted later.[13] But we may dismiss all the rest of knowledge, the entire subconcept of nonpropositional knowledge, all the knowings how (skills), the knowings to (adaptations), the knowings of person and places (recognitions), the knowings of one thing from another (discriminations) with this (admittedly conspicuous) presumption: given the full range of theories continuous with physics—set theory, evolutionary theory, reinforcement theory, and the like—one can parse all sentences in the nonpropositional concept of knowledge in terms that *are* continuous with physics. One compelling argument for the grandiose claim about nonpropositional knowledge—adaptations, skills, and so forth—is that we recognize their existence in species far earlier than Homo sapiens on the evolutionary scale, species whose emergent properties are, our theory of evolution assures us, continuous with physics. We suffer no ontological qualms as we allow the concept of nonpropositional knowledge, whole and entire, into the Realm of Being.

But propositional knowledge presents a problem. What sorts of

---

12. Jonas F. Soltis, *An Introduction to the Analysis of Educational Concepts*, 2d ed. (Reading, Mass.: Addison-Wesley Publishing Co., 1978).

13. Thomas F. Green, *The Activities of Teaching* (New York: McGraw-Hill, 1971), pp. 124-29. See also, Wilfrid Sellars, "Some Problems about Belief," in *Words and Objections: Essays on the Work of W. V. Quine*, ed. Donald Davidson and Kaarlo J. J. Hintikka (Dordrecht: D. Reidel, 1975), pp. 186-205, and also Quine's reply, ibid., pp. 337-40.

entities are we ontologically committed to when we say that B knows that s? Let us put in our quantifiers and see. Consider:

> Sentence 3': $(\exists y)(\exists x)\quad (y = B)$ and $(x = s)$ and Kyx

where 'Kyx' is read 'y knows that x', or, substituting, 'B knows that s'. Taking Sentence 3' as the quantified schema defining the concept of propositional knowledge, consider the following argument: Let B = Georgia; $s = (5 + 7 = 12)$.

> Sentence 4: Georgia knows that five plus seven equals twelve.

Given the quantification of Sentence 3', Sentence 4 means that we are committed to there being things like organisms named Georgia and sentences asserting arithmetical truths. Nothing ontologically suspicious here, not on first glance. Organisms and sentences are continuous with physics, organisms being measurable on cgs scales and a sentence being the sort of thing, like $\sqrt{2}$, that is definable as a set (of symbols, signs, inscriptions) obeying certain rules. Sentence $s = (5 + 7 = 12)$ is, let us think, a set that joins the set $= 5$ to the set $= 7$ by the operation of addition yielding a set $= 12$, all according to a formalized system of logical rules generating what I understand are called "set-theoretic" definitions of natural numbers, operations, and so forth.

But here the trouble begins, for within any set theory that can generate Sentence s above, there is, I shall assume, another Sentence $s' = (7 + 5 = 12)$. I shall assume further that, according to that same set theory, $s = s'$. By the rule known as "Leibniz's Law," the "identity of indiscernables," if $s = s'$, then *anywhere* s appears you can substitute s'. Therefore Sentence 4 = Sentence 5.

> Sentence 5: Georgia knows that seven plus five equals twelve.

Now ordinarily, the truth of Sentence 4 marches together with the truth of Sentence 5. But they *could* diverge. Imagine a chimpanzee named Georgia who has learned that five plus seven equals twelve. (On presentation of visual cue "$5 + 7 = 12$," Georgia takes set [string?] of beads from box marked "5" and counts them, takes set from box marked "7" and counts them also, turns them in together at chute labeled "12" and expects reinforcement.) But, by some accident of reinforcement, Georgia has not learned that seven plus five equals twelve. (On the cue "$7 + 5 = 12$," Georgia scrambles about aimlessly, appears at chute "12" empty-handed, exhibits agitation and distress.) Here is a situation we should most naturally describe with the assertion of Sentence 4 and the denial of Sentence 5; thus the truth values of Sentence 4 and Sentence 5 are not necessarily the same, as the logical rules generating s and s' require them to be.

And thus a problem for the austere ontology of our theory of the world. If you take it, as Sentence 3' does, that Sentence 3 commits us to there *being* an object of knowledge as well as a knower, then a sentence is about the only candidate there is for the job of "being an object of knowledge continuous with physics" for propositional knowledge. But the problem generated by Sentences 4 and 5 in the chimpanzee example shows that such an interpretation will not work everywhere in our concept of knowledge. Therefore, lots of unacceptable conclusions *can* be drawn, for example, that epistemology has achieved ontological autonomy from physics, that the enterprise of first philosophy has failed, and so forth.

But before *we* draw any conclusions, let us step back and reconsider the whole question from within the standard Platonic analysis of knowing. Thus,

Sentence 6: If B knows that s, then
6.1: B believes that s, and
6.2: B has adequate warrant for s, and
6.3: s is True.

Do the concepts of belief, warrant, and truth require ontological commitments beyond physics?[14] Let us look at each.

Sentence 6.1. "B believes that s" is to be read as "believes-that-s is true of B" or "B is disposed to treat s as true in any instance of practical reasoning such that s appears in B's consciousness." The concept of belief is thus enclosed in the concept of disposition. For

---

14. See David M. Armstrong, *Belief, Truth, and Knowledge* (Cambridge: Cambridge University Press, 1973), chap. 10.

example, B is asked point blank, given a situation in which B wants to tell the truth, whole and nothing but: Is s true? If B believes that s, B is disposed to answer "yes," by word or gesture. Notice that the formula does not *entail* that B so answer in fact. A slip of the tongue does not negate the disposition.

What *is* a disposition? It is like brittleness in glass—a structural material state describable as a conditional: if struck, will shatter (usually). Being disposed to answer affirmatively to "Is s true?" is only more complicated in structural detail than being disposed to shatter when struck, but it is equally a material state.

Then what *is* consciousness? It is the material state we are all in when we are conscious, as distinguished from the material state we are in when we are unconscious. It is defined, roughly, as being able to receive input from all operating senses and to muster full central nervous system energy to override any incipient response of localized origin. Consciousness is what enables 'possums and pugilists to feign *un*consciousness in the hope of escaping further blows. Nothing here that requires ontological commitments beyond physics.[15]

Sentence 6.2. To treat "warrant" at the desperate speed of our tour through "belief" is too dangerous even for one who would essay first philosophy. I believe that its analysis will require ontological commitment to the abstract entities required by theories of probability and research design *and* a "community" (following Quine) capable of rank ordering warrants, that is, strength of belief on evidence, all of which we find in physics. It is a complicated notion but not, so far as I can see, ontologically suspicious.

Sentence 6.3. And the same logic that underlies set theory, evolutionary theory, reinforcement theory, and so forth will define sentences and allow quantification over truth values without inconsistencies. Since physics consists of sentences having truth values, we find this feature of Knowledge no problem for our theory of Being.

Now where has that *problem* with the concept of propositional

---

15. For an example of what the subjective experience of consciousness might look like as a mathematical entity, see Ralph Abraham, "Vibrations and the Realization of Form," in *Evolution and Consciousness: Human Systems in Transition*, ed. Erich Jantsch and Conrad H. Waddington (Reading, Mass.: Addison-Wesley, 1976), pp. 134-39.

knowledge disappeared to? Down the drain from which it emerged, through the fallacy of partial quantification, to oblivion. To know something is to be in a particular material state, that of believing something; to have been materially caused to be in that state through a sequence of perceptions and logical operations, those constituting the warrant for the belief; the "something" one believes being interpreted as a sentence *and* everything logically equivalent, as in Sentence 3'. Thus the entire concept of propositional knowledge is now defined in terms that are continuous with physics. Since the same conclusions held in respect to the concept of nonpropositional knowledge, we have demonstrated that there is amplitude in our ontology sufficient for an epistemology that can account for itself. Our first philosophy has come home safely. Whew!

Which is not to say that everything is in order in the epistemology we glanced through so briefly. Western philosophers draw distinctions between the analytic and synthetic, the logical and empirical, the a priori and the a posteriori, the necessary and the contingent, the this and the that. They will find it difficult to break the habit. In the effort to construct a logically consistent system of concepts for mental predicates, such problems as synonymy, translatability, transitivity of meanings, and so forth do appear singularly intractable if one is not allowed to invent "intensional objects," "meanings," and other such entities that obey neither the law of gravity nor the law of identity. Frankly speaking, however, I should not want such unruly things running loose in *my* system of concepts. Would you? So it is hard to take seriously any epistemological scheme that tries to contain them; propositional learning can be explained without their aid.[16]

It should be clear now why Sentence 3' is an incorrect quantification of propositional knowledge. Having propositional knowledge is a complicated notion indeed, combining a material disposition to act on certain contingencies with objective *relational* conditions of warrant and truth. We can recognize an evolutionary advantage accruing to a human group having that complex concept at hand: the chief asks the scout, "Do you *know* that there is game

16. James E. McClellan and Thomas Costello, "Quine's Roots of Reference," *Educational Theory* 26 (Summer 1976): 310-18.

in the valley?" The prosecutor asks the witness, "Do you *know* that the accused left the house at 5 A.M.?" But our quantification schema must never *identify* the sentence that B is disposed to treat as true with the sentence that must *be* and be true if B knows something. The course of education (including growth in self-knowledge, skill in reasoning, and so forth) should have as its goal increasing isomorphism between B's '*s*', the sentence that is true-for-B in B's practical reasoning, and the *s* that is simply true in our theory of the world. But there is nothing in logic, physics, or psychology to justify their ontological identification.

MATERIALISM

Dare we call the first philosophy here sketched materialism? Only if we first recognize certain arguments against using that label, among others that some whose works advance it specifically reject "materialism" as the correct label for this first philosophy.[17] It *is* counterintuitive to call such things as rainbows, afterimages, magnetic fields, probability operators, $\sqrt{2}$, and so forth, "material objects," even though all such entities exist and *are* continuous with physics in one way or another.

I would, if there were space, present the defense:

1. *Political.* The philosophical struggle against idealism, including traces of Cartesianism, is but part of the ongoing process of human liberation alive in the world today. The only theories to guide that larger revolutionary struggle that are both scientifically interesting and practically useful are varieties of Marxism-Leninism all of which proclaim an ontology of "Historical Materialism." I do not know whether certain elements in Marxism-Leninism (for example, "Dialectical," "Labor Theory of Value") will hold up to the rather strict ontological and epistemological criteria sketched here. So I call it lower-case "materialism." I add, for benefit of any comrade in the revolutionary struggle who might look askance at this deviation, that if Marx were alive today he would follow the logic of W. V. O. Quine, not G. W. F. Hegel. *Nicht wahr?*

2. *Historical.* From Democritus to the present, the central

---

17. Hilary Putnam, *Mathematics, Matter, and Method* (Cambridge: University Press, 1975), p. vii.

point of materialism has been what I have been calling "ontological continuity with physics," *not* the content of specific physical theories, which varies from one historical epoch to another.[18]

For upholders of intuitions I add that it is like revising our intuitions of space and time, matter and energy, and so forth. "Ontological Relativity" enters our individual and collective consciousness with the same painful slowness that other theories of relativity are revising the "roots" of our physical concepts.[19] But we learn to adjust our intuitions or else adjust to (because we understand it) an occasional jolt of counterintuition in the practice of a scientific first philosophy, rather like a shot of static electricity to a worker in the electronics laboratory.

CONCEPTUAL SPECULATIONS

Can such a snippet from a first philosophy convey any understanding of it as a whole? No more, alas, than the snippets in previous sections of this chapter convey Aristotle and Descartes. Perhaps a further thought or two might tempt the serious educator to pursue the arguments beyond these pages and the limitations of the present author. Suppose we ask how this particular animal species happened to invent a science like physics. The materialist wants to understand that process from an evolutionary point of view, going back (*in principle*, one must add) to the origin of the universe itself. At that exact moment—more or less—some of the basic *matter* of the world went evolutionary, evolving over time from the truly elementary particle, whatever that may turn out to be, into subatomic particles ... electrons ... elements (hydrogen, helium, and so forth) ... then molecules ... compounds ... organisms ... mammals ... Homo sapiens ... physics. The chain is unbroken; nothing has been added, nothing taken away.

Did abstract entities evolve also? There is a sense in which some abstract entities depend on others. When a number, n, is defined as the nth iterative of succession from 0, then n, by definition *in that*

18. Keith Campbell, "Materialism," in *Encyclopedia of Philosophy*, vol. 5, ed. Paul Edwards (New York: Macmillan and The Free Press, 1967), pp. 179-88.

19. Willard V. O. Quine, *Ontological Relativity and Other Essays* (New York: Columbia University Press, 1968), pp. 26-28.

system presupposes, depends on, the existence of 0. (Relativity rules.) But no *n* ever actually evolves, for evolution entails change over time, while these abstract entities—the infinite infinitude of them—were there in the first instant of this universe's Being and will be there at its last, if alpha or omega there be for a universe as a whole. Such an inoffensive Pythagoreanism seems the most sensible attitude to hold toward those nonevolving entities we define and thus confine in formal systems.

What seems to have happened is that in Homo sapiens the abstract and evolutionary entities came together again on this planet.[20] A species evolved that carried its theory of the world not in genetically fixed circuits but in languages. Every human language consists of elements such that in learning to speak the language, a child is also learning the elements of a universal logic, a logic that eventually enabled us to use abstract entities quite consciously in the production of material goods and the destruction of material enemies. It is as if we had learned to generalize the enormously advanced vector-calculating operations of our brachiating ancestors. This Piagetian shift from concrete to formal operations would have been impossible were we not tuned in to some facet of existence out of the frequency range of competitor species. Whether we will use the power thus given us to the advantage of our species or to our self-destruction depends on the outcome of a worldwide political struggle now entering its most critical phase, a struggle in which every American educator takes an active part, wittingly or no.

Practical Applications

Every step on the path that brought us to this point is fraught with peril. Perhaps a serious technical error has crept into the exposition such that the claim staked here will prove barren. So be it: science guarantees that such errors will be discovered in due course. But let us assume that any technical difficulties on the way to this point can be overcome. If so, first philosophy is a very useful tool

---

20. See the special issue on evolution in *Scientific American* 23 (September 1978). See also Karl R. Popper and John C. Eccles, *The Self and Its Brain: An Argument for Interactionism* (Boston: Springer International, 1979) for an alternative epistemology built on the same evolutionary ontology.

indeed. We can hold up any theory that we accept as guiding our practice and we can ask of it:

1. Does it include ontological commitments not continuous with physics, that is, does it quantify over entities that obey neither the laws of mechanics (including quantum) nor the laws of logic (including, it may turn out, certain restrictions that constitute quantum logic)?[21]

2. Does it contain (or as a whole constitute) a knowledge claim that cannot be justified on a materialist analysis of "B know(s) _____ X"?

The trick, of course, is in stating the theories that we in fact do act upon with sufficient precision to enable first philosophy to apply. That is the point where philosophers and practitioners must meet. In some aspects of educational practice (for example, in educational research), theories should be stated in such form that their ontological and epistemological claims are obvious; in any case "The Logical Foundations of Educational Research" have received sustained scrutiny ever since B. Othanel Smith's doctoral dissertation on that topic forty years ago.[22] I once gained the impression, however, that those who advanced the "central tendency" research reported in publications of the American Educational Research Association were less concerned than perhaps they should have been for philosophical soundness in the theories they followed, and some occasionally appeared more concerned than was seemly to attract money and power to their particular establishments. Perhaps all that has changed in the last few years.

Apart from quantitative research, we may find it difficult to state our operating theories in a form that enables us to determine exactly what ontological and epistemological claims they commit us to. We have a net excess of theories in education and a sad deficit of precision in stating the principles that we do, in fact, follow in our professional practice. Application of the criteria of

21. Putnam, *Mathematics, Matter, and Method*, pp. 174-97.

22. See Edward G. Rozycki, "Human Behavior: Measurement and Cause" (doct. diss., Temple University, 1973). See also, Harry S. Broudy, Robert H. Ennis, and Leonard I. Krimerman, eds., *Philosophy of Educational Research* (New York: John Wiley and Sons, 1973).

first philosophy to our *actual* theories of esthetic development, our *actual* theories of political authority, and so forth waits upon a higher level of collective self-consciousness in our actions than we have so far attained. The utility of the analytic mode in philosophy is in supplying us with a *form* to articulate that collective self-consciousness. Kerr's brilliant analysis of standard arguments in educational policy is a model that leads directly to questions of first philosophy.[23]

Let us take one step more. Suppose we find that the theories we in fact follow in our educational practice cannot be reconciled with our scientific theory of the world. What do we do then? Hook's answer is "humility" and "toleration": "Philosophy is the discipline which considers fundamental questions in such a way that no matter what answers one makes to them, one can give reasons or grounds for belief or disbelief."[24] That answer leads to political passivity, to acceptance of theories that require us to treat young members of species Homo sapiens—the smartest animals God ever waddled a gut in—as if they were cretins. The correct answer, as perhaps Professor Hook once knew and later forgot, is to organize with the working class to seize the means of production and smash the capitalist state. But that is another story.

23. Donna Kerr, *Educational Policy* (New York: David McKay Co., 1976).

24. Sidney Hook, "Does Philosophy Have a Future?" in *What Is Philosophy of Education?* ed. Lucas, p. 55.

Name Index

Abraham, Ralph, 282
Abrams, Morris H., 129
Adler, Mortimer J., 19, 36
Andris, James F., 75
Antz, Louis, 21
Aquinas, Saint Thomas, 203
Archambault, Reginald D., 29, 38
Aristotle, 203, 206, 212, 265, 266, 267, 268, 269, 270, 271, 273, 274, 275, 285
Armstrong, David M., 281
Arnstine, Donald, 114
Axtelle, George 21, 142

Bakke, Allen, 35
Bantock, G. H., 66
Barrow, Robin, 40, 48
Bayles, Ernest, 19, 60
Beck, Clive M., 10, 184, 185, 195
Bell, Clive, 129
Bell, Griffin, 222
Benn, Stanley I., 245
Benne, Kenneth, 21, 142
Bentham, Jeremy, 205, 206, 207, 231
Berger, Peter L., 99
Bernstein, Basil, 46
Bertocci, Peter A., 184
Bierman, Arthur K., 30
Blanshard, Brand, 13, 21, 22, 33, 35
Bode, Boyd, 212, 262
Bohr, Niels, 244
Bowles, Samuel, 220
Brameld, Theodore, 21, 263
Breed, Frederick S., 19, 262
Brent, Allen, 40, 47, 55
Brodbeck, May, 236, 268
Bronfenbrenner, Urie, 191
Broudy, Harry S., 3, 9, 12, 13, 24, 31, 36, 38, 60, 114, 116, 262, 287
Brown, Harold I., 239
Brubacher, John S., 12, 18, 19, 20, 21
Bruner, Jerome S., 36, 38, 63
Bullough, Edward, 132
Burke, Kenneth, 20
Burnett, Joe R., 36, 38
Butler, James D., 184

Cagan, Elizabeth, 56

Cahn, Edmond, 222
Campbell, Keith, 285
Cézanne, Paul, 130
Childs, John, 184
Chomsky, Noam, 82
Clark, Kenneth, 221, 223, 224, 225
Clark, Stephen R. L., 56
Cohen, Robert S., 20
Cole, Michael, 247
Coleman, James, 223, 224, 225
Comenius, Johann A., 15
Conant, James, 157
Conrad, Joseph, 130
Costello, Thomas, 283
Counts, George, 212
Creighton, J. E., 22
Cronbach, Lee J., 83, 161, 162, 238, 249
Cunningham, William F., 262

Dahl, Robert, 52
Danto, Arthur C., 73, 76, 78
Darwin, Charles 108, 259
Daveney, T. F., 85
Dearden, R. F., 38
de Castell, Suzanne, 66
Descartes, Rene, 261, 268, 269, 270, 271, 272, 273, 274, 275, 285
Dewey, John, 4, 12, 19, 23, 51, 60, 106, 114, 124, 136, 142, 184, 187, 188, 189, 191, 206, 207, 208, 212, 236, 238, 260, 262, 272, 273, 274
Diller, Ann, 37, 56
Doyle, William G., 226, 227
Durant, Will, 261
Dworkin, Ronald, 232

Eccles, John C., 286
Ecker, David W., 114
Einstein, Albert, 108, 244, 259
Elkind, David, 110
Elliott, R. K., 127
Ennis, Robert H., 9, 19, 29, 31, 44, 86, 142, 143, 146, 287
Epps, Edgar G., 235
Eysenck, H. G., 257

NAME INDEX

Feibleman, James K., 21
Feigle, Herbert, 20, 23
Fenstermacher, Gary, 237
Feyerabend, Paul K., 254, 255, 256, 257, 258, 261
Fisch, Max, 266
Frankena, William, 47
Freeman, Helen, 66
Frege, Gottlob, 275
Freire, Paulo, 30
Freud, Sigmund, 248
Friedenberg, Edgar Z., 30
Froebel, Friedrich, 15
Furth, Hans G., 109

Gage, N. L., 63, 64, 66, 80, 90, 91, 237
Gagné, R. M., 82
Gardner, Howard, 139, 140
Geiger, George R., 20
Gellner, Ernest, 245, 248
Ginsberg, Morris, 208, 209
Gintis, Herbert, 220
Glock, Nancy, 37, 56
Gödel, Kurt, 275
Gombrich, Ernst, 136, 137
Goodman, Nelson, 122, 124, 125
Goodman, Paul, 30
Gould, James A., 30
Gowin, D. Bob, 256
Green, Thomas F., 72, 279
Greene, Maxine, 9, 114, 115
Greene, Theodore M., 20
Greif, Esther B., 259
Gribble, James, 40

Hare, Richard, 189
Harmin, Merrill, 194
Harper, Ralph, 20
Harré, Romano, 238, 256
Hegel, G. W. F., 284
Heidegger, Martin, 23
Henkel, Ramon E., 256
Henle, Robert J., 19, 262
Herbart, Johann F., 15, 96
Hirst, Paul H., 9, 25, 38, 39, 40, 41, 42, 43, 44, 45, 46, 47, 48, 49, 50, 51, 52, 53, 54, 55, 64, 65, 94, 104, 105, 106, 119, 250, 251, 252
Hobbes, Thomas, 204, 205, 206
Holt, John, 30
Hook, Sidney, 263, 264, 265, 273, 275, 288
Horne, Herman H., 19, 262
Hough, Graham, 121

Howison, G. H., 22
Hullfish, H. Gordon, 19, 60, 142
Hume, David, 275
Husserl, Edmund, 23
Hutchins, Robert M., 36

Illich, Ivan, 30
Inhelder, Bärbel, 82
Isenberg, Arnold, 122

Jackson, Philip W., 256
James, William, 22, 23, 32, 134, 237, 261
Jarvie, I. C., 242, 243, 244, 245, 249
Jeffrey, Ronald P., 31
Jencks, Christopher, 220
Jensen, Arthur J., 257

Katz, Michael B., 119
Kerlinger, Fred N., 256
Kerr, Donna H., 9, 60, 61, 75, 288
Kierkegaard, Søren, 23
Kieslar, Sara B., 256
Kilpatrick, William H., 19, 60, 96, 212
Kneller, George, 60, 262
Kohlberg, Lawrence, 10, 184, 188, 189, 191, 193, 195, 199, 246, 247, 248, 258, 259, 260
Komisar, B. Paul, 19
Kozol, Jonathan, 30
Krimerman, Leonard I., 31, 287
Kuhn, Thomas S., 10, 38, 41, 82, 108, 111, 236, 238, 239, 240, 241, 242, 244, 253, 257, 261
Kurtines, William, 259

Lakatos, Imre, 76, 108, 253, 254, 256, 257, 258, 260, 261
Langer, Susanne K., 129
Langford, Glenn, 54
Lewis, W. W., 72
Lickona, Thomas, 195
Lindsay, A. D., 51
Locke, John, 82, 96, 261
Luckmann, Thomas, 99
Lumsdaine, Arthur A., 82

Mackenzie, Brian D., 238, 242
Macpherson, C. B., 51, 52
Marcuse, Herbert, 130, 140, 141
Margolis, Joseph, 127
Maritain, Jacques, 20, 36, 262
Martin, Jane Roland, 9, 36, 37, 66, 85, 105, 251

NAME INDEX

Martin, Michael, 37
Martin, W. Oliver, 26
Marx, Karl, 4, 284
Masterman, Margaret, 240
Matthews, Michael, 41
McClellan, James E., 10, 19, 80, 262, 263, 264, 283
McGucken, William J., 19
Meehl, Paul, 249
Merleau-Ponty, Maurice, 130, 131, 133
Mill, John Stuart, 22, 51, 205
Millman, Jason, 256
Morris, Van Cleve, 60, 262
Morrison, Denton, E., 256
Mortimore, G. W., 245
Murphy, Arthur E., 22, 23
Musgrave, Peter W., 40, 251

Nelson, Beatrice, 37
Nelson, Thomas W., 28
Newell, John M., 72
Newmann, Fred, 192
Newton, Sir Isaac, 244, 259, 266
Nicolayev, Jennie, 237, 258
Noddings, Nel, 89, 237
Nozick, Robert, 86

O'Conner, D. J., 64
Oliver, Donald, 192

Peters, Richard S., 25, 38, 50, 54, 84, 104, 184, 188, 189, 191, 250, 251, 252
Pettigrew, Thomas, 226
Phenix, Philip H., 25, 36, 38, 94, 104, 117, 184, 250, 251
Phillips, Denis C., 10, 40, 81, 108, 236, 237, 250, 251, 258
Piaget, Jean, 27, 82, 83, 94, 109, 110, 111, 170, 191, 263
Plato, 15, 75, 77, 96, 184, 203, 212, 260, 267
Polanyi, Michael, 101, 106, 107, 113, 134
Popper, Karl R., 243, 249, 257, 261, 286
Price, Kingsley, 12
Putnam, Hilary, 284, 287

Quine, Willard V. O., 245, 275, 276, 279, 284, 285

Rader, Melvin, 139
Raths, Louis E., 194
Raup, R. Bruce, 21, 142

Rawls, John, 27, 189, 212, 219, 229, 230, 232, 233
Reid, Louis Arnaud, 120
Reisner, Edward H., 18
Rousseau, Jean Jacques, 15
Royce, Josiah, 22
Rozycki, Edward G., 287
Rugg, Harold, 114
Russell, Bertrand, 241, 275, 277
Ryle, Gilbert, 25, 42, 68, 101, 102, 119

Sartre, Jean-Paul, 127
Schapiro, Meyer, 131
Scheffler, Israel, 25, 29, 44, 55, 60, 86, 94, 118, 188, 244
Schumpeter, Joseph, 52
Schutz, Alfred, 125, 126
Schwab, Joseph J., 36, 236, 250, 251
Scriven, Michael, 236
Secord, Paul F., 238, 256
Sellars, Wilfred, 279
Shahab, Syed, 252
Simon, Sidney B., 194
Skinner, B. F., 70, 71, 102, 191, 248
Smith, B. Othanel, 25, 29, 36, 38, 60, 142, 287
Smith, Christiana M., 31
Smith, Philip G., 142
Smith, Ralph, 114
Smythe, Ormond, 42
Snow, Richard E., 63, 83
Socrates, 77
Soltis, Jonas F., 1, 9, 47, 75, 95, 106, 279
Steiner, George, 137
Stevens, Wallace, 138
Strike, Kenneth A., 10, 82, 86, 212, 213, 217, 222, 227
Suppe, Frederick, 239

Thomas, Lawrence G., 14, 256
Toulmin, Stephen, 95, 108, 244, 245, 249
Tufts, James, 208
Tyack, David B., 119

Ulich, Robert, 21, 114
Urbach, Peter, 258

Walsh, Dorothy, 138
Warren, Earl, 215, 216, 219, 221
Wasserman, Elsa, 195
Watt, A. J., 40
Weimer, Walter B., 261

NAME INDEX

Weisbrod, Burton, 219
Weitz, Morris, 129, 130
Wenley, Robert M., 22
Westermarck, Edward, 209
White, John P., 40, 55, 250, 251, 252
Whitehead, Alfred N., 32, 36, 114
Wild, John, 20
Wilson, Bryan R., 245
Wilson, John, 184, 190, 191

Winch, Peter, 189, 241, 242, 243, 244, 245, 249
Withall, John, 72
Wittgenstein, Ludwig, 23, 166, 241, 242, 244, 249
Wittrock, M. C., 82
Woolf, Virginia, 137, 141
Worrall, John, 254

Zelditch, Morris, Jr., 245

Subject Index

Action, analysis of, 73-74, 76
Aesthetic education: aesthetic literacy as goal of, 119-20; art education and art appreciation contrasted with, 120-21; lack of attention to, in schools, 116-19; needed emphases in, 132; requirements for teachers of, 133; satisfaction as primary aim of activity in, 125
Aesthetic experience, as a form of understanding, 124
Aesthetic literacy: conditions required for achievement of, 123; qualitative perceiving as fundamental to, 133-34; role of imaginative awareness in, 137-39; role of perception in, 134-37
American Educational Research Association, 287
American Philosophical Association, 21
Art appreciation, forms of, in schools, 120-21
Artistic-aesthetic domain: as a province of meaning, 125-27; "doing of" philosophy in, 123-28; modes of attending in, 127-28, 130; need for overlapping perspectives in, 130; role of percipient in, 127
Arts: increased public interest in, 115-16; lack of attention to, in schools, 116-18; problem of defining, 128-30; various theories of, 128-30
Attending, modes of: in artistic-aesthetic domain, 127-28, 130; role of subsidiary awareness in, 134-35

Bakke decision, 34-35
Basic human values, in relation to values education, 196-98
Brewer v. Norfolk, 226
Brown v. Board of Education of Topeka, 154, 155-59, 160, 213, 214, 215-16, 217, 219, 220-22, 226, 227-28, 232, 234; concern of, for consequences of segregation, 216; effects of decision in, 213; failure of, to answer philosophical questions clearly, 214; interpretation of, based on principle of equal humanity of all persons, 227-28; use of social science data in, 221-22
Brunson v. Board of Trustees, 226

Cartesian dualism, need for removing traces of, in philosophy, 102, 271-73
Commission on the Function of Philosophy in Liberal Education (Blanshard Commission), report of, 21-24, 33
Civil Rights Act (1964), 222
Coleman Report (1966), 223
Conceptual frameworks, changes in: implications of, for educators, 111; views of, as radical or evolutionary, 108-111. See also, Paradigms
Control groups, use of, in research design, 164-65
Credibility (of statements), criteria for judging, 146-47
Criticism, nature and purpose of, in the arts, 121-23
Cross-cultural (external) criticism, requirements for, according to Winch, 241-43
Cross-cultural study, issues in, 245-48
Curriculum: changes in, 30; content and objectives of, not determined by structure of knowledge, 51; implications for, under Hirst's conception of liberal education, 47-48, 250-53; need for a more general paradigm for, 57-59; neglect of, by contemporary philosophers of education, 37-38; persistent character of, 37
Curriculum organization, in relation to forms of knowledge theory, 39-40

Definition, kinds of, 177

293

Decision making, relevant reasons for, 217-18
Desegregation (of schools): different views of, 214; two moral views of, 228-29. See also, Segregation
Detroit, desegregation plans in, 225
Dilemmas, discussion of, in values education, 193-94
Distributive justice: concepts of, related to principle of equal humanity of persons, 229-32; desegregation as a problem in, 228-29; self-respect in relation to, 233-34

Education: as initiation into forms of knowledge, 104; new problems of, since mid-1960s, 29-30; obligation of, under sociocentric perspective of knowledge, 103, 107-8, 113; tendency of, to ignore broader dimensions of knowledge, 112
Educational research, criticisms of, 255-57
Environment versus heredity, rival programs of research on, 257-58
Epistemological fallacy, in forms of knowledge theory, 47, 49, 50, 58
Equality, notions of, 227
Equal humanity of persons, principle of, 227, 229, 231, 232, 235
Equivocation fallacy, examples of, 151
Ethics: dependence of reflective values education upon, 210; reflective approach to, 186; various philosophical views of, in relation to reflective ethics, 203-9

First philosophy: applications of, 286-88; contemporary example of, 275-86; definition of, as union of epistemology and metaphysics, 263; essential role of natural science in the practice of, 273-75; examples of, from Aristotle and from Descartes, 265-71
Forms of knowledge theory: conception of liberal education in, 39, 40, 41-45, 48-50, 51, 53; conception of mind in, 44, 49, 51, 53; criticisms of, 40-41, 42, 45-46, 105-6; "developmental" and "equilibrium" democracy in relation to, 52; emotion and action ignored by, 41-42, 46; epistemological fallacy in, 47, 49, 50, 58; forms of knowledge in, 39, 105; nature of liberally educated persons under, 44-45, 49, 53; relevance of, to curriculum issues, 250-53; value judgments in, 48, 51. See also, Liberal education
Fourteenth Amendment, equal protection clause of, 216

Good judgment, importance of, in rational thinking, 147, 149, 150, 166, 167, 183

Imagination, phases of, 139
Impact equivocation, example of, 152
Indoctrination, in relation to moral education, 189-90
"Isms," importance of study of, 32

Knowledge: broadened concept of, under sociocentric perspective, 103-4; forms of, according to Hirst, 39, 105; implications of new views of science for the nature of, 260-61; knowledge-in-use as part of the concept of, 110-11; sociocentric versus egocentric perspective on, 97-99; various conceptions of, in relation to teaching and education, 95-96
Kuder-Richardson formulas, 163

Language, role of, in dealing with human knowledge, 99-102
Liberal education: Hirst's concept of, 39, 40, 41-45, 48-50, 51, 53, 105-6; proposed alternative to Hirst's paradigm for, 53-59. See also, Forms of knowledge theory
Life success: connection of segregation with (figure), 221; function of schools in contributing to (figure), 220

Milliken v. Bradley, 224-25
Mind, concept of, in Hirst's theory of liberal education, 44, 49-50, 105
Moral behavior, components of, 191
Moral development, criticism of stage theory of, 246-48, 258-60
Moral education: affective components in, 190-92; definition of, as critical and open-ended inquiry, 187-89; indoctrination in relation to, 189-90

Moral views of desegregation: 228-29

National Institute of Education, 29
National Society for the Study of Education: former name of, 273; yearbooks of, on philosophy of education, 14, 18-21

Paradigms: common elements in, 244-45; evolutionary view of changes in, 108-9; relevance of issue of incommensurability of, to educational research, 245-52; role of, in scientific inquiry, 240-43
Philosophers of education: difficulties of, in communicating with educators, 17-18; increased training of, in discipline of philosophy, 5-6; new problems addressed by, 30-31; recent emphases of, on "doing of" philosophy, 4-5. See also, Philosophy of education
Philosophy: "doing of," in the artistic-aesthetic domain, 123-28; increasing specialization in, 10; organization of, by subareas of philosophical inquiry, 7
Philosophy of education: changes in, since 1965, 15-18, 25-26; courses in, in professional programs, 16, 25-26, 32-33; criticisms of, 22-25; dual audiences of, 15-16; educators' rights of expectation from, 33-35; failure of, to meet philosophical expectations of educators, 2-3; movement of, away from "isms" approach, 25-26, 28; new emphases in, 27-28; traditional defining questions of, 264; shifts in the field of, 3-7
Philosophy of Education Society, 17, 19, 21
Plans for teaching: available means and resources in relation to, 84; immediate action context in relation to, 86-87; moral and political context in relation to, 84-86; recognition of need for changes in, 87-88; teachers' understanding of subject matter in relation to, 81; teachers' view of learning and particular learners in relation to, 81-84
Plessy v. Ferguson, 157, 215, 222, 228

Problem-centered approach, in values education, 198-200
Propaganda, problems in definition of, 149-50, 152-53
Provinces of meaning, use of, in interpretation of reality, 126
Psychic distance, concept of, in aesthetic literacy, 132

Quality in teaching: considerations relevant in the judging of, 79-80; tests of subjective and objective adequacy of, 77-78; theoretical description of structure of, 76-89. See also, Plans for teaching

Race, as irrelevant reason for distribution of social rewards, 218
Racial balance, in schools, as goal of desegregation, 224
Rand Corporation, 249
Rational thinker, components of (figure), 145
Rational thinking: aspects of, employed in analysis of an editorial on segregation, 160-61; detailed outline of proficiencies required for, 166-82
Reasoning skills, in values education, 192-93
Reflective approach, to values education: nature and definition of, 198, 200; problem-centered character of, 198-200; philosophical roots of, 202-9; role of basic human values in, 196-98; ways of implementing, in schools, 200-2
Reflective ethics, 186
Relativism, emergence of, 243
Relevant reasons, theory of, 217-18
Reliability, definitions of, 161-62
Reliability of tests, 162-63

School organization and atmosphere, in relation to values education, 195
Schools, function of, in contributing to life success, 219-20
Science, new views of the nature of, 238-39
Scientific revolution, as the development of new paradigms, 240
Scientific research: assessment of programs of, as either progressive or degenerative, 253-55; need for rival programs in, 257-60

Segregation: analysis of an editorial on, 154-61; as state-sponsored attack on the full humanity of blacks, 228; contrasting views of, related to remedies for, 223-24; intentional and statistical senses of, 156-57; presumed connection of, with life success, 221. *See also*, Desegregation

Self-respect, role of, in distributive justice, 202-4

Social goods, principle for distribution of, on relevant grounds, 216-17

Social changes (after mid-1960s), impact of, on schools, 29-31

Social science evidence: challenge to relevance of, in judicial deliberations, 222, 226; cited in *Brown v. Board of Education of Topeka*, 221-22

Sociometric perspective on knowledge, implications of, 97-99

Stage theory of moral development: cross-cultural work on, 246-48; hard-core assumptions of, 258-59

Subject matter, importance of understanding nature of, in choosing learnings, 81

Teachers, role of, in aesthetic education, 133, 136-37, 141

Teaching: factors involved in evaluation of, 89-90; factors related to excellence in, 89; importance of understanding nature of, 62; needed components in program of professional preparation for, 92; range of research relevant to, 90-91; theoretical description of, 72-75; three component actions of, 74-75

Teaching actions, considerations relevant in judging quality of, 79-80

Teaching events, description of: desirability of using nonmetaphorical and action language in, 69-72; ordered components used in, 75; problems related to, 68-70

Theory of teaching: reasons for inadequate development of, 62-67; relationship of, to theory of practice, 65-66

United States Commission on Civil Rights, 249-50

United States Department of Health, Education, and Welfare, 29

United States Supreme Court: 213, 215-16, 220-22, 224-25, 227

Utilitarianism, 229

Values clarification, as an approach to values education, 194

Values education: approaches to, in schools, 19-95; cognitive and affective aspects of, 185-86

INFORMATION ABOUT MEMBERSHIP IN THE SOCIETY

From its small beginnings in the early 1900s, the National Society for the Study of Education has grown to a major educational organization with more than 4,000 members in the United States, Canada, and overseas. Members include professors, researchers, graduate students, and administrators in colleges and universities; teachers, supervisors, curriculum specialists, and administrators in elementary and secondary schools; and a considerable number of persons who are not formally connected with an educational institution. Membership in the Society is open to all persons who desire to receive its publications.

Since its establishment the Society has sought to promote its central purpose—the stimulation of investigations and discussions of important educational issues—through regular publication of a two-volume yearbook that is sent to all members. Many of these volumes have been so well received throughout the profession that they have gone into several printings. A recently inaugurated series of substantial paperbacks on Contemporary Educational Issues supplements the series of yearbooks and allows for treatment of a wider range of educational topics than can be addressed each year through the yearbooks alone.

Through membership in the Society one can add regularly to one's professional library at a very reasonable cost. Members also help to sustain a publication program that is widely recognized for its unique contributions to the literature of education.

The categories of membership, and the dues in each category for 1980, are as follows:

Regular. The member receives a clothbound copy of each part of the two-volume yearbook (approximately 300 pages per volume). Annual dues, $15.

Comprehensive. The member receives clothbound copies of the two-volume yearbook and the two volumes in the current paperback series. Annual dues, $28.

Retirees and Graduate Students. Reduced dues—Regular, $12; Comprehensive $24.
The above reduced dues are available to (a) those who have retired or are over sixty-five years of age and who have been members of the Society for at least ten years, and (b) graduate students in their first year of membership.

Life Membership. Persons sixty years of age or over may hold a Regular Membership for life upon payment of a lump sum based upon the life expectancy for their age group. Consult the Secretary-Treasurer for further details.

New members are required to pay an entrance fee of $1, in addition to the dues, in their first year of membership.

Membership is for the calendar year and dues are payable on or before January 1. A reinstatement fee of $.50 must be added to dues payments made after January 1.

In addition to receiving the publications of the Society as described above, members participate in the nomination and election of the six-member Board of Directors, which is responsible for managing the business and affairs of the Society, including the authorization of volumes to appear in the yearbook series. Two members of the Board are elected each year for three-year terms. Members of the Society who have contributed to its publications and who indicate a willingness to serve are eligible for election to the Board.

Members are urged to attend the one or more meetings of the Society that are arranged each year in conjunction with the annual meetings of major educational organizations. The purpose of such meetings is to present, discuss, and critique volumes in the current yearbook series. Announcements of meetings for the ensuing year are sent to members in December.

Upon written request from a member, the Secretary-Treasurer will send the current directory of members, synopses of meetings of the Board of Directors, and the annual financial report.

Persons desiring further information about membership may write to

> KENNETH J. REHAGE, Secretary-Treasurer
> National Society for the Study of Education

5835 Kimbark Ave.
Chicago, Ill. 60637

PUBLICATIONS OF THE NATIONAL SOCIETY FOR THE STUDY OF EDUCATION

1. The Yearbooks

NOTICE: Many of the early yearbooks of this series are now out of print. In the following list, those titles to which an asterisk is prefixed are not available for purchase.

*First Yearbook, 1902, Part I—*Some Principles in the Teaching of History.* Lucy M. Salmon.
*First Yearbook, 1902, Part II—*The Progress of Geography in the Schools.* W. M. Davis and H. M. Wilson.
*Second Yearbook, 1903, Part I—*The Course of Study in History in the Common School.* Isabel Lawrence, C. A. McMurray, Frank McMurry, E. C. Page, and E. J. Rice.
*Second Yearbook, 1903, Part II—*The Relation of Theory to Practice in Education.* M. J. Holmes, J. A. Keith, and Levi Seeley.
*Third Yearbook, 1904, Part I—*The Relation of Theory to Practice in the Education of Teachers.* John Dewey, Sarah C. Brooks, F. M. McMurry, et al.
*Third Yearbook, 1904, Part II—*Nature Study.* W. S. Jackman.
*Fourth Yearbook, 1905, Part I—*The Education and Training of Secondary Teachers.* E. C. Elliott, E. G. Dexter, M. J. Holmes, et al.
*Fourth Yearbook, 1905, Part II—*The Place of Vocational Subjects in the High-School Curriculum.* J. S. Brown, G. B. Morrison, and Ellen Richards.
*Fifth Yearbook, 1906, Part I—*On the Teaching of English in Elementary and High Schools.* G. P. Brown and Emerson Davis.
*Fifth Yearbook, 1906, Part II—*The Certification of Teachers.* E. P. Cubberley.
*Sixth Yearbook, 1907, Part I—*Vocational Studies for College Entrance.* C. A. Herrick, H. W. Holmes, T. deLaguna, V. Prettyman, and W. J. S. Bryan.
*Sixth Yearbook, 1907, Part II—*The Kindergarten and Its Relation to Elementary Education.* Ada Van Stone Harris, E. A. Kirkpatrick, Marie Kraus-Boelté, Patty S. Hill, Harriette M. Mills, and Nina Vandewalker.
*Seventh Yearbook, 1908, Part I—*The Relation of Superintendents and Principals to the Training and Professional Improvement of Their Teachers.* Charles D. Lowry.
*Seventh Yearbook, 1908, Part II—*The Co-ordination of the Kindergarten and the Elementary School.* B. J. Gregory, Jennie B. Merrill, Bertha Payne, and Margaret Giddings.
*Eighth Yearbook, 1909, Part I—*Education with Reference to Sex: Pathological, Economic, and Social Aspects.* C. R. Henderson.
*Eighth Yearbook, 1909, Part II—*Education with Reference to Sex: Agencies and Methods.* C. R. Henderson and Helen C. Putnam.
*Ninth Yearbook, 1910, Part I—*Health and Education.* T. D. Wood.
*Ninth Yearbook, 1910, Part II—*The Nurses in Education.* T. D. Wood, et al.
*Tenth Yearbook, 1911, Part I—*The City School as a Community Center.* H. C. Leipziger, Sarah E. Hyre, R. D. Warden, C. Ward Crampton, E. W. Stitt, E. J. Ward, Mrs. T. C. Grice, and C. A. Perry.
*Tenth Yearbook, 1911, Part II—*The Rural School as a Community Center.* B. H. Crocheron, Jessie Field, F. W. Howe, E. C. Bishop, A. B. Graham, O. J. Kern, M. T. Scudder, and B. M. Davis.
*Eleventh Yearbook, 1912, Part I—*Industrial Education: Typical Experiments Described and Interpreted.* J. F. Barker, M. Bloomfield, B. W. Johnson, P. Johnson, L. M. Leavitt, G. A. Mirick, M. W. Murray, C. F. Perry, A. L. Stafford, and H. B. Wilson.
*Eleventh Yearbook, 1912, Part II—*Agricultural Education in Secondary Schools.* A. C. Monahan, R. W. Stimson, D. J. Crosby, W. H. French, H. F. Button, F. R. Crane, W. R. Hart, and G. F. Warren.
*Twelfth Yearbook, 1913, Part I—*The Supervision of City Schools.* Franklin Bobbitt, J. W. Hall, and J. D. Wolcott.
*Twelfth Yearbook, 1913, Part II—*The Supervision of Rural Schools.* A. C. Monahan, L. J. Hanifan, J. E. Warren, Wallace Lund, U. J. Hoffman, A. S. Cook, E. M. Rapp, Jackson Davis, J. D. Wolcott.
*Thirteenth Yearbook, 1914, Part I—*Some Aspects of High-School Instruction and Administration.* H. C. Morrison, E. R. Breslich, W. A. Jessup, and L. D. Coffman.
*Thirteenth Yearbook, 1914, Part II—*Plans for Organizing School Surveys, with a Summary of Typical School Surveys.* Charles H. Judd and Henry L. Smith.
*Fourteenth Yearbook, 1915, Part I—*Minimum Essentials in Elementary School Subjects—Standards and Current Practices.* H. B. Wilson, H. W. Holmes, F. E. Thompson, R. G. Jones, S. A. Courtis, W. S. Gray, F. N. Freeman, H. C. Pryor, J. F. Hosic, W. A. Jessup, and W. C. Bagley.
*Fourteenth Yearbook, 1915, Part II—*Methods for Measuring Teachers' Efficiency.* Arthur C. Boyce.
*Fifteenth Yearbook, 1916, Part I—*Standards and Tests for the Measurement of the Efficiency of Schools and School Systems.* G. D. Strayer, Bird T. Baldwin, B. R. Buckingham, F. W. Ballou, D. C. Bliss, H. G. Childs, S. A. Courtis, E. P. Cubberley, C. H. Judd, George Melcher, E. E. Oberholtzer, J. B. Sears, Daniel Starch, M. R. Trabue, and G. M. Whipple.

*Fifteenth Yearbook, 1916, Part II—*The Relationship between Persistence in School and Home Conditions.* Charles E. Holley.
*Fifteenth Yearbook, 1916, Part III—*The Junior High School.* Aubrey A. Douglass.
*Sixteenth Yearbook, 1917, Part I—*Second Report of the Committee on Minimum Essentials in Elementary-School Subjects.* W. C. Bagley, W. W. Charters, F. N. Freeman, W. S. Gray, Ernest Horn, J. H. Hoskinson, W. S. Monroe, C. F. Munson, H. C. Pryor, L. W. Rapeer, G. M. Wilson, and H. B. Wilson.
*Sixteenth Yearbook, 1917, Part II—*The Efficiency of College Students as Conditioned by Age at Entrance and Size of High School.* B. F. Pittenger.
*Seventeenth Yearbook, 1918, Part I—*Third Report of the Committee on Economy of Time in Education.* W. C. Bagley, B. B. Bassett, M. E. Branom, Alice Camerer, J. E. Dealey, C. A. Ellwood, E. B. Greene, A. B. Hart, J. F. Hosic, E. T. Housh, W. H. Mace, L. R. Marston, H. C. McKown, H. E. Mitchell, W. V. Reavis, D. Snedden, and H. B. Wilson.
*Seventeenth Yearbook, 1918, Part II—*The Measurement of Educational Products.* E. J. Ashbaugh, W. A. Averill, L. P. Ayers, F. W. Ballou, Edna Bryner, B. R. Buckingham, S. A. Courtis, M. E. Haggerty, C. H. Judd, George Melcher, W. S. Monroe, E. A. Nifenecker, and E. L. Thorndike.
*Eighteenth Yearbook, 1919, Part I—*The Professional Preparation of High-School Teachers.* G. N. Cade, S. S. Colvin, Charles Fordyce, H. H. Foster, T. S. Gosling, W. S. Gray, L. V. Koos, A. R. Mead, H. L. Miller, F. C. Whitcomb, and Clifford Woody.
*Eighteenth Yearbook, 1919, Part II—*Fourth Report of Committee on Economy of Time in Education.* F. C. Ayer, F. N. Freeman, W. S. Gray, Ernest Horn, W. S. Monroe, and C. E. Seashore.
*Nineteenth Yearbook, 1920, Part I—*New Materials of Instruction.* Prepared by the Society's Committee on Materials of Instruction.
*Nineteenth Yearbook, 1920, Part II—*Classroom Problems in the Education of Gifted Children.* T. S. Henry.
*Twentieth Yearbook, 1921, Part I—*New Materials of Instruction.* Second Report by Society's Committee.
*Twentieth Yearbook, 1921, Part II—*Report of the Society's Committee on Silent Reading.* M. A. Burgess, S. A. Courtis, C. E. Germane, W. S. Gray, H. A. Greene, Regina R. Heller, J. H. Hoover, J. A. O'Brien, J. L. Packer, Daniel Starch, W. W. Theisen, G. A. Yoakam, and representatives of other school systems.
*Twenty-first Yearbook, 1922, Parts I and II—*Intelligence Tests and Their Use,* Part I—*The Nature, History, and General Principles of Intelligence Testing.* E. L. Thorndike, S. S. Colvin, Harold Rugg, G. M. Whipple, Part II—*The Administrative Use of Intelligence Tests.* H. W. Holmes, W. K. Layton, Helen Davis, Agnes L. Rogers, Rudolf Pintner, M. R. Trabue, W. S. Miller, Bessie L. Gambrill, and others. The two parts are bound together.
*Twenty-second Yearbook, 1923, Part I—*English Composition: Its Aims, Methods and Measurements.* Earl Hudelson.
*Twenty-second Yearbook, 1923, Part II—*The Social Studies in the Elementary and Secondary School.* A. S. Barr, J. J. Coss, Henry Harap, R. W. Hatch, H. C. Hill, Ernest Horn, C. H. Judd, L. C. Marshall, F. M. McMurry, Earle Rugg, H. O. Rugg, Emma Schweppe, Mabel Snedaker, and C. W. Washburne.
*Twenty-third Yearbook, 1924, Part I—*The Education of Gifted Children.* Report of the Society's Committee. Guy M. Whipple, Chairman.
*Twenty-third Yearbook, 1924, Part II—*Vocational Guidance and Vocational Education for Industries.* A. H. Edgerton and others.
*Twenty-fourth Yearbook, 1925, Part I—*Report of the National Committee on Reading.* W. S. Gray, Chairman, F. W. Ballou, Rose L. Hardy, Ernest Horn, Francis Jenkins, S. A. Leonard, Estaline Wilson, and Laura Zirbes.
*Twenty-fourth Yearbook, 1925, Part II—*Adapting the Schools to Individual Differences.* Report of the Society's Committee. Carleton W. Washburne, Chairman.
*Twenty-fifth Yearbook, 1926, Part I—*The Present Status of Safety Education.* Report of the Society's Committee. Guy M. Whipple, Chairman.
*Twenty-fifth Yearbook, 1926, Part II—*Extra-Curricular Activities.* Report of the Society's Committee. Leonard V. Koos, Chairman.
*Twenty-sixth Yearbook, 1927, Part I—*Curriculum-making: Past and Present.* Report of the Society's Committee. Harold O. Rugg, Chairman.
*Twenty-sixth Yearbook, 1927, Part II—*The Foundations of Curriculum-making.* Prepared by individual members of the Society's Committee. Harold O. Rugg, Chairman.
*Twenty-seventh Yearbook, 1928, Part I—*Nature and Nurture: Their Influence upon Intelligence.* Prepared by the Society's Committee. Lewis M. Terman, Chairman.
*Twenty-seventh Yearbook, 1928, Part II—*Nature and Nurture: Their Influence upon Achievement.* Prepared by the Society's Committee. Lewis M. Terman, Chairman.
Twenty-eighth Yearbook, 1929, Parts I and II—*Preschool and Parental Education,* Part I—*Organization and Development.* Part II—*Research and Method.* Prepared by the Society's Committee. Lois H. Meek, Chairman. Bound in one volume. Cloth.
*Twenty-ninth Yearbook, 1930, Parts I and II—*Report of the Society's Committee on Arithmetic.* Part I—*Some Aspects of Modern Thought on Arithmetic.* Part II—*Research in Arithmetic.* Prepared by the Society's Committee. F. B. Knight, Chairman. Bound in one volume.
*Thirtieth Yearbook, 1931— Part I—*The Status of Rural Education.* First Report of the Society's Committee on Rural Education. Orville G. Brim, Chairman.
Thirtieth Yearbook, 1931, Part II—*The Textbook in American Education.* Report of the Society's Committee on the Textbook, J. B. Edmonson, Chairman. Cloth, Paper.

*Thirty-first Yearbook, 1932, Part I—*A Program for Teaching Science.* Prepared by the Society's Committee on the Teaching of Science. S. Ralph Powers, Chairman.
*Thirty-first Yearbook, 1932, Part II—*Changes and Experiments in Liberal-Arts Education.* Prepared by Kathryn McHale, with numerous collaborators.
*Thirty-second Yearbook, 1933—*The Teaching of Geography.* Prepared by the Society's Committee on the Teaching of Geography. A. E. Parkins, Chairman.
*Thirty-third Yearbook, 1934, Part I—*The Planning and Construction of School Buildings.* Prepared by the Society's Committee on School Buildings. N. L. Engelhardt, Chairman.
*Thirty-third Yearbook, 1934, Part II—*The Activity Movement.* Prepared by the Society's Committee on the Activity Movement. Lois Coffey Mossman, Chairman.
Thirty-fourth Yearbook, 1935—*Educational Diagnosis.* Prepared by the Society's Committee on Educational Diagnosis. L. J. Brueckner, Chairman. Paper.
*Thirty-fifth Yearbook, 1936, Part I—*The Grouping of Pupils.* Prepared by the Society's Committee. W. W. Coxe, Chairman.
*Thirty-fifth Yearbook, 1936, Part II—*Music Education.* Prepared by the Society's Committee. W. L. Uhl, Chairman.
*Thirty-sixth Yearbook, 1937, Part I—*The Teaching of Reading.* Prepared by the Society's Committee. W. S. Gray, Chairman.
*Thirty-sixth Yearbook, 1937, Part II—*International Understanding through the Public-School Curriculum.* Prepared by the Society's Committee. I. L. Kandel, Chairman.
*Thirty-seventh Yearbook, 1938, Part I—*Guidance in Educational Institutions.* Prepared by the Society's Committee. G. N. Kefauver, Chairman.
*Thirty-seventh Yearbook, 1938, Part II—*The Scientific Movement in Education.* Prepared by the Society's Committee. F. N. Freeman, Chairman.
*Thirty-eighth Yearbook, 1939, Part I—*Child Development and the Curriculum.* Prepared by the Society's Committee. Carleton Washburne, Chairman.
*Thirty-eighth Yearbook, 1939, Part II—*General Education in the American College.* Prepared by the Society's Committee. Alvin Eurich, Chairman. Cloth.
*Thirty-ninth Yearbook, 1940, Part I—*Intelligence: Its Nature and Nurture. Comparative and Critical Exposition.* Prepared by the Society's Committee. G. D. Stoddard, Chairman.
*Thirty-ninth Yearbook, 1940, Part II—*Intelligence: Its Nature and Nurture. Original Studies and Experiments.* Prepared by the Society's Committee. G. D. Stoddard, Chairman.
*Fortieth Yearbook, 1941—*Art in American Life and Education.* Prepared by the Society's Committee. Thomas Munro, Chairman.
Forty-first Yearbook, 1942, Part I—*Philosophies of Education.* Prepared by the Society's Committee. John S. Brubacher, Chairman. Paper.
Forty-first Yearbook, 1942, Part II—*The Psychology of Learning.* Prepared by the Society's Committee. T. R. McConnell, Chairman. Cloth.
*Forty-second Yearbook, 1943, Part I—*Vocational Education.* Prepared by the Society's Committee. F. J. Keller, Chairman.
*Forty-second Yearbook, 1943, Part II—*The Library in General Education.* Prepared by the Society's Committee. L. R. Wilson, Chairman.
Forty-third Yearbook, 1944, Part I—*Adolescence.* Prepared by the Society's Committee. Harold E. Jones, Chairman. Paper.
*Forty-third Yearbook, 1944, Part II—*Teaching Language in the Elementary School.* Prepared by the Society's Committee. M. R. Trabue, Chairman.
*Forty-fourth Yearbook, 1945, Part I—*American Education in the Postwar Period: Curriculum Reconstruction.* Prepared by the Society's Committee. Ralph W. Tyler, Chairman.
Forty-fourth Yearbook, 1945, Part II—*American Education in the Postwar Period: Structural Reorganization.* Prepared by the Society's Committee. Bess Goodykoontz, Chairman. Paper.
*Forty-fifth Yearbook, 1946, Part I—*The Measurement of Understanding.* Prepared by the Society's Committee. William A. Brownell, Chairman.
*Forty-fifth Yearbook, 1946, Part II—*Changing Conceptions in Educational Administration.* Prepared by the Society's Committee. Alonzo G. Grace, Chairman.
*Forty-sixth Yearbook, 1947, Part I—*Science Education in American Schools.* Prepared by the Society's Committee. Victor H. Noll, Chairman.
*Forty-sixth Yearbook, 1947, Part II—*Early Childhood Education.* Prepared by the Society's Committee. N. Searle Light, Chairman. Paper.
Forty-seventh Yearbook, 1948, Part I—*Juvenile Delinquency and the Schools.* Prepared by the Society's Committee. Ruth Strang, Chairman.
Forty-seventh Yearbook, 1948, Part II—*Reading in the High School and College.* Prepared by the Society's Committee. William S. Gray, Chairman. Cloth, Paper.
Forty-eighth Yearbook, 1949, Part I—*Audio-visual Materials of Instruction.* Prepared by the Society's Committee. Stephen M. Corey, Chairman. Cloth.
*Forty-eighth Yearbook, 1949, Part II—*Reading in the Elementary School.* Prepared by the Society's Committee. Arthur I. Gates, Chairman.
*Forty-ninth Yearbook, 1950, Part I—*Learning and Instruction.* Prepared by the Society's Committee. G. Lester Anderson, Chairman.
*Forty-ninth Yearbook, 1950, Part II—*The Education of Exceptional Children.* Prepared by the Society's Committee. Samuel A. Kirk, Chairman.
Fiftieth Yearbook, 1951, Part I—*Graduate Study in Education.* Prepared by the Society's Board of Directors. Ralph W. Tyler, Chairman. Paper.
Fiftieth Yearbook, 1951, Part II—*The Teaching of Arithmetic.* Prepared by the Society's Committee. G. T. Buswell, Chairman. Cloth, Paper.
Fifty-first Yearbook, 1952, Part I—*General Education.* Prepared by the Society's Committee. T. R. McConnell, Chairman. Cloth, Paper.

PUBLICATIONS

Fifty-first Yearbook, 1952, Part II—*Education in Rural Communities.* Prepared by the Society's Committee. Ruth Strang, Chairman. Cloth, Paper.

*Fifty-second Yearbook, 1953, Part I—*Adapting the Secondary-School Program to the Needs of Youth.* Prepared by the Society's Committee: William G. Brink, Chairman.

Fifty-second Yearbook, 1953, Part II—*The Community School.* Prepared by the Society's Committee. Maurice F. Seay, Chairman. Cloth.

*Fifty-third Yearbook, 1954, Part I—*Citizen Cooperation for Better Public Schools.* Prepared by the Society's Committee, Edgar L. Morphet, Chairman.

*Fifty-third Yearbook, 1954, Part II—*Mass Media and Education.* Prepared by the Society's Committee. Edgar Dale, Chairman.

*Fifty-fourth Yearbook, 1955, Part I—*Modern Philosophies and Education.* Prepared by the Society's Committee. John S. Brubacher, Chairman.

Fifty-fourth Yearbook, 1955, Part II—*Mental Health in Modern Education.* Prepared by the Society's Committee. Paul A. Witty, Chairman. Paper.

*Fifty-fifth Yearbook, 1956, Part I—*The Public Junior College.* Prepared by the Society's Committee. B. Lamar Johnson, Chairman.

*Fifty-fifth Yearbook, 1956, Part II—*Adult Reading.* Prepared by the Society's Committee. David H. Clift, Chairman.

Fifty-sixth Yearbook, 1957, Part I—*In-service Education of Teachers, Supervisors, and Administrators.* Prepared by the Society's Committee. Stephen M. Corey, Chairman. Cloth.

Fifty-sixth Yearbook, 1957, Part II—*Social Studies in the Elementary School.* Prepared by the Society's Committee. Ralph C. Preston, Chairman. Cloth, Paper.

Fifty-seventh Yearbook, 1958, Part I—*Basic Concepts in Music Education.* Prepared by the Society's Committee. Thurber H. Madison, Chairman. Cloth.

*Fifty-seventh Yearbook, 1958, Part II—*Education for the Gifted.* Prepared by the Society's Committee. Robert J. Havighurst, Chairman.

*Fifty-seventh Yearbook, 1958, Part III—*The Integration of Educational Experiences.* Prepared by the Society's Committee. Paul L. Dressel, Chairman. Cloth.

Fifty-eighth Yearbook, 1959, Part I—*Community Education: Principles and Practices from World-wide Experience.* Prepared by the Society's Committee. C. O. Arndt, Chairman. Cloth, Paper.

*Fifty-eighth Yearbook, 1959, Part II—*Personal Services in Education.* Prepared by the Society's Committee. Melvene D. Hardee, Chairman.

*Fifty-ninth Yearbook, 1960, Part I—*Rethinking Science Education.* Prepared by the Society's Committee. J. Darrell Barnard, Chairman.

*Fifty-ninth Yearbook, 1960, Part II—*The Dynamics of Instructional Groups.* Prepared by the Society's Committee. Gale E. Jensen, Chairman.

Sixtieth Yearbook, 1961, Part I—*Development in and through Reading.* Prepared by the Society's Committee. Paul A. Witty, Chairman. Cloth.

Sixtieth Yearbook, 1961, Part II—*Social Forces Influencing American Education.* Prepared by the Society's Committee. Ralph W. Tyler, Chairman. Cloth, Paper.

Sixty-first Yearbook, 1962, Part I—*Individualizing Instruction.* Prepared by the Society's Committee. Fred T. Tyler, Chairman. Cloth.

Sixty-first Yearbook, 1962, Part II—*Education for the Professions.* Prepared by the Society's Committee. G. Lester Anderson, Chairman. Cloth.

Sixty-second Yearbook, 1963, Part I—*Child Psychology.* Prepared by the Society's Committee. Harold W. Stevenson, Editor. Cloth.

Sixty-second Yearbook, 1963, Part II—*The Impact and Improvement of School Testing Programs.* Prepared by the Society's Committee. Warren G. Findley, Editor. Cloth.

Sixty-third Yearbook, 1964, Part I—*Theories of Learning and Instruction.* Prepared by the Society's Committee. Ernest R. Hilgard, Editor. Paper, Cloth.

Sixty-third Yearbook, 1964, Part II—*Behavioral Science and Educational Administration.* Prepared by the Society' Committee. Daniel E. Griffiths, Editor. Paper.

Sixty-fourth Yearbook, 1965, Part I—*Vocational Education.* Prepared by the Society's Committee. Melvin L. Barlow, Editor. Cloth.

*Sixty-fourth Yearbook, 1965, Part II—*Art Education.* Prepared by the Society's Committee. W. Reid Hastie, Editor.

Sixty-fifth Yearbook, 1966, Part I—*Social Deviancy among Youth.* Prepared by the Society's Committee. William W. Wattenberg, Editor. Cloth.

Sixty-fifth Yearbook, 1966, Part II—*The Changing American School.* Prepared by the Society's Committee. John I. Goodlad, Editor. Cloth.

Sixty-sixth Yearbook, 1967, Part I—*The Educationally Retarded and Disadvantaged.* Prepared by the Society's Committee. Paul A. Witty, Editor. Cloth.

Sixty-sixth Yearbook, 1967, Part II—*Programed Instruction.* Prepared by the Society's Committee. Phil C. Lange, Editor. Cloth.

Sixty-seventh Yearbook, 1968, Part I—*Metropolitanism: Its Challenge to Education.* Prepared by the Society's Committee. Robert J. Havighurst, Editor. Cloth.

Sixty-seventh Yearbook, 1968, Part II—*Innovation and Change in Reading Instruction.* Prepared by the Society's Committee. Helen M. Robinson, Editor. Cloth.

Sixty-eighth Yearbook, 1969, Part I—*The United States and International Education.* Prepared by the Society's Committee. Harold G. Shane, Editor. Cloth.

Sixty-eighth Yearbook, 1969, Part II—*Educational Evaluation: New Roles, New Means.* Prepared by the Society's Committee. Ralph W. Tyler, Editor. Paper.

Sixty-ninth Yearbook, 1970, Part I—*Mathematics Education.* Prepared by the Society's Committee. Edward G. Begle, Editor. Cloth.

Sixty-ninth Yearbook, 1970, Part II—*Linguistics in School Programs.* Prepared by the Society's Committee. Albert H. Marckwardt, Editor. Cloth.

Seventieth Yearbook, 1971, Part I—*The Curriculum: Retrospect and Prospect.* Prepared by the Society's Committee. Robert M. McClure, Editor. Paper.

PUBLICATIONS

Seventieth Yearbook, 1971, Part II—*Leaders in American Education*. Prepared by the Society's Committee. Robert J. Havighurst, Editor. Cloth.
Seventy-first Yearbook, 1972, Part I—*Philosophical Redirection of Educational Research*. Prepared by the Society's Committee. Lawrence G. Thomas, Editor. Cloth.
Seventy-first Yearbook, 1972, Part II—*Early Childhood Education*. Prepared by the Society's Committee. Ira J. Gordon, Editor. Paper.
Seventy-second Yearbook, 1973, Part I—*Behavior Modification in Education*. Prepared by the Society's Committee. Carl E. Thoresen, Editor. Cloth.
Seventy-second Yearbook, 1973, Part II—*The Elementary School in the United States*. Prepared by the Society's Committee. John I. Goodlad and Harold G. Shane, Editors. Cloth.
Seventy-third Yearbook, 1974, Part I—*Media and Symbols: The Forms of Expression, Communication, and Education*. Prepared by the Society's Committee. David R. Olson, Editor. Cloth.
Seventy-third Yearbook, 1974, Part II—*Uses of the Sociology of Education*. Prepared by the Society's Committee. C. Wayne Gordon, Editor. Cloth.
Seventy-fourth Yearbook, 1975, Part I—*Youth*. Prepared by the Society's Committee. Robert J. Havighurst and Philip H. Dreyer, Editors. Cloth.
Seventy-fourth Yearbook, 1975, Part II—*Teacher Education*. Prepared by the Society's Committee. Kevin Ryan, Editor. Cloth.
Seventy-fifth Yearbook, 1976, Part I—*Psychology of Teaching Methods*. Prepared by the Society's Committee. N. L. Gage, Editor. Paper.
Seventy-fifth Yearbook, 1976, Part II—*Issues in Secondary Education*. Prepared by the Society's Committee. William Van Til, Editor. Cloth.
Seventy-sixth Yearbook, 1977, Part I—*The Teaching of English*. Prepared by the Society's Committee. James R. Squire, Editor. Cloth.
Seventy-sixth Yearbook, 1977, Part II—*The Politics of Education*. Prepared by the Society's Committee. Jay D. Scribner, Editor. Paper.
Seventy-seventh Yearbook, 1978, Part I—*The Courts and Education*, Clifford P. Hooker, Editor. Cloth.
Seventy-seventh Yearbook, 1978, Part II—*Education and the Brain*, Jeanne Chall and Allan F. Mirsky, Editors. Cloth.
Seventy-eighth Yearbook, 1979, Part I—*The Gifted and the Talented: Their Education and Development*, A. Harry Passow, Editor. Cloth.
Seventy-eighth Yearbook, 1979, Part II—*Classroom Management*, Daniel L. Duke, Editor. Cloth.
Seventy-ninth Yearbook, 1980, Part I—*Toward Adolescence: The Middle School Years*, Mauritz Johnson, Editor. Cloth.
Seventy-ninth Yearbook, 1980, Part II—*Learning a Second Language*, Frank M. Grittner, Editor. Cloth.
Eightieth Yearbook, 1981, Part I—*Philosophy and Education*, Jonas F. Soltis, Editor. Cloth.
Eightieth Yearbook, 1981, Part II—*The Social Studies*, Howard D. Mehlinger and O. L. Davis, Jr., Editors. Cloth.

Yearbooks of the National Society are distributed by
UNIVERSITY OF CHICAGO PRESS, 5801 ELLIS AVE., CHICAGO, ILLINOIS 60637

Please direct inquiries regarding prices of volumes still available to the University of Chicago Press. Orders for these volumes should be sent to the University of Chicago Press, not to the offices of the National Society.

2. The Series on Contemporary Educational Issues

In addition to its Yearbooks the Society now publishes volumes in a series on Contemporary Educational Issues. These volumes are prepared under the supervision of the Society's Commission on an Expanded Publication Program.

The 1981 Titles

Psychology and Education: The State of the Union (Frank H. Farley and Neal J. Gordon, eds.)

Selected Issues in Mathematics Education (Mary M. Lindquist, ed.)

The 1980 Titles

Minimum Competency Achievement Testing: Motives, Models, Measures, and Consequences (Richard M. Jaeger and Carol K. Tittle, eds.)

Collective Bargaining in Public Education (Anthony M. Cresswell, Michael J. Murphy, with Charles T. Kerchner)

The 1979 Titles

Educational Environments and Effects: Evaluation, Policy, and Productivity (Herbert J. Walberg, ed.)

Research on Teaching: Concepts, Findings, and Implications (Penelope L. Peterson and Herbert J. Walberg, eds.)

The Principal in Metropolitan Schools (Donald A. Erickson and Theodore L. Reller, eds.)

The 1978 Titles

Aspects of Reading Education (Susanna Pflaum-Connor, ed.)

History, Education, and Public Policy: Recovering the American Educational Past (Donald R. Warren, ed.)

From Youth to Constructive Adult Life: The Role of the Public School (Ralph W. Tyler, ed.)

The 1977 Titles

Early Childhood Education: Issues and Insights (Bernard Spodek and Herbert J. Walberg, eds.)

The Future of Big City Schools: Desegregation Policies and Magnet Alternatives (Daniel U. Levine and Robert J. Havighurst, eds.)

Educational Administration: The Developing Decades (Luvern L. Cunningham, Walter G. Hack, and Raphael O. Nystrand, eds.)

The 1976 Titles

Prospects for Research and Development in Education (Ralph W. Tyler, ed.)

Public Testimony on Public Schools (Commission on Educational Governance)

Counseling Children and Adolescents (William M. Walsh, ed.)

The 1975 Titles

Schooling and the Rights of Children (Vernon Haubrich and Michael Apple, eds.)

Systems of Individualized Education (Harriet Talmage, ed.)

Educational Policy and International Assessment: Implications of the IEA Assessment of Achievement (Alan Purves and Daniel U. Levine, eds.)

The 1974 Titles

Crucial Issues in Testing (Ralph W. Tyler and Richard M. Wolf, eds.)

Conflicting Conceptions of Curriculum (Elliott Eisner and Elizabeth Vallance, eds.)

Cultural Pluralism (Edgar G. Epps, ed.)

Rethinking Educational Equality (Andrew T. Kopan and Herbert J. Walberg, eds.)

All of the above volumes may be ordered from

McCutchan Publishing Corporation
2526 Grove Street
Berkeley, California 94704

The 1972 Titles
Black Students in White Schools (Edgar G. Epps, ed.)
Flexibility in School Programs (W. J. Congreve and G. L. Rinehart, eds.)
Performance Contracting—1969–1971 (J. A. Mecklenburger)
The Potential of Educational Futures (Michael Marien and W. L. Ziegler, eds.)
Sex Differences and Discrimination in Education (Scarvia Anderson, ed.)

The 1971 Titles
Accountability in Education (Leon M. Lessinger and Ralph W. Tyler, eds.)
Farewell to Schools??? (D. U. Levine and R. J. Havighurst, eds.)
Models for Integrated Education (D. U. Levine, ed.)
PYGMALION Reconsidered (J. D. Elashoff and R. E. Snow)
Reactions to Silberman's CRISIS IN THE CLASSROOM (A. Harry Passow, ed.)

The 1971 and 1972 titles in this series are now out of print and are no longer available.